The
Dreaded Broccoli
Cookbook

A

**Good-Natured Guide
to Healthful Eating,
with 100 Recipes**

Barbara and Tamar Haspel

Scribner

SCRIBNER
1230 Avenue of the Americas
New York, NY 10020

Designed by Barbara M. Bachman
Set in Optima and Franklin Gothic

Manufactured in the United States of America
10 9 8 7 6 5 4 3 2 1
Library of Congress Cataloging-in-Publication Data
Haspel, Barbara.
The dreaded broccoli cookbook : a good-natured guide to healthful
eating, with 100 recipes / Barbara and Tamar Haspel.
p.   cm.
1. Low-fat diet—Recipes. 2. Nutrition. 3. Coronary heart
disease—diet therapy. I. Haspel, Tamar. II. Title.
RM237.7.H386   1999
641.5'63—dc21   98-46902
CIP

ISBN 0-684-85454-6

The publisher gratefully acknowledges permission to reprint from
One Fish, Two Fish, Red Fish, Blue Fish by Dr. Seuss. TM and copy-
right © 1960 and renewed 1988 by Dr. Seuss Enterprises, L.P.
Reprinted by permission of Random House, Inc.

In Memoriam

JACOB HASPEL

Son and Brother,

Friend and Colleague

1965 – 1998

ACKNOWLEDGMENTS

OVER THE SIX YEARS SINCE *Dreaded Broccoli*'s inception as a newsletter, many people have helped give it the momentum it needed to become a book. We're grateful to all *Dreaded Broccoli* subscribers; we still haven't quite gotten over being astonished that people are willing to send us actual, genuine money to do us the honor of reading what we write. We'd also like to thank all the newspaper and magazine editors who deemed *Dreaded Broccoli* newsworthy and said nice things about us in print.

Our graphic designer, Lisa Tranter Sibony, was also an integral part of our newsletter's success. Her whimsical illustrations and eye-catching layout encouraged people to pick it up and read it. Lisa, we're delighted that you've stuck with us all this time, and hope you'll be working with us for a long time to come.

We've also gotten a lot of help with the book itself. Thanks to our agent, Susan Lescher, and to Carolyn Larson from Susan's office, for helping us navigate the publishing waters. At Scribner, we'd like to thank Matthew Thornton, who handled the day-to-day detail with attention, patience, and intelligence, and Marah Stets, whose enthusiasm for the project helped carry the day.

There would be no book without our editor, Maria Guarnaschelli. From our very first meeting, Maria understood what we were trying to do, and helped us do it better. We count ourselves among the most fortunate of food writers for having her support, backing, and input. And her friendship—no small thing.

But we wouldn't be here thanking Maria if it hadn't been for Chas Edwards, who introduced us to her. Chas, by making that phone call, you changed the course of *Dreaded Broccoli,* and we are in your debt.

All along the way we've had help from many, many friends. They've given us marketing ideas, they've edited our prose, they've come to our tastings, and they've forgiven us for writing about them. Our particular thanks to Susan Toth, Frank and Polly Papsadore, Lisa Menna, Michael Goodman, and Susan Beningson.

This has been a family venture, bolstered by the help of all Haspels and Haspels-by-association. Our thanks to Chuck, Lisa Wilhelmi, Aaron, and Jacob. Chuck's willingness to hold a real job made *Dreaded Broccoli* possible. Jake's exacting standards and careful editing made this a better book.

CONTENTS

PART ONE

1.

Dreaded Broccoli Explained

IN 1989, EVERY RESTAURATEUR in Manhattan felt duty bound to offer a vegetable of the day. But it was the menu's stepchild. No one gave it much thought, and when some eccentric, nutrition-obsessed patron ordered it, the lowest of the sous chefs, already overwhelmed with other duties, was given the job of readying it for the table.

"Watch out," I'd hiss to my husband, "it's Dreaded Broccoli," and Chuck would cast up his eyes in mock despair as the waiter placed the plate in front of him. There it was: a dull-green, sullen-looking object resembling a small tree. Chuck was trying to adhere to his low-fat, high-vegetable diet when he ate in restaurants. It wasn't easy. It didn't help that the vegetable of the day every day in every restaurant seemed to be broccoli.

From a restaurateur's point of view, broccoli makes an almost perfect vegetable of the day. It's available year-round, keeps well, looks substantial (VERY substantial) on a plate, and back then could usually be palmed off in any condition from nearly raw to gray and limp.

These days, at least in New York, vegetables have attained higher status. Meals are likely to be conceived with special attention to the vegetables on the plate. Vegetarian entrées are staples of mainstream restaurants. Broccoli, when it appears, is usually at its bright green best, steamed to crisp-tenderness. The dark, sullen tree, except in second-class establishments, has pretty much disappeared. But not before it bore fruit: our title.

The broccoli of the title isn't the actual broccoli of our old marital joke. It's stuff that's good for you, that you know you should be eating, and that you haven't a clue how to get into your diet. It's all those vegetables and whole grains you keep hearing about.

It's hard to enjoy your morning chocolate doughnut with the Angel of Death smirking hideously at you over your coffee cup. "Lots of fat in that," he croaks, "not much fiber. Guess YOU won't be getting your five servings of fruits and vegetables today." The Broccoli may not be real, but the Dread certainly is.

The kitchen seems to have become the least-frequented room in a lot of homes in recent years. Of course, that's partly due to the rise of the two-career family, but I think the profusion of confusing—not to mention scary—dietary advice also plays a role. Cooking, for many of us, has always meant producing the old standbys: macaroni and cheese, meat loaf, pot roast. These things taste good, and our families, if they're not into nutritional correctness, applaud when they appear on the table. Unfortunately, even a cursory glance at the nutrition news is enough to convince you this stuff is terrible for you. Don't even bother to eat it. Just pack it right into your coronary arteries. Few of us are comfortable serving food that we know doesn't do our bodies any good. Feeding ourselves and others implies more than just satisfying the appetite. When we cook we want to increase both the short- and long-term well-being of our near and dear, not sentence them to an early grave.

But as soon as we look around for something different to cook, we run right into another major intimidator: the gourmet trend. The American culinary scene has become a minefield of strange ingredients and elaborate preparations. The country teems with super-chefs, all of whom seem to have written recipe books designed to make the average home cook feel inferior.

Many of their recipes work well for serious weekend chefs, hobbyists who want to truly master the culinary arts, and for whom complex and painstaking preparation is a taken-for-granted part of the cooking experience. There are many such people. We recently ate a Chinese banquet, meticulously prepared by our editor's husband, that absolutely blew us away. Clearly, the art of fine cooking is in no danger, but the craft of everyday home cooking may be. After you look in a few gourmet cookbooks, and eat in a top-tier restaurant or at the home of a talented amateur, you're ready to throw in the towel. If you don't have all day to cook, and there's no lemongrass or porcini mushrooms at your local A&P, you figure you might as well run down to McDonald's.

We're convinced, though, that you don't have to let either the dietitians or the chefs—or even your busy lifestyle—keep you out of your kitchen. *Dreaded Broccoli* won't make you into an expert nutritionist or an awesome gourmet chef. Nor will you find in its index references to every food you might ever want to prepare. If it's something Tamar or I don't cook and eat fairly regularly, it's not in here. This is a shamelessly quirky book full of our food enthusiasms. We think it will help you produce good-tasting healthful meals you can share happily with your family and friends—all without spending endless hours in front of the stove.

When Tamar and I began to cook low-fat/high-veggie meals, we learned that just tweaking our old favorites wasn't the way to go. Most of our traditional menus and favorite dishes had been designed to capitalize on the flavors and textures of meats and on the emulsions and liaisons created by saturated fats. Learning to appreciate a lot of new foods was the only way we could make significant, lasting changes in the way we ate. Obviously we needed new preparation methods for the new foods. We experimented, working from a foundation of stocks and basic flavors. We found recipes that helped us make these changes, but we also discovered that a lot of discrete recipes weren't all that useful as a guide for everyday cooking.

You too, if you turn out meals on a regular basis, have general strategies, even if your menus are an unvarying meat-potato-2 veg. You visualize dinner. You know what foods belong in it. You know which of these foods are essential and which are incidental, which should be cooked and which can remain raw. You have a few cooking techniques that you use over and over again. To cook and eat more healthfully you need to examine and evaluate the foods you prepare and the way you prepare them, and then make fundamental alterations, beginning with your basic concept of what constitutes dinner. No way are you going to do that because a dietitian hands you a few recipes.

You will, however, find recipes in this book. Every time I write one, I hear a still, small voice whisper that there are already too many recipes in the world. I answer that all I'm doing is telling people that this is how I cooked something one day. I'm just letting them know, by providing instructions organized into a familiar pattern, that they can cook it, or something like it, too. I hope you'll treat no recipe in this book as a sacred text. Imagine us mucking around in our tiny kitchens wondering what to do with whatever's in the refrigerator or the pantry. When you make something that this book has inspired, it won't be mine and it won't be Tamar's—it will be your own.

This book is about taking back your kitchen from the guys in white, whether they're wearing chefs' toques or lab coats. It's about recipe independence; it's about cooking as a craft for every day; it's about improvisation; it's about making one meal segue into the next; and it's about techniques for making healthful food palatable. It's also about Tamar and me, our family and friends, and the foods we love.

2.

Who We Are and the Way We Cook Now

Barbara's Story

Late one afternoon in the spring of 1989 the phone rang just as I was shutting down the computer in my midtown Manhattan office. It was my husband, who had been feeling vaguely unwell for several days. He was at home, where he had gone after his doctor informed him he'd had a heart attack. He was scheduled to meet Dr. M. at the hospital at 8:00 P.M. and be admitted for more tests. "Well," I said, rather as though he'd committed us to visiting some cranky old relative, "I'll come home right away. I'll have time to make us some pasta. It only takes ten minutes to get to Mt. Sinai in a cab."

That's about as dramatic as most stories in which I have a major role ever get. I'd like to think it's because I keep my head when all about me are losing theirs, but I'm afraid I'm just a phlegmatic person with an abnormally slow reaction time. That afternoon, I finished putting stuff away, locked up the office, and headed for the subway. It was raining, and I regretted my earlier generosity. My boss had gone to a job interview, and as she was walking out in her big fuzzy white coat, I had said, "Better wear my Burberry. That coat's got no *gravitas*. " Now, in the spring drizzle, her frivolous garment rapidly developed the odor of a wet dog. I went down the subway stairs and inserted my token, only to be met by a wave of disgruntled patrons leaving the station, having just been informed there were no trains. Some mobbed the token booths, intent on getting their fares refunded, but most of us returned immediately to the street in search of taxis. Getting a taxi in the rain at five o'clock in Midtown is always a near impossibility. If the subway isn't running, it's a wild fantasy.

Now, at last, my adrenaline began to flow. It seemed vitally important that I get to West 92nd Street, more than three miles away. A bus would take nearly an hour. I began to walk, encumbered by a large bag and what felt like twenty pounds of smelly white wool. If I had given up hope of a cab, I could have moved a lot faster. But I was more than hopeful. I was irrationally confident. I had to get home. There must be a taxi. Sure enough, at 8th Avenue and 50th, a cab with his light on drew to a stop a few feet in front of me. But just as my heart lifted at the sight, I realized it wasn't my cab. The man who was opening the door to get in had been there ahead of me. I didn't pause for moral reasoning. I zipped around behind him as he was closing his umbrella and slid in, leaving him standing in the wet street in the classic pose of a helpful doorman. Hell hath no fury like a New Yorker robbed of a taxi on a rainy day. That man was not about to go quietly. He held on to the door, demanding that I decab instantly. "I'm sorry," I said, in a tone that I'm afraid implied very little regret, "but I really need to get home."

Then the taxi driver spoke. "Hey, buddy," he said. "It was the lady I saw." He turned toward me, leering slightly. (Fortunately, I seemed to be downwind of him.) "I noticed her beautiful white coat. It's her cab." And the dear good man took me home.

I have rarely told anyone this story because I'm ashamed of what I did. It is inconsistent with anything I or those who know me believe to be my character. Recently, when I told it to my daughter (who is thirty-five and should have lost all illusions about her mother), her eyes got as big as saucers. "YOU stole a cab?!" She couldn't have been much more surprised if I had meant it literally—that I had expelled the driver and sped uptown, running red lights and scattering pedestrians. The reason I'm going public now is that my memory of myself engaged in profoundly uncivil behavior while disguised in a flashy white coat remains startlingly vivid, somehow representing for me the watershed in my life that day was to become. Before that afternoon, if you had asked me, I could certainly have told you that there was a bedrock, indissoluble connection between me and my husband. I also could have explained my belief that lots of information and profound skepticism should be part of every health-care consumer's arsenal. And I was committed to a prudent lifestyle: regular exercise and healthful eating, based on the best and most up-to-date information. Furthermore, whatever the gurus said we should be eating, I was sure I could make it taste really good. What changed was that these issues suddenly captured my full attention and remained its focus for many months. To a large degree they still are. You might say that I went home in a cab one rainy spring afternoon in 1989 and never left again.

But that day I had no clue that my life was irrevocably changed. Once I had seen my husband in the flesh, looking normal if perhaps a little pale, and had hung my woolly disguise in the bathroom to dry, I became myself again. First, I served pasta in tomato sauce, which we ate rather quietly. We were both somewhat subdued, but by no means distraught. Chuck wasn't really sick, and it was hard to believe anything all that serious was happening. Then we went to the hospital where an angiogram showed his three coronary arteries to be respectively 100 percent, 90 percent, and 65 percent blocked, and the doctors looked at him in much the same way the veterinarian had regarded our dog a few years before. (He had peered at the printout of blood values, then at the lively animal standing on his examination table. "That dog," he said, incredulously, "ought to be dead— moribund at the very least." Since the dog had gone on to live to a ripe old age, this parallel was actually mildly encouraging.)

Immediate coronary bypass surgery was recommended. We asked all the questions we could think of and did our best to examine the options dispassionately. Chuck could see no choice but to go ahead. An initially rapid recovery was followed by endless complications and discomfort culminating in the discovery just six months post-op that one of the four bypass grafts had closed and another had never worked at all. Hypertension, rapid heartbeat, and arrhythmia reared their ugly heads. Beta-blocking drugs were turning him into a zombie. And, despite his having eliminated nearly every dietary source of saturated fat, his cholesterol was too high.

Meanwhile, I was reading everything I could get my hands on about coronary artery disease. One of the first things I learned was that his experience was a common one. The results of bypass surgery were frequently disappointing. It was anything but a magic bullet. And I learned that all the drugs available to treat hypertension, arrhythmia, and high cholesterol had serious side effects. None of this information was making either of us very happy.

I was also reading everything I could get my hands on about nutrition.

My neighborhood bookstore stocked a mind-numbing load of material that purported to deal with nutrition and good health. Most of these books featured bad science, tasteless recipes, or turgid writing. Many featured all three. Nobody who knew more than I did about what constituted a healthful diet for a cardiac patient—let alone how to make it palatable—seemed to have written anything. What was respectable was old. What was new was disreputable. But I knew that there was some real research going on in nutrition science, so I got a friend with access to a medical library to check out current journals for me. That's how I learned about Dr. Dean Ornish.

By now you've probably heard of Dean Ornish, America's favorite cardiologist. He may well qualify as the father of *Dreaded Broccoli.* In 1975, while he was still in medical school, he became convinced that lifestyle changes offered more hope for coronary artery disease patients than standard medical interventions. By the time he had completed his residency, he had already conducted several small studies that indicated that radical dietary changes could not only alleviate symptoms of heart disease but could actually improve the heart's ability to pump blood. By 1989 he had demonstrated in a controlled study that his program of diet, exercise, and stress reduction reduced the blockages in the coronary arteries of the participants, while the condition of those patients following the standard recommendations of the American Heart Association (30 percent of calories from fat) worsened.

I soon learned that a book was in the works: *Dr. Dean Ornish's Program for Reversing Heart Disease* (Random House, 1990). Maybe that's not such a catchy title as *Dreaded Broccoli,* but it was exactly what I was looking for. Through connections at Random House, I wangled an advance copy. I read it cover to cover in a few hours. There wasn't as much hard data in it as I would have liked, but there was enough to convince me that the program was performing as advertised. So the only question was how we were going to implement it at our house.

The stress reduction part of Ornish's program involves a lot of meeting in groups and leans pretty heavily on New Age jargon. (Or maybe it's just California psychobabble—I don't keep up very well in this field.) I—and, more to the point, my husband—found Ornish's stress reduction recommendations not only off-putting but mildly embarrassing. Only a lobotomy would prepare Chuck to Visualize his Inner Teacher. On the other hand, exercise was no problem. Chuck had been physically active for years and, while the heart attack and subsequent surgery had lowered his exercise tolerance, he was still doing regular resistance training and walking several miles nearly every day.

That left the diet. Ornish's diet is even more limited than a standard diet restricted solely to vegetable products because no vegetable oils (except, of course, those actually contained in the vegetables and grains) or nuts or seeds are permitted. It also forbids high-fat vegetable foods such as avocados, coconuts, and cocoa products. The only animal products permitted are skim milk, nonfat yogurt, and egg whites.

Ornish's stated goal is a diet with approximately 10 percent of its calories from fat and fewer than 5 milligrams of cholesterol a day. (In fact, if you follow this diet, even less than 10 percent of your calories will come from fat unless you eat an awful lot of soybeans—just about the only relatively high-fat item permitted.) However, having designed this rather daunting regimen, he did a very smart thing. He got some serious food professionals (chefs, not dietitians) like Deborah Madison, Alice Waters, and Mollie Katzen to create recipes working within the constraints of his diet.

Many of the recipes are excellent, but the reason it was really clever of him to involve people known for their respect for and skill at preparing food was that it made people like me think, "Well, if Deborah Madison can do this and her sneer muscles don't go into spasm, maybe I can too."

So I tried it, and most of the stuff I made tasted pretty good. I tinkered a little with the constraints. I ignored those of Ornish's strictures that seemed to me arbitrary. For example, I used more fat-free dairy products than he allows. We ate small amounts of fish at the beginning (we've increased the portion sizes in the last couple of years in response to all the good news about omega3 fatty acids). We occasionally eat a little poultry or ultra-low-fat meat, and I use animal-based stocks (which, properly defatted, contain no fat or cholesterol) in soups and sauces. I also use small amounts of oil in salad and cooking, in the beginning less than an ounce per person per week, now perhaps twice that.

After three months of the modified Ornish diet Chuck had lost ten pounds. He had been fairly lean to begin with. Now he was really thin. His cholesterol was 209, his blood pressure was normal without beta-blockers, and he was no longer troubled by arrhythmia. He could exercise much longer and more vigorously without experiencing either chest pain or a dramatically elevated heart rate. After six months he was able to exercise even more vigorously, his weight was down to 150 and his cholesterol 197 with an LDL/HDL ratio of less than three. These numbers have been fairly stable for about eight years. I also weigh somewhat less than I did when I began to eat the same meals my husband does. (At home, that is. Elsewhere, I cheat. As Chuck has often remarked, he is the guinea pig, I am just the pig.)

In the last few years some pretty good studies have been publicized indicating that monounsaturated fats like the ones in olive and canola oils may protect the heart. As a result we've increased our use of olive oil just a little. But whenever I think how nice it would be to use all the oil I want when I cook, I remember how much easier it is to maintain a desirable weight when your diet is very low in fat. I also remember that the Mediterranean diet—low animal/high vegetable, with lots of olive oil—is what my husband was eating in 1989, pre-Ornish, when he was sick as a dog.

Chuck and I both have low triglycerides and high HDL (the good cholesterol), which is apparently not always the case with people on high-carbohydrate/low-fat diets. We seem to thrive eating this way, but some recent data hints that this isn't true of everyone. *Nutrition Action News,* the organ of the Center for Science in the Public Interest, states a sensible bottom-line solution to the controversy. "For most people, the healthiest diet is a low-fat one that's full of grains, fruits, vegetables, and beans and that uses olive oil as the main source of fat. If you are slim and have low HDL, a diet rich in monounsaturated fat (like olive oil) may protect your heart. If you have a tendency to gain weight, a diet rich in monounsaturated fat may make you fatter, which can raise your risk of heart disease." Dr. Ornish, however, isn't about to make any wimpy compromises. The eating plan in his newer books hasn't deviated one whit from the original.

A famous essay by Isaiah Berlin begins: "There is a line among the fragments of the Greek poet Archilochus which says: 'The fox knows many things, but the hedgehog knows one big thing.'" Berlin claims that writers and thinkers can be divided loosely into foxes and hedgehogs. Foxes are those whose thought moves on many levels, evaluating ideas and experiences for their inherent value without trying to fit them into any unitary whole, any overarching principle. For hedgehogs unity is everything; they "relate everything to a single central vision . . . in terms of which alone all that they are and say has significance." All my own favorite authors are among the foxes; Berlin himself was the quintessential fox. I love surprises, suppleness of thought, openness to experience.

Exasperated, I have watched Dean Ornish stubbornly refuse to change his eating plan—continue to insist in the face of mounting evidence to the contrary that ultra-low-fat eating is the only true path to health. He persistently denies the validity of perfectly good data that points to the value of monounsaturated fats in the diet. But he's still the guy with the good-sized, long-term database that associates a particular diet with actual reduction of plaque in the coronary arteries of its adherents. And we've done well here for nearly a decade eating an only slightly modified version of the diet he recommends. Dr. Ornish is a hedgehog, but the one big thing he knows may have saved my husband's life.

DREADED BROCCOLI AND HOW IT GREW

The last decade of our lives, ushered in dramatically by Chuck's heart attack, was by no means the beginning of our search for a healthful lifestyle. We didn't know *Dreaded Broccoli* was on its way, but its evolution has been similar to that of many of Earth's life-forms, at least according to the most recent theories. That is, it evolved gradually over many years, punctuated by several short bursts of rapid change in response to stressful events. (In evolutionary biology this theory is known as Punctuated Equilibrium. According to one of its originators, Stephen J. Gould, it is affectionately nicknamed Punk Eke by its proponents. Its detractors call it Evolution by Jerks.)

The *Dreaded Broccoli* plan is the product of my husband's unfortunate genetic inheritance. The men in Chuck's family tend to have heart attacks at early ages. One of his uncles dropped dead at thirty. Chuck, a prudent man with a healthy desire to survive to a ripe old age, has always been willing to take whatever measures might serve to evade the family curse.

Not much was known about preventing coronary artery disease back in 1960. You could figure you shouldn't smoke and that you ought to exercise and keep your weight down. That not only seemed logical—an extra margin of safety for the body In good shape—but it was borne out by the sorry condition of most of the people who had heart attacks. So Chuck did all those things—and the years passed.

Gradually, during the late sixties and early seventies, news about the existence of such things as cholesterol and different kinds of fat began to filter down to the public, and I began to use more polyunsaturates and less butter and cream. As we grew older and more inclined to gain weight, I became more careful about total fat content. (Note the first-person singular pronoun. I should make one thing clear right now. I do and have always done, except for an occasional conscription of slave labor, all the cooking in our family. "Aha," you say, "patriarchy's tyranny!" Just try to come into my kitchen and I'll show you tyranny!)

Certainly our post-1970 diet did not get more than 30 percent of its total calories from fat. In other words, it fell within the current American Heart Association guidelines for a healthy diet. We always ate a lot of fruits, vegetables, and grains. Chuck actually prefers these foods up to a point (a point he passed long ago, poor man). As for me, in spite of my inordinate fondness for meat, I am a bit squeamish about eating my fellow creatures, especially my close relatives, the large mammals. So as the years went by we tended to eat less red meat and more chicken, fish, and Mediterranean-style vegetable preparations. Pasta dishes were favorites of all our children so we had them often. A few of them were pretty heavy on the oil and cheese but most were fairly lean. We stayed thin and fit. We figured we were doing our best.

Then came the eighties—the cholesterol-screening years. In 1980 Chuck's cholesterol was measured at nearly 300. (Don't ask me mine. You don't want to know. I was wise enough to choose the proper ancestors.) Time to bite the bullet—not much else to bite, we quipped. (Sorry. Our diet may have improved with the passing years, but our jokes have never gotten any better.) No more red meat. No more egg yolks. No more cheese or whole milk. I still used a fair amount of oil in food preparation, but my concern with total calories kept me moderate and certainly no more than 25 percent of our calories came from fat. Chuck's cholesterol fell to 189 in two months. Jubilation! He was then introduced to the syndrome that is dishearteningly familiar to anyone whose liver is a truly efficient cholesterol factory. In spite of his adhering conscientiously to his diet, his cholesterol crept up inexorably and hovered between 200 and 250.

And he really didn't cheat. I can vouch for my husband. He is an honest, sensible, and well-disciplined man. Our daughter's theory is that his cholesterol is like a colony of New York cockroaches. You can foil it for a while, keep it down with some new strategy, but it adapts and outwits you and comes back as strong as ever—stronger in fact, because you've used up yet another weapon in your arsenal. No ordinary, moderate measures work. I think the Tamar Haspel Cockroach Syndrome is poorly understood by doctors who do not believe that their patients are eating what they say they are. This belief helps to justify the wholesale prescribing of powerful cholesterol-lowering drugs. Doctors are convinced that people will simply not stick to restricted diets.

We tried oat bran—remember oat bran? The miracle food of 1989. It really is good stuff, all kidding aside. Soluble fiber is good for you and oat bran has a lot of it. It is also fairly bland and absorbent, not nearly as assertive and, well, *woody* as wheat bran. It makes a decent high-fiber muffin or even a quick bowl of hot cereal. And it did lower Chuck's cholesterol. But three months later it had crept back up to 220 again. Just like the cockroaches.

By this time Chuck was ready to admit that diet alone would not work for him. He had reduced the fat content of his diet to under 20 percent. Lots of that fat came from fatty fishes with omega3 fatty acids, which were—and still are—reputed to be cholesterol lowering. Most of the rest came from olive oil, which being monounsaturated was also supposed to have a favorable effect on lipid profiles. He had increased his exercise level (a three-mile walk to work nearly every day in addition to four aerobics classes a week). These measures raised his HDL cholesterol (the good kind) so that his ratio of LDLs to HDLs was less than three, a ratio so favorable that it is thought by many to effectively counteract the risk posed by a high total cholesterol reading. Nevertheless, he really wanted his cholesterol level to be under 200, and in March of 1989 he made an appointment with a cardiologist to discuss whether he ought to try a cholesterol-lowering drug. But he didn't keep that appointment. Instead, he had his heart attack and we fumbled around for solutions until we found Dr. Ornish. And it has been only this most recent, and most radical, set of changes that has seemed to make a significant difference to my husband's health.

When the modified Ornish program began producing dramatic results—not to mention satisfying meals—at our house, our daughter became interested. She too was concerned about healthful eating and effective weight control. And, like all good cooks, she enjoys a culinary challenge. It amused her to produce low-fat meals that garnered high praise from mainstream eaters. When I began to write up some of my recipes and kitchen strategies, she joined me and, in 1992, we inaugurated a quarterly food newsletter called *Dreaded Broccoli,* dedicated to making low-fat cooking and eating feasible, perhaps even pleasurable.

When I'm asked what it's like to work closely with my daughter, I usually just remark that I could go farther and do worse, but now that I seem to be committed to letting it all hang out, I guess I should say more. There's no one I know, or can even imagine, who would be a better partner. She is intelligent, humorous, reliable, and absolutely to be trusted—not to mention being a fine cook and writer. In the next section she's going to be saying some nice things about her family of origin. But her father and I take no credit for our daughter's fine qualities. They belong to her alone. But we're glad we had her.

Tamar's Story

The naturalist and sociobiologist Edward O. Wilson, in his autobiography, writes about finding a jellyfish in the Gulf of Mexico when he was seven years old. The creature captivated him and he knew, even then, that he would spend his life studying animals. I am awed by the combination of drive, focus, and prescience that gives an occupation the force of a calling.

At seven, not only had I not figured out what I wanted to be, it hadn't even occurred to me that I would one day have to be something. I didn't have time for questions like that; I was too busy coming up with new and creative ways to terrorize my little brother. But directionlessness is to be expected when you're seven. It only starts to be a problem fifteen years and an expensive education later, when you're still in the dark.

I have friends who, through some combination of insight, foresight, and blind luck, landed right out of college in careers that suit them. They do work they find interesting and satisfying, and they're good at it. For many of us, though, it takes trial, error, and time to find a suitable niche.

It has saddened me not to know what to be. I wanted very much to be called—it wouldn't much matter to what. Science, maybe. Or math. Medicine. Teaching. It could be almost anything, as long as it was honorable and as long as it spoke to me. Perhaps it is a function of the nature of my interests, which are wide and shallow, that no one thing seemed to be mine.

My mother is like me in that her interests are of the wide-and-shallow variety (although her shallow is deeper than mine) and, like me, she has no calling. When I was in college she worked as the assistant to a well-known writer. The position had been advertised in the *New York Times* as an often interesting but sometimes tedious job with "no future." Mom applied, writing that it sounded perfect for a woman with "no ambition." Naturally, she was hired.

Her interests crystallized when my father had a heart attack, the aftermath of which was *Dreaded Broccoli*'s inception. Please don't think me callous if I admit that I wish I had as good a story.

I would like to report that my interest in *Dreaded Broccoli* originated in a lightbulb moment, when all of a sudden my career and my future were illuminated and I knew what I had to do. But that's not what happened. Instead, it was a confluence of many interests and influences. Food, writing, and independence were all things I enjoyed. And then there was Mom.

It wasn't until I went to college that I realized my parents were unusual. From the time my brothers and I were old enough to reason, our opinions and wishes were taken seriously. As we grew up, we were increasingly entrusted with the decisions that shaped our lives. We were autonomous and our interests were encouraged. Almost everything was open for discussion. I remember telling my mother, when I was about twenty-five, that I don't remember her ever telling me I couldn't do something I wanted to do. She said, "Well, you never asked to do anything unreasonable."

And while all this was going on, they were also setting an example of what it was to be responsible, interesting, involved adults. They told the truth, to us and to others. They were active in community and political organizations. They gave money to a variety of causes. They read books and magazines and newspapers. They were well-versed in many subjects and truly expert in several. I learned to think critically, to behave responsibly, and to laugh easily.

To be sure, there were lots of things I didn't learn at home. Interior decorating. Lawn care. I can't play soccer and I throw like a girl. And I wasn't the only one who was incompletely educated. One day when my brother Aaron was about seven, my family went to visit some friends. We were all gathered in their living room, and Aaron found a stack of coasters. He took one off the stack, looked at it, turned it over, and brought it over to my mother. "Mom," he asked, "what are these?"

My parents' lifestyle meant that we didn't fit seamlessly into our little suburban enclave. We were the eggheads of Jean Drive. Our neighbors thought, not without some justification, that we just did things differently from other people. I certainly remember my parents doing things other parents didn't. Some of those things, like co-chairing the Mid-Hudson chapter of the ACLU and making regular trips to New York City, were still well within the range of normal.

Others were, I will admit, a little strange. One example of my parents' unique approach to problem solving involved our mailbox. It was a typical suburban mailbox, a compartment with a door and a flag, planted on a post at the end of our driveway. It had been there since we moved into the house, and it was beginning to fall apart. First, the box came loose from its post, so you could just lift it off. It proved an irresistible target for low-rent suburban vandalism, and it would occasionally disappear. We would find it halfway down the block and put it back. Eventually, the post also came loose, and one day the entire mailbox disappeared. It reappeared the next day, but my parents were getting tired of hunting for it.

The solution? You'd think a new mailbox would be in order and, eventually, we did get one. In the meantime, however, my mother simply kept the mailbox in the garage. She brought it out in the morning and took it in with the mail. If we were a little late getting it out, or the mailman was a little early, we'd have to go racing to the curb, mailbox in hand. If you timed it right, you didn't even have to put the mailbox in the ground— you simply held it out for the mailman. No one else on our block did that.

It isn't surprising that our Poughkeepsie neighbors thought we were a little weird. Fortunately, I've since discovered that what's weird in Poughkeepsie translates better elsewhere.

As an adult, I've always enjoyed spending time with my parents, partly because they treat me and my brothers like adult friends, not like children, but mostly because they're two of the most interesting people I know. So it's hard to imagine a better business partner than my mother. We're often asked whether it's difficult for a mother and daughter to work together, but only by people who don't know Mom.

When I tell people I work with my mother, I almost always get a raised eyebrow, but I've found that mothers of grown daughters have a different reaction from the daughters themselves. Mothers tend to think a mother-daughter business is a wonderful thing, and several have told me (and several more have told Mom) that they wish they had that kind of relationship with their daughters. Daughters, however, usually say, "You work with your *mother*?"

The potential source of conflict isn't that we're mother and daughter—it's that we're both kitchen autocrats. We reign supreme in our respective kitchens and no interference is tolerated (unless, of course, it takes the form of a willingness to peel shallots or slice tomatoes). We circumvent this problem easily: We don't cook together. We each regard dinner as a one-person job. She does it at her house and I do it at mine.

We cook and write separately, but we talk almost every day. We talk about food. We talk about things we try and what works and what doesn't. We read about food and we talk about what we read. We edit each other's work and we talk about that. *Dreaded Broccoli* allows us to indulge our interest in food to an almost embarrassing degree. Normally, I might think that spending so much time focused on eating was frivolous, but, hey, this is business!

My mother and I have, independently and in very different circumstances, developed similar styles of cooking. It would be reasonable to assume that my mother taught me to cook, but she didn't. I undoubtedly absorbed some of her techniques and biases by eating at her table all my life, but there was never instruction. I learned the same way she did: by paying close attention to food, deconstructing what was fed to me, reading, and experimenting.

That our attitudes about food and cooking are remarkably similar comes as something of a relief to me. Ever since I was quite small, my family teased me about being my father's clone. I look like him, I talk like him, I beat dead horses like him. I am ridiculously punctual and I like ships. But my kitchen proclivities prove that I am undoubtedly the product of two parents. Sometimes I don't really understand why my mother does certain things until I find myself doing them. For instance, when we were growing up we never cleared the table after a meal; we simply left the dishes for Mom to deal with. I always took for granted it was one of the many things Mom just did. It wasn't until I started feeding people myself that I realized I was actually annoyed by having people clear the dishes. They put them in the wrong place, they stack them precariously, and they generally interfere with the smooth running of my kitchen. And it doesn't save me any time. Now, like Mom, I insist that my guests leave their dishes right where they are. "Aha!" I said to myself when I first figured this out, "I am my mother's daughter. Even if I do like ships."

And, like my mother, I haven't overcome my wide-and-shallow nature by specializing. For the expert authentic Italian or Mexican or Indian meal, we go elsewhere. We owe a debt of gratitude to the food writers who have spent their lives exploring and codifying those cuisines because we borrow from them all the time (sometimes in unorthodox ways, but we hope they'll forgive us).

The advantage to not being a specialist is that you get to be a generalist. We cook everything and we'll try anything. The cooking we do is improvisational and imprecise. We invent combinations and substitute ingredients and vary quantities not just with equanimity but with glee. This isn't a science, as Mom points out, it's a craft.

In her many years of meal preparation, my mother has been known to take improvisation to extremes. In their New York apartment, for example, they have no balcony or backyard, so there is no place to put a barbecue grill. They do, however, have a fireplace. One night my parents decided they wanted grilled fish, so they opened the flue, put the hibachi in the fireplace, and grilled up a nice piece of swordfish. The family reaction to what soon became a regular practice was skeptical. My brother Jake came over one afternoon and spotted the grill in the fireplace. "If that was okay to do," he asked, "wouldn't other people be doing it?"

Most of the improvisation that goes on in our kitchens is more conventional, and stems from a combination of independence and irreverence. Being a kitchen autocrat means not just that you don't let other people help make dinner, but also that you're not a slave to a recipe. The idea that you have to follow someone else's instructions deflates the spirit of cooking. Small wonder that the take-home food industry is booming when doing it yourself means finding a recipe, making a list, shopping for ingredients, and following directions. That's no fun. It's a chore.

My mother is fond of telling the story of one of my first words. One day when I was about eight months old (I talked early but made up for it by being remarkably slow to understand the conventions of social discourse), she got some clothes out and started to dress me. She did this every morning, only this morning I wasn't having it. I took the clothes away from her with an independent gleam in my eye and said, emphatically, "Self!" I got my pants on my head but I was determined to dress myself.

This unfortunate need to assert myself has not lessened with time, and although it didn't serve me well in the corporate world, I've found that it's less of a liability in the kitchen. You'll probably annoy your boss if you don't follow directions; your asparagus, however, will never know.

And so *Dreaded Broccoli* is for the insurrectionist in all of us. It's about improvisation and experimentation. It's about developing and trusting your own judgment. And it's about vegetables.

PART TWO

THE BASICS

Concepts, Techniques, Strategies, and (Yes!) Food

OVER THE LAST COUPLE OF YEARS I've bought several pieces of furniture from Ikea, the Swedish furniture manufacturer. They have a big warehouse of a showroom in New Jersey where you can see what all the furniture looks like assembled. This is important because everything you buy from Ikea comes unassembled in big flat boxes that are very, very heavy.

Since they don't deliver, half the battle of buying from Ikea is procuring a car, schlepping to New Jersey, tying the big heavy boxes to whatever part of the car will best accommodate them (Ikea provides both the beefy guys and the miles of twine required for this), driving them back to Manhattan, and getting them upstairs to your apartment. The other half is assembling them.

Believe it or not, assembling is the fun part. Ikea has great instructions. They're completely pictorial, a policy I assume they adopted when they realized that instructions in Swedish wouldn't fit in with their global marketing plans.

(Swedish is a strange-sounding language. It really does sound like the Swedish Chef, a Muppet character who insouciantly makes a huge mess in his Muppet kitchen while warbling nonstop faux Swedish. In fact, when I went to see Ingmar Bergman's *Fanny and Alexander,* I temporarily blanked on Bergman's nationality and when the dialogue began I leaned over to my mother, puzzled, and said, "What language are they speaking? It sounds like the Swedish Chef." Then the lightbulb went on.)

The steps in Ikea instructions are numbered clearly, the diagrams of the parts look like the actual parts, and actions are represented by arrows and pictures of tools (a hammer and screwdriver are usually all that's required). I start with the first step, do what the picture shows, then move on to the second, and so on until, miraculously, the box of wood and screws and pegs turns into a night table.

But when I'm finished, although I have a night table, I don't have a clue about how a night table is really built. If you gave me all the pieces without the directions, I might be able to do it again, but if you gave me the pieces for, say, a chair, I would be stymied.

Recipes are often like that. You buy the ingredients, you follow the instructions, grateful that they're not in Swedish, and if you've done it right, you end up with a risotto or a stew or a cake. But it's hard to extract general principles applicable to tomorrow's dinner or Saturday's lunch from recipes. They are designed to do one thing—show you how to duplicate the steps the author took to make the dish.

For many cooks, this is just fine. If you cook about as often as I assemble furniture, you're probably not interested in extracting general principles. If, however, you cook every day and aspire to some degree of recipe independence, general principles help. In this section we've tried to outline some of the basic ideas and skills that are fundamental to what we do in the kitchen.

3.

Vegetables: The Raw and the Cooked

"Soon after people become vegetarians, they are likely to make a marvelous discovery: vegetables."

—*The New Laurel's Kitchen*

AS **TAMAR PROMISED,** this book is about vegetables. We're going to confront the root, the stalk, the leaf, and the pod. Vegetables are probably the one category of food most of us don't eat too much of. Restaurant entrées and desserts seem to get larger every year. Movie popcorn comes in tubs you could take home and use to bathe your baby. Soft drinks are served in half-gallon cups. Bagels and muffins tip the scales at nearly half a pound. Not surprisingly, we are a fat nation. Vegetables, however, despite their manifold nutritional virtues, haven't played much of a role in our collective feeding frenzy. Lots of people claim they don't like vegetables.

What an odd claim that is! Of all the major food categories, vegetables range over the broadest spectrum of tastes, colors, shapes, and textures. What does a green bean have in common with a beet, or a broccoli floret with a carrot? We speak of foods being meaty or fishy or fruity, and it's clear what we're talking about. My dictionary does list the adjective "vegetably," but it's not in common use—perhaps because it's devilishly hard to pronounce but more likely because no one would know whether you were saying that something resembled a potato, a green pea, or a stalk of asparagus. The set of what we know as vegetables (which includes impostors like tomatoes and mushrooms) has more members than any other food group. Not only that, but most of them are inexpensive, easy to cook, and taste good over a wide range of doneness.

Many of the folks who say they hate vegetables, of course, are talking about cooked ones. Most people can deal with a carrot stick or a moderate portion of green salad. But if these are your only veggies, you should try to branch out. If you depend on salads and crudités, you are unlikely ever to eat enough to make vegetables a cornerstone of your diet.

Consider, for example, the Great Dreaded One itself: broccoli. It has twenty-four calories a cup if you eat it raw, forty-six if you cook it. This is not because calories lurk in your saucepans just waiting for a chance to migrate into your broccoli, but because cooking reduces its volume by approximately half. Cooking also makes it easier and quicker to eat—just in case you have something to do today besides eating your broccoli. And while some nutrients either are partially destroyed by heat or wind up in the cooking water, others become more available to the body.

Leafy greens change in cooking even more dramatically than sturdier vegetables, reducing to less than a quarter of their original volume. Three cups of raw spinach cooks down to about half a cup of well-drained cooked spinach. I like spinach salad, but 3 cups of raw spinach is a *lot* of spinach. Both Chuck and I are likely to stop after a cup or two and fill up on whatever else is on the table, or later on snacks of bread and fruit. Salad, whole grains, fruit, modest amounts of animal protein—there's nothing wrong with such a diet. It's a lot better than the one being scarfed up by most of your fellow countrymen, but you can almost certainly improve it by expanding your repertoire to include cooked vegetables.

Tamar and I do like both raw and cooked vegetables. (Read about some we like a lot in Chapter 8, Fun with Vegetables.) This is no surprise to anyone who knows us. We try to convince ourselves we're serious gourmets with discriminating palates, but the truth is we can eat just about anything and enjoy it. If we're not near the food we love, we love the food we're near.

Our main goal in this book is to convince you—even if you don't share our predisposition to happily scarf up anything that comes along—that some of the healthful foods we cook and eat would work at your house. Before we can actually eat vegetables, however, we have to confront my worst culinary nightmare.

Veggie Prep (The Horror! The Horror!)

One of the jobs that got rotated in my college co-op house was officially known as "Vegetable Preparation," and it was the one I would do almost anything to get out of. I was famous for my willingness to swap my veggie prep for a whole week of dishwashing or bathroom cleaning. The thought of an afternoon spent cutting radish roses and scraping carrots was enough to make me lose my will to live. Still is.

Denial of veggie prep's tedium is an annoying characteristic of a lot of recipes, those purportedly written by famous chefs being the worse offenders. "1 large celery root, julienned." "20 cloves of garlic, peeled and finely sliced." Yeah, right! Every vegetable presents its own special challenges, which we address in this book whenever appropriate, but it's helpful to be aware of some basic guidelines.

1. SIMPLIFY.

Never peel potatoes, carrots, or zucchini. Just brush the dirt off mushrooms. Don't be compulsive about picking things over. So the boss's wife gets a rotten blueberry. She'll live. (I know, that's fruit prep. It's included under veggie prep just like it was when I was in college. I thought it was unfair then too.) This example, however, brings us to a necessary corollary of the "simplify" guideline. If there is a peach pit in the compote, a pebble in the lentil soup, or a spotted potato in the pot, it will end up on the plate of either A) The guest you most wanted to impress, or B) A person of exquisite gastronomic sensitivity who will be put off the dish in question for life. This person is almost always a child who will apply the traumatic lesson not just to peaches, lentils, and potatoes but to all compotes, soups, and pots of vegetables.

Besides, certain applications of this guideline may render food unattractive, unpalatable, or even inedible. Most cucumbers, for example, should be peeled. Use caution.

2. GET A FOOD PROCESSOR AND USE IT CONSTANTLY.

Alternatively, get a set of large sharp knives and become very skillful. Many gourmets recommend this as the only acceptable option. In a food processor, they say, the flavorful juices bleed out of your chopped onions. Your garlic becomes oxidized. All your vegetables are bruised and abused rather than cleanly cut. Maybe a blind tasting could distinguish my sautéed onions and garlic from theirs, although I doubt it. The bottom line, however, is that I am a world-class klutz and am afraid of large sharp knives.

I have been known to activate the food processor solely for the purpose of slicing a dozen mushrooms. I find this appliance virtually indispensable. (Tamar, whose knife skills are better than mine, swears by hers too.) I use the slicing blade for everything from tomatoes for sauce to garlic for stir-frying. The S-shaped chopping blade is excellent for the herbs I use in enormous quantities—parsley, cilantro, basil, mint. Most of my meal preparations begin with slicing and end with chopping. I recommend the purchase of a food processor if you can possibly afford one without indenturing your children. An acceptable one can be had for less than $100, a good one for less than $200. Select a simple model. You don't need eighteen different blades. I picked up an off-brand food processor for $10 at a thrift shop to use in my Florida apartment. It works fine.

3. PREPARE AS MUCH AS POSSIBLE AT ONE TIME.

It's just as easy to wash four days' worth of salad greens as one. Thoroughly dried, they will keep very well in plastic bags in the refrigerator. Cloth bags are even better, but if you don't have them, a paper towel in the plastic bag will help. Brown paper bags work okay if your vegetables are well dried. (Incidentally, these bags are excellent for storing mushrooms, which should never, never be put in plastic bags. They drown in their own juices in a matter of hours. In paper bags they will usually keep for more than a week. They may become slightly dried out but they taste fine. We all know dried mushrooms are a delicacy.)

A salad spinner is very good for drying greens, and you can just leave them in it for refrigerator storage if you have room. If you don't have room, you can do what I do and just balance it precariously on top of other stuff, where it will fall out every time you open the refrigerator. It doesn't weigh much and won't injure your foot, although it may startle your dog the first couple of times. Check your greens every day for signs of rot and dispose of offending leaves.

4. USE SLAVE LABOR.

It will do your heart good to see your four-year-old bent over a sinkful, or a bathtubful, of floating spinach leaves. Four is an excellent age for compulsively removing all the sand and thick stems, though you must be prepared for a lot of, "Is this one too thick? Should I take this one off?" It's easy to convince a four-year-old this is an important job, because it is. If you don't believe me, you've never eaten sandy spinach with the tough stems left on. You could have had some at my house from time to time before I learned that Guideline #1 doesn't apply to cleaning greens. If you haven't a handy four-year-old at your house, older children, roommates, and spouses who aren't fast enough on their feet can also be enlisted. None of these people should be referred to as slaves. The correct term is "sous chef."

5. BUY FRESH PRODUCE FROM PEOPLE WHO CLEAN IT.

The price will most likely be higher, but if your time is worth anything at all, the extra cost is justified. Most things you'll have to wash again, but not nearly so thoroughly as you would if they were encrusted with dirt. Also, cleaned produce has usually been culled of its inedible parts and rotten bits, so the amount you save by purchasing unwashed vegetables may be more apparent than real. I buy all my greens in New York in summer from two New York greenmarket vendors, the proprietors of Windfall Farms and Mountain Sweet Farms, who wash and trim them carefully. They sell wonderful mixtures of tender young greens that make a perfect salad. Many a heartfelt blessing have I sent their way at dinner time. They do not spray their greens with pesticides—another important consideration for anyone contemplating minimal washing time. (Since a link was established between a recent outbreak of *E.coli* and a batch of greens from California, I do give all the greens I buy in bulk—even from vendors I've trusted for years—an additional immersion at home.)

Similar salad green mixtures are now available in the produce sections of many supermarkets. If you can find one that looks good—with no yellow or wilted leaves—it will probably taste better than a prepackaged salad mixture in a plastic bag. The bulk greens do have the disadvantage of needing a wash, but the bagged ones, although they may look terrific, seem to have a flavor that I can only describe as dead. They should be labeled "past season," like the clothes I buy at the discount store.

Even using the above guidelines, fresh vegetables are the most tedious part of food preparation. They are also messy and I am a legendary messy cook. Stems, leaves, and peels accumulate as I work and seem to adhere to every available surface. My landlord once came into my kitchen just after I'd prepared a large stir-fry and asked if there'd been an explosion. Even my less dramatic veggie prep leaves behind shreds of parsley and (my particular nemesis because it gets tracked all over the house) the peels of garlic and onions. However, there is an upside here.

An unexpected benefit of low-fat cookery is ease of cleanup. Those juicy meats and buttery sauces that are so luscious and mouthwatering at the table are just plain old grease at dishwashing time. I remember grease! The stuff that used to precipitate a *crise de conscience*. Can I let it all go down the drain or must I find a suitable disposable container so it can harden in the refrigerator before going into the garbage?

I might have had a career in philosophy or politics had I not spent so many hours wondering, "Is that pot too slimy to put back on the shelf?" or "How did these plates get greasy on the *bottom*?"

It's true that these days I have to deal with food's tendency to stick to pots for lack of an oil-slicked surface, but hot liquid solves the problem readily. If you decide to go low-fat/high-veggie, you'll never have a truly disgusting cleanup chore again. Despite the vegetable debris, your stovetop, kitchen counters, walls, floors, cookbooks, etc., will be cleaner than you ever dreamed possible.

Shopping for Produce

Salad greens and the more perishable fresh vegetables should be purchased as close to the day you use them as possible. Whenever you can, buy your produce before you plan your menu so as to take advantage of whatever looks best at the market. The basic dishes we discuss in this book can be adapted to a variety of vegetables. Most fresh produce declines in flavor and nutritional value very quickly, so try to buy from local growers.

Produce from local growers, even at the height of its season, is rarely available at the supermarket. Farmers' markets have proliferated in recent years and there's almost certainly one in your area. But in winter, pickings can be slim. If the only available fresh peas come from a remote third-world country and look like they rolled most of the way to you, it's better, and almost certainly cheaper, to buy frozen ones.

Organic produce, grown without the use of pesticides or chemical fertilizers, is now widely available. Unfortunately it is usually expensive and, in many supermarkets and health food stores, it is often past its prime. I find that, when it can be purchased in good condition, organic produce is usually the best tasting, but I doubt that is connected with pesticide-free growing methods.

I suspect that organic farmers are growing old-fashioned strains of fruits and vegetables that are not practical for large commercial growers. Conversations I have had with organic farmers who vend produce at the New York City greenmarkets support this belief. Also, organic farmers, because they do not use chemical fertilizers, must pay considerable attention to soil quality. I come from a family of Minnesota farmers who firmly believed that the soil affected the taste of the produce. My great-aunt Dagmar used to smell and sometimes taste the soil in different parts of her garden before she decided what to plant where in any given year. So buy organic if you've got a good source and can afford it and, of course, if you think you can trust Aunt Dag.

GREENMARKET

I'M AN INVETERATE CITY DWELLER. It takes a lot of coaxing, and sometimes out-and-out bribery, to get me to go anywhere the subway doesn't. For the most part, trees, flowers, shrubs, and other green things I can't eat hold few charms for me.

But the green things I *can* eat are another story entirely. Asparagus, mesclun, and fresh herbs interest me inordinately. While I feel absolutely no spiritual connection to Mother Earth, I connect in the most tangible way with the edibles that spring from her soil. In fact, one of the reasons I like to go to the greenmarket is that it's the only reminder I get that fruits and vegetables don't grow at the A&P.

Although it's been almost three years since I moved back to New York from California, I still think the San Francisco greenmarket sets the standard. I do love New York's Union Square market, and I frequent the smaller markets near my apartment, but the variety and year-round availability of produce in California make it difficult for New York markets to measure up.

The San Francisco market is small. It has to be since it fits between the north- and south-bound lanes of the Embarcadero, the main thoroughfare that runs along the eastern edge of San Francisco. During the week, the space is a parking lot, but on Saturday morning it goes into its phone booth and emerges as Greenmarket—bringing genuine farmers and fresh produce to jaded city dwellers.

Actually, the city dwellers who frequent the greenmarket don't look so jaded. Birkenstocks and string bags predominate, as does a feeling of goodwill, even kinship. Everyone's relieved of some of their weekly stress by the mere sight of the dirt under the fingernails of the Mushroom Guy. These are people brought together by food and that's a tie that binds. That's why you never hear about greenmarket brawls. People don't even butt in line.

The greenmarket inspires. It's a weekly reminder of all the great things that can be encompassed by a healthful diet. Life doesn't, after all, end at cheesecake. The sight of so many vegetables makes me want to cook, to experiment, to eat. It even helps me fight my weekend inclination to sloth, which runs strong and deep.

The greenmarket is also a reminder that things grow in seasons. If you go in the spring, there's lots of asparagus. Summer is for peaches, plums, and nectarines. Fall is for apples. I'll never forget the time I went to the greenmarket in the dead season between summer and fall—too late for peaches, too early for pears. All they had were persimmons. Piles and piles of persimmons which, needless to say, were priced to move. True to form, I bought persimmons. I looked for interesting things to do with persimmons, but I wasn't very successful. Persimmons are now on the (very short) list of produce I don't really like. In fact, the only other item on that list that springs to mind is jícama. If you're not familiar with jícama, just gnaw on your Styrofoam coffee cup and you'll get the general idea. Fortunately, I've never seen jícama at the greenmarket.

What have I seen? The San Francisco market has a tremendous variety of stuff. There's produce, but there's also bread from Acme (a great local bakery), fresh fish and meat from local providers, eggs, pasta, and the Best Yogurt in the World (they don't call it that—that's my name for it). The Best Yogurt in the World is from Redwood Hill Farm, in Sebastopol, California, and it's made from goat's milk. It has the same kind of tang you get in goat cheese (of which they also make several varieties). But their coup de grâce is the vanilla, which is flavored by vanilla (obviously) and just a little bit of maple syrup. It's, well, the Best Yogurt in the World. (To my delight, this yogurt is now available at Fairway, right around the corner from me on the Upper West Side.)

The aforementioned Mushroom Guy was also one of my regular stops. He's usually got a couple of grades of shiitakes, oyster mushrooms, portobellos, the regular white kind, and a few other goodies.

There are several dried-fruit vendors that sell a variety of dried figs, apples, pears, apricots, and whatever else is in season. One of the local farms also has a kind of apple that I've never found anywhere else. They're dehydrated. They look like regular run-of-the mill dried apples, but they're crunchy. Not poker-chip crunchy like those awful dried banana chips that masquerade as healthful food, but crunchy almost like a corn chip. They're flavored with cinnamon and extremely addictive. You're liable to eat the whole bag in one sitting, which isn't a bad thing, since they're very sensitive to humidity and lose their crunch quickly.

The San Francisco market almost always has a good selection of vegetables and fruits in season from many different local farms. The farms represented (and their offerings) vary from week to week. But even if you live in a less produce-friendly region, chances are there's a farmers' market near you. Once you find it, I'm willing to bet you'll visit it regularly. Go for the produce. Go for the goodwill. And, whatever you do, don't butt in line.

Cooking Vegetables: Sauté, Steam, Bake

DARE WE CALL IT SAUTÉING?

"Ask the waiter if your vegetables can be sautéed in wine," suggests Dean Ornish in his discussion of healthful eating in restaurants. Well, Ornish is a doctor and can presumably stitch up the waiter after the chef assaults him with a cleaver. The rest of us should probably not ask that question. While it's fine to request alternative preparations, we should watch our terminology. Most traditionally trained chefs will tell you—usually in rather rude terms—that vegetables can no more be sautéed in wine than they can be deep-fried in water.

The chemistry involved in cooking food in hot butter or oil is entirely different from cooking it in liquid. We won't get technical. (Tamar will address this issue in somewhat more detail in her discussion of sauces, Chapter 6.) Just think about the difference between boiled potatoes and french fries and you'll see what I mean. Foods can be steamed or boiled in liquid. They can't be sautéed or fried. What I try to do, and want to teach you how to do, in this chapter is to mimic the process of sautéing using as little oil as possible. If you want to use more, you can get good results with less skill. If, like Ornish, you insist on using none, you can't even come close.

The basic method outlined below can be used for any quick-cooking vegetable or combination. What you're doing is starting with a small amount of oil—just enough to coat and soften the first ingredients. Then, instead of adding more oil as your vegetables cook, as you would have done in the days prior to nutritional enlightenment, you add small amounts of liquid, stirring to moisten the vegetables and scraping to deglaze the pan. Your additions of liquid should be poured directly onto the hottest part of the pan. If the liquid doesn't immediately start to bubble, you've either added too much or your pan isn't hot enough. (Roasted or steamed vegetables can be reheated using the same technique.)

I've made the instructions below fairly detailed, not because anything complicated is going on, but because I have found it somewhat difficult to organize this process in my minuscule kitchen. The recipe is my description of how I do it. I'm trying to give you the benefit of my experience, not all of which has been pleasurable, but I don't mean to make this sound like rocket science. All you're really doing is frying up a bunch of stuff using hardly any oil.

STIR-FRY
This, on a bed of rice or pasta, can be your whole dinner.
Makes 2 to 4 servings

½ pound mixed greens (2 or more of the following—or any others that turn up in your market or your yard: spinach, kale, mustard greens, turnip greens, chard, beet greens, dandelion, purslane)

½ pound broccoli

3 to 6 garlic cloves

1 large chunk fresh ginger to taste

1 bunch scallions or 2 onions

3 carrots

1 red, yellow, or green bell pepper

1 pound mushrooms

½ cup bean sprouts

1 cup sugar snap, snow, or shelled fresh (or frozen) peas

1 large bunch cilantro or small bunch Italian parsley

2 teaspoons sesame, canola, or mild-tasting olive oil, or a combination

¼ to ½ cup dry white wine

1 to 2 tablespoons fresh oregano leaves, or 1 teaspoon dried

Chinese hot pepper oil, minced hot peppers such as jalapeños, or red pepper flakes to taste

1 small can water chestnuts, drained (optional; omit if Tamar is coming to dinner)

1 tablespoon reduced-sodium soy sauce (optional)
1 tablespoon rice or white wine vinegar, or more to taste
Salt to taste

STAGE 1

This can be done several hours, or even a whole day, in advance.

1. Wash the greens well and cut the large leaves to bite size, always re-membering they'll take up less room in your mouth when they're cooked. Any stems that seem edible but too fibrous to be cooked by brief steaming can be sliced in the food processor with the broccoli stalks (see Notes). Set the greens aside to dry.
2. Remove the stalks from the broccoli (you'll slice them with the veg-gies in the next step) and discard the very fibrous portions. Separate the florets into more or less bite-size pieces.
3. Prepare the vegetables to be sliced in the food processor as follows: Peel the garlic, and the ginger if you want. Strip the outer leaves from the scallions. Scrape the carrots if desired. Cut the pepper into large chunks. Immerse the mushrooms in water briefly or clean them with a brush or damp paper towel. Trim and discard any inedible or dubi-ous-looking portions of everything. Wash the bean sprouts and peas if necessary. You may want to remove stem ends from pea pods. Wash the cilantro or parsley and set aside to dry.

STAGE 2

When you are ready to cook (see Notes).

1. Insert the slicing blade into your food processor.
2. Heat a large wok over medium heat and add the oil. Be careful not to overheat, especially if you're using sesame oil, which burns easily. This stir-fry will not cook as quickly as a traditional oily one.
3. While the oil heats, slice the garlic and scallions or onion in the processor. Add them to the wok and cook, stirring frequently, until they are soft and have released their moisture. (This process is aptly known as sweating.) When they stick, which they will, add a little wine and stir to loosen. Add the oregano and hot pepper oil (or what-ever source of heat you're using).
4. Slice and add to the wok the carrots, broccoli stalks, bell pepper, gin-ger, mushrooms, and water chestnuts more or less in that order. You'll probably have to put in the mushrooms a few at a time and wait for each addition to cook down before adding more. Increase the heat slightly and cook, stirring often and moistening with a little wine if

necessary, for about 5 minutes or until the vegetables are thoroughly cooked.

5. Push the contents of the wok up the sides, leaving the middle, the hottest part, fairly empty and add the broccoli florets, bean sprouts, and peas. (Should you want to prepare a stir-fry containing a little meat or chicken, cut it into strips and add it at this point. Shellfish like shrimp or scallops is another option.) Cook 2 to 3 minutes until the broccoli is bright green. Stir all ingredients together. If at any point more than about a tablespoon of liquid accumulates at the bottom of the wok, pour or spoon it off.

6. Steal an odd moment from stirring to switch your processor to its chopping blade (no need to wash the work bowl) and chop the cilantro fairly fine.

7. Add the greens, the vinegar, the soy sauce, and the salt (if using), and incorporate them into the stir-fry as you would toss a salad. As soon as the greens begin to wilt, remove the wok from the heat and add the cilantro, continuing with the tossing motion. Taste for seasoning.

8. Serve immediately over brown rice or soba noodles.

N O T E S : If you prefer, cut up everything before you start to cook. The space constraints of my kitchen make it more efficient for me to work as I describe.

If your greens are rather mature or strong-tasting—or if your wok is overcrowded—you may want to steam them briefly before adding them to the stir-fry. Just wash them, chop them, put them in a covered pot, and let them cook about 3 minutes in the water clinging to them. Save any liquid they exude for soup.

This recipe is susceptible to any number of variations. Of course, any vegetable that cooks fairly quickly is fair game. Also, there is no law restricting this technique to the flavorings we associate with Chinese food. If you use olive oil, tomatoes, and (preferably preroasted or grilled) eggplant and omit things like ginger, bean sprouts, and vinegar, you can use your wok to create an excellent sauce for pasta. An Indian stir-fry can be seasoned with cumin, coriander, and turmeric, and tastes good served over a combination of basmati rice and lentils.

A wok is a virtual necessity in a low-fat kitchen. (Get the largest one your kitchen can accommodate. A wok can't be too big.) Its shape enables you to use a small amount of oil and sauté your ingredients one after another, pushing the ones that have finished cooking up the sides where they will not burn or overcook. All the sautéing takes place in the small hot spot in the bottom of the wok. No one tasting this stir-fry will believe that it contains only 2 teaspoons of oil. I also own a stir-fry pan that is actually a modified wok with a nonstick surface. It is much smaller than my wok and has a flat enough bottom so that it doesn't require a ring to support it on my stove burner. It is extremely convenient for preparing vegetable side dishes, or even stir-frys that don't contain any very bulky vegetables.

200 calories, 3 grams fat, 1 gram saturated fat per serving of 4

STEAMED VEGETABLES

You probably don't need this section unless you either haven't been cooking vegetables at all or have been boiling them. Next time you consider immersing a vegetable in water: think. There may be a better way.

When you're cooking almost any vegetable that's not a root, steaming is the method you're most likely to choose. It requires no fat, doesn't make a mess, preserves vital nutrients, and takes very little effort. You need only pay enough attention to make sure your veggie doesn't overcook.

Vegetables can be steamed with or without a steamer. All you really need is a pot with a tight cover. Many vegetables contain enough water, in combination with the washing water that clings to them, to steam in their own juices. However, a vegetable steamer is an extremely handy gadget; it contributes to even cooking and makes it easy to monitor the process. It's merely a collapsible basket on legs that fits into any pot, and it's available cheaply anywhere housewares are sold.

Unless, like asparagus spears, they have a natural structure you want to preserve, vegetables should be cut bite size before steaming. If you're using a steamer, put an inch or two of water in the bottom of a saucepan—if possible one large enough so that the steamer basket can open to accommodate all your vegetables in a fairly thin layer.

Put the vegetables in the steamer over the water, cover the pot, and bring to a boil over medium heat. (Steam will escape and the pot lid will rattle.) Then reduce the heat to keep the water simmering. Most vegetables will be fully cooked in about 5 minutes from this point. I find that my nose is a reliable guide to when a steamed vegetable is done, but it takes a bit of practice to develop a reliable olfactory sense. Meanwhile, just raise the lid periodically and check.

To steam without benefit of a steamer, put the vegetables in a heavy pot with a close-fitting lid. You may want to add an ounce or so of water if they seem fairly dry. Place the pot over low heat and keep your ears and nose alert. Loud sizzling is undesirable—it means the liquid is cooking away to nothing and your dinner is about to be sacrificed to the fire gods. Steaming *sans* steamer takes a bit longer but gives you a lot more room in the pot. It's especially good for cooking greens.

YOUR OVEN AND YOU

Your Oven: Steambath or Sauna? I'd always referred to the clay-pot vegetables described on page 46 as "roasted" until it was called to my attention that to label a procedure that involves a significant amount of liquid "roasting" is equivalent to calling foods cooked in wine "sautéed," a locution I got pretty snide about a few pages back.

Roasting is a dry heat technique. When you add liquid your food is being baked or oven-steamed. In defense of my error, however, I will point out that home cooks were playing fast and loose with the term "roasting" long before most of them knew that "sautéing" was even a word.

When Chuck and I had been married only a week or two, I decided to celebrate the move into our first apartment by making a roast beef. I was aware that my new husband wasn't a fan of rare meat, but I certainly wasn't going to cook the nice ribeye, which had cost a small fortune at the kosher butcher shop, until it was gray and petrified. And Chuck had told me he liked roast beef, so I assumed that he found pink in the middle acceptable. He could eat the outside pieces. As soon as he cut into it, though, we both knew he wasn't going to eat it. It just didn't look like food to him.

"If your mother's roast beef is cooked all the way through," I asked with some acerbity, after we'd adjourned to the pizza parlor, "how does she keep it from drying out?"

"How do I know? Ask her."

I asked her. She sent me a recipe for pot roast.

I was outraged. Everything I knew about cooking I had learned from books. My skills were limited, my repertoire was small, but my grasp of cooking terms was excellent. "Just because," I explained to Chuck, "your mother wrote 'Roast Beef' at the top of this recipe, doesn't mean that's what it is."

That was back in 1960. Even then my mother-in-law was not alone. "Roasting" was a term that got no respect. A couple of years later I noticed a recipe on my box of aluminum foil for "roast" turkey. The procedure was to enclose the turkey in an airtight foil wrap for nearly the whole cooking time—opening it for browning during the last half hour. I shook my head in disbelief. Then a friend told me she had tried it and noticed very little difference from the conventional method. I decided she could no longer be viewed as a serious eater. The next year, however, I found myself involved in a project that would take me out of the house during the crucial turkey-basting hours. So I bought a box of heavy-duty foil, wrapped up the bird, and left it to its own devices in the oven. The only serious deficiency I detected was the lack of good drippings for gravy. How could this be?

The answer, I decided, lies in the nature of a standard home oven. When you cook a large, moist object like a turkey in a small, enclosed space, you raise the humidity too much to achieve true roasting. So added liquids, covered "roasting" pans, and even tight foil wraps don't make nearly as much difference to the results as you might think. It's no wonder home cooks have given up making a distinction between wet and dry oven cookery. I suppose the only truly roasted turkey I can claim responsibility for is the one I once roasted on a spit. (It tasted very good, but it was a rather messy, labor-intensive procedure. I can only recommend it to possessors of very high quality equipment.)

This incapacity of your oven to provide dry heat holds true for any food that contains significant moisture, unless you're making an extremely small portion. Root vegetables, which give up their moisture slowly, do develop a roasted flavor in the oven. Try the Root Roast on page 185, to which I add only enough stock to prevent serious sticking. If you want to use an extra tablespoon or two of olive oil, even that much liquid shouldn't be necessary.

The recipe on page 46, however, designed to be baked in either a clay pot or covered pan, does not (pace my mother-in-law and the manufacturer of my clay pot) produce roasted vegetables. Whatever you call them, though, they taste pretty good.

The Clay Pot. When it's winter in New York, except for a few rather pitiful specimens that come from far, far away, fresh vegetables are scarce. 'Tis the season of the root—the potato, the sweet potato, the carrot, the onion, the turnip. And don't forget the tasteless, indestructible squashes. My favorite technique for dealing with winter vegetables is to cook a lot of them together in my clay pot.

Clay-pot veggies can be recycled as many times as the political life of Richard Nixon, with generally better results. Of course, vegetables can be baked without a clay pot, but to my mind, nothing brings out the flavor of roots like the Römertopf, and the vegetable broth it produces surpasses all others.

First you need a clay pot. I've often wished for an enormous clay pot, one that would hold a turkey and several pounds of veggies, but I've always suspected it would be too heavy to lift and, due to uneven distribution of stress when it was lifted, rather fragile. Also there is the problem of my tiny oven. But in Elizabeth David's *French Provincial Cooking* I found the pot I want. It is designed for cooking *tripe à la mode de Caen* and is called, appropriately enough, a *tripière*. It is earthenware and looks rather like a flattened-out version of my Römertopf. According to Elizabeth, it was traditionally carried to the local bakery to be cooked in the oven after the bread had been taken out. Escoffier recommends putting into the *tripière*—along with the four feet and most of the stomach of an ox—4 pounds of onions, 3 pounds of carrots, 2 pounds of leeks, 2 quarts of cider, and a half-pint of brandy. So we're talking a *big* pot here. I'm sure such pots are no longer to be found, even in Normandy. Nor do I know where I would keep such a monster and, as I've already admitted, it wouldn't fit in my oven. (But I want one anyway.)

I recommend, however, not a *tripière,* but an ordinary Römertopf (Roman pot), a clay pot of German manufacture that is widely available in this country. If you can't find one where you live, order one from Williams-Sonoma or the Chef's Catalog (page 300). Even if you're a single person, get a large Römertopf—the 4-quart size. If it's big enough to roast a whole week's worth of vegetables, all the better. (I suppose if you're very little and weak you might consider a smaller one. The 4-quart job is fairly heavy when it's full.)

A clay pot must be treated with some care. Always soak it for at least 15 minutes before using it and never put it into a preheated oven no matter what the recipe says. Deborah Madison has at least one recipe that tells you to do this, so I assume she must do it herself, but I maintain she'll be sorry some day. Also exercise some care when you remove it from the oven. It's not a good idea to put it (or its lid) down on a cold metal surface while it's hot. I have exercised these precautions and have had my large Römertopf for more than twenty years, but I know two people who have been less careful and have had theirs crack in the oven.

CLAY POT VEGETABLES
Makes 6 to 8 servings

Suggested vegetables: In approximate order of importance.

- Potatoes, whole or halved
- Carrots, cut into thirds
- 1 or 2 onions, whole or halved
- 1 or 2 whole heads of garlic (remove some of the papery outer coating, but don't separate the cloves)
- Sweet potatoes, whole or halved
- Mushrooms, whole (bury these under other veggies, or they'll shrivel a little)

- Fennel bulb, well trimmed
- Young, small turnips, whole
- Parsnips, whole but with dirty-looking parts scraped away
- Winter squash, quartered and seeds removed

All vegetables should be washed, but there is no need to peel anything.

Hint on proportions: I like to use enough potatoes to fill about a third of the pot, enough carrots and sweet potatoes to fill another third, and then I do what I want with the final third.

Suggested liquids: Use no more than 1 or 2 cups of liquid, enough to leave a little broth, but not so much as to create a stew.

- Chicken stock
- Soaking liquid from dried mushrooms
- Beer
- Vegetable stock
- Leftover cooking liquid from grains, dried beans, or vegetables

1. Fill the presoaked clay pot with the vegetables, pour in the liquid, cover the pot, and place it in a cold oven. Set the oven at 400°F and bake for about 1¼ hours.
2. Serve the vegetables directly from the pot with whole-grain bread and a green salad. I don't add much in the way of flavor enhancers to the pot. I like the vegetables to be adaptable to whatever mode of preparation I choose when I recycle them. If, like me, you choose a plain preparation, serve it with plenty of condiments. Pommery mustard, chutney, and salsa are all good. But it's really the discrete tastes of the various vegetables that provide the main enjoyments of this dish. Of course, the garlic helps a lot. One of the great pleasures of this meal is to play with the garlic. Eaters can extrude the cloves onto the bread and vegetables. A bean salad complements this meal nicely. So does a fine Cabernet.

No Clay Pot? If you don't own a clay pot, the same mix of vegetables and liquid can be placed in a large, shallow pan, more or less in a single layer. Cook, covered, at 350°F for about 30 minutes, using only about ½ cup of liquid. Then uncover and continue to bake, turning and basting the vegetables occasionally.

For a truly roasted veggie, try an eggplant. Whole eggplants can be roasted at 350°F. Pierce them with a fork in several places and roast them until they are quite soft—usually 45 minutes or so. They can then be turned into a tasty purée with seasonings of your choice or sliced and re-heated. The same technique will also produce a roasted zucchini or sum-mer squash in a shorter time—15 to 25 minutes, depending on size. They, as well as the roasted eggplant, can be used in the Ratatouille In-catenata (page 158) or the Roasted Eggplant Dip below. None of these high-moisture vegetables cooks well in the clay pot.

ROASTED EGGPLANT DIP OR SPREAD
Serves 4 as an appetizer

1 large eggplant, roasted as above, peel removed
1 chunk peeled fresh ginger (about the size of a baby's thumb—
　　or your thumb if you really like ginger)
1 clove raw garlic, or 3 to 4 cloves roasted
1 small bunch fresh cilantro, washed, large stems removed
¼ teaspoon red pepper flakes (optional)
1 tablespoon vinegar
Salt to taste

1. Purée all ingredients in a blender or food processor. This dip is best served at room temperature.

40 calories, 0 grams fat, 0 grams saturated fat per serving

The Leafy Greens Dichotomy

Dark leafy greens are just about the most nutritious foods, calorie for calo-rie, you'll ever eat, and more and more varieties keep turning up at the mar-ket. This can get confusing, especially since some people seem to think each variety requires its own particular mode of preparation. For example, recently the words "Asian greens" caught my eye in an article title. It turned out the author meant things like bok choy, mustard greens, and mizuna, but her use of the term led me to consider my own greens categories. Asian-schmasian! By me there are two kind of greens—little and big.

Little greens are easy. The only problem is getting them. Mostly you put them in your salad (see The One and Only Green Salad, page 51), but you can also throw some into your soup or stir-fry at the very end. They are one of the great pleasures of spring. I tend to like fairly strong-flavored greens. I look for mesclun mixtures that are heavy on baby mus-tard greens, watercress, and arugula.

Actually, "mesclun mixtures" is a redundancy. "Mesclun" is a variant of "maslin," an old word that refers to mixtures of all kinds and of which there once were countless dialectic variations. Words like "mash" and "mess" are among its offspring, but the *Oxford English Dictionary* expresses doubt about whether it is derived from the same Latin root as "miscellany." I haven't been able to discover who decided to use the word "mesclun" to mean a mixture of baby lettuces and herbs, but that now seems to be the universal term.

Only in the last few years have I been able to say something like, "I look for mesclun mixtures that . . ." In New York, mesclun used to be available only in summer at the farmers' markets. Gradually it crept into specialty food stores and finally into supermarkets. At first the quality of store-bought mesclun was abysmal, but now I can find decent versions at several stores in my neighborhood. They seem to be available all year, although in both the coldest and hottest weather their quality tends to suffer.

Then there are the big greens, of which I must acknowledge, there really are two categories: the raw and the cooked. The raw are the big lettuces: heads of leaf lettuce and romaine. You can cook these lettuces too. The big outside leaves are fine in the soup pot or added to a stir-fry. Spinach is another green that works well both in salad and as a cooked vegetable. Just don't try cooking lettuces like Boston or Bibb or (especially) iceberg. You'll be left with a barely discernible scrap of wilted greenery.

When I say big greens, however, I'm really thinking about the daunting ones: those enormous bunches of kale and collards and mustard greens that we all know are wondrously nutritious but so few of us want to cook and eat. It's easy to tell what's a truly BIG GREEN. You taste it raw and find it inedible. Making it fit to eat is no easy matter, especially now that you've given up cooking with the fatty substances that pervade Southern-style greens—or the creamed greens that were a staple of my childhood. I once ate so much creamed spinach at Thanksgiving dinner that I had no room for pumpkin pie, much to the amusement of all my relatives. It was an intelligent choice. My Aunt Marie's creamed spinach was vastly superior to her pumpkin pie. (Fortunately I was old enough at the time to know I had to endure my family's ridicule without blurting out tactless comparisons.)

If you like creamed greens, are still eating a little butter, and make a good traditional white sauce, try substituting evaporated skim milk for the cream and cutting back on the butter. The assertiveness of the greens masks the slightly cooked taste that makes evaporated skim milk less than ideal for sauces. Tamar and I have found that, by adding the flour very gradually, you can make an acceptable white sauce with about one part butter to two parts flour, but no less. (One-to-one is the traditional way—often with a little extra butter swirled in at the finish.)

But big greens need not be creamed. Once you get comfortable with big greens, you'll find you can use them in lots of places where you're used to using less intimidating vegetables like green beans, asparagus, and peppers. They're good additions to a stir-fry (bok choy is particularly good, and seems to need less oil than most other greens), which can be given an Asian flavor with ginger and coriander, or five-spice powder, or fermented black beans. If you serve it with rice noodles or bean threads (a.k.a. glass noodles), it's almost authentic.

There are other uses for greens further down the Asian continent— greens curry well. Cook up some greens and the legume of your choice (chickpeas and lentils are my favorites), and then combine them in a large skillet with curry seasonings. You can serve it as a side dish, or combine it with a grain (rice or barley, perhaps) and make it a main dish.

Assertive greens, like chard, mustard greens, and broccoli rabe also combine well with pasta. Not only do the flavors work well, the shapes do too. The greens tend to get tangled up in the pasta, making it that much easier to eat.

The following Nippy Greens recipe may help you produce some low-fat meals featuring Dreaded Big Greens. Serve your greens combined with rather smooth bland foods like beans, potatoes, and pasta to mellow the taste and provide textural contrast. You'll note that this recipe calls for some olive oil. Less assiduous fat cutters can increase the amount to good effect. If you must prepare absolutely oil-free dishes in the style of Ornish or Pritikin, I suggest you stick to small (or smallish) greens, mostly raw. In the spring and fall when fresh spinach is really good, you might enjoy a fat-free version of the Nippy Greens. But the kitchen that is totally free of oil should also be free of *really big greens*. If you buy a bunch or two, you'll probably find them going yellow in your refrigerator and taking up an inordinate amount of space while they're doing it.

Even those of you who feel free to use some olive oil or (gasp!) butter should introduce big greens to your cooking repertoire gradually. Get too enthusiastic and your refrigerator can fill up with rotting, guilt-inducing produce. Think about your eating public and you may decide they're not ready for serious cooked greens. In that case, don't hesitate to leave the shrubbery in the market. Greens are good for you. Guilt is not.

NIPPY GREENS
This recipe generally serves 4 to 6 people, or 2 to 3 like me. I like it best as a pasta topping, with a few white beans or chickpeas thrown in.

2 pounds mixed greens (spinach, Swiss chard, mustard greens, collards, whatever), large stems removed

2 teaspoons olive oil

2 to 4 garlic cloves, minced

¼ cup chopped feathery fennel tops (that's the greens on the bulb
that may be called anise in your market—an all-around
useful veggie) or chopped cilantro leaves

¼ to ½ teaspoon red pepper flakes (or whatever other source of
heat you favor)

Salt and freshly ground black pepper to taste

2 tablespoons lemon juice

1. Thoroughly wash the greens to remove any sand. (I'm afraid total immersion is required. Just rinsing in a colander will not do.) Cut them into approximately 3-inch pieces but don't dry them.
2. Heat the oil briefly in a pot large enough to hold the greens. (If you have no such pot, you can wilt half of them, then add the rest. They shrink instantly.) Sauté the garlic in the oil just until it becomes fragrant, then add the greens. Cover the pot and cook over medium heat until the greens wilt, no more than a minute or two.
3. Stir in the chopped fennel tops or cilantro, pepper flakes, and salt and black pepper. Cook the mixture, stirring, for about 4 minutes.
4. Remove from the heat and toss the greens with the lemon juice.
5. To serve as an independent vegetable, rather than as an ingredient in a pasta dish, before you add the lemon juice, place the greens in a colander and press out some of the liquid. (Once this is done, they will keep well for a few days in the refrigerator and can be recycled in a number of ways, including as a topping for pizza.)

60 calories, 2 grams fat, 0 grams saturated fat per side-dish serving of 6

THE ONE AND ONLY GREEN SALAD

Let me tell you about the salad of my dreams, my heart's desire. First of all, it consists of a variety of perfectly fresh young greens. My favorites are arugula, mustard greens, purslane, watercress, and tiny delicate lettuces—no spongy old ones. Some young herbs should be included—I especially like chervil. Some edible flowers—like nasturtiums—make a nice color contrast.

All the greens should be thoroughly washed and scrupulously dried. They should not be cut up. If a leaf is larger than bite size, it doesn't belong in my dream salad. The ingredients should be placed in a bowl that is large enough for effective tossing. Then they should be dressed with a tablespoon of vinaigrette for every two cups of salad. A little less is all right, but *no more.*

To my mind the best—and certainly the simplest—vinaigrette is made as follows: Mince or press one clove of garlic into the large spoon with which you will toss and serve your salad. Immediately pour a tablespoon of the best and freshest extra-virgin olive oil you can get into the spoon. Let it rest at least five minutes, then toss the garlic-infused oil with the salad. Add a tablespoon of fine red wine vinegar, sprinkle with freshly ground pepper, and toss again. That's enough dressing for four cups of my perfect salad—a reasonable serving for two.

There are many traditionalists who would insist that vinaigrette should be made with a much higher proportion of oil to vinegar. But I must tell you that a number of these purists have taken second and third helpings of salad at my table. So have lots of people who habitually eat iceberg lettuce drowned in bottled "lite" dressing. Now let's look at the acceptable modifications to the ideal salad and why we make them.

1. PUTTING IN OTHER STUFF.

There are a lot of bad greens in the world. Some of them started out being good, but good young greens are highly perishable. So if you live anywhere where your greens must be trucked in during the winter, the only options your market may offer may be one of the virtually indestructible lettuce varieties such as romaine or (shudder) iceberg. The only excuse I can think of for serving iceberg lettuce is the presence of children in your household. ("There's *green* lettuce in this salad," Jake used to say reproachfully.) One of the several advantages of having your children grow up and move out is that you never have to eat iceberg lettuce again.

In New York City in winter I use a lot of chicory, escarole, and spinach. Usually they are so mature that they are better cooked than raw, but I can often find some young, tender parts that are fine in salad. And sometimes the mesclun from California is all right. But lots of days I must depend on romaine, Boston, and Bibb lettuces of dubious quality. Hot weather is also the enemy of tender young greens. I can really only produce my ideal, totally green salad in the spring and fall. The rest of the time I have to put in other stuff.

In summer it's no problem to augment the greens with other veggies. Tomatoes, cucumbers, sweet peppers in all colors, radishes, and scallions are all available in profusion. It's tougher in winter. I use a lot of raw mushrooms, dried tomatoes (we get ours from Just Tomatoes, see page 302), bean sprouts, chickpeas, and thinly sliced carrots, as well as cucumbers, radishes, and scallions from faraway places. Not everyone considers it a hardship to have to put things that aren't leafy and green into their salads. I know I'd have to make these mixed salads occasionally to keep Chuck happy even if I lived in San Francisco, where I could get proper greens year-round. After a week or so of eating The One and Only Green Salad, he is prone to talk a lot about the low energy levels of animals that subsist on leaves. "You know why the sloth is called a sloth," he says, and I know it must be time to put some other stuff in the salad.

2. CUTTING DOWN ON THE OIL.

You will note that when you eat two cups of my ideal salad you will take in approximately 60 fat calories. If you're eating 2,000 calories a day that's 3 percent of the total—not insignificant if you're trying to follow, for example, the Ornish diet. You can modify this salad. Try using only one tablespoon of dressing for every four cups of salad and alter the proportions—using only one teaspoon of oil and two teaspoons of vinegar.

That little bit of oil is the difference between eating real salad and eating wet raw veggies. It coats the leaves just enough so that the flavors of the vinegar and garlic and pepper cling to them. There are acceptable vinaigrette variants: adding some herbs chopped in the food processor along with a little Dijon or Pommery mustard works well and is one way to produce a slightly moister salad. A small amount of nonfat yogurt is a good addition, especially for those who like their salad fairly heavily dressed, as it will promote a thorough coating of the leaves without adding either a lot of oil or a mouth-puckering amount of vinegar.

A little of a dried herb can marinate in the oil on the spoon along with or in place of the garlic. Balsamic vinegar makes a slightly mellower salad than the red wine variety; lemon juice makes for a sharper taste. If you really find the flavor too strong or the salad too dry, add part of a puréed tomato, or a few drops of wine, or a teaspoon of tomato juice, or even bean broth. But be careful. Salad can go from too dry to too wet very quickly. You didn't spend all that time drying your salad greens just so you could drown them.

WHEN IS A SALAD NOT A SALAD?

(WARNING: This is a rant. Skip to the end of the chapter if you want to.)

Where is it written that the correct amount of dressing for two cups of salad is an entire ounce—two tablespoons? The answer: All over, that's where. But don't believe it. As we just discussed, *one* tablespoon for *four* cups of salad gives a presentable result. No one should use more than two.

No good restaurant or self-respecting home cook will ever, ever bring to the table a pint of salad drowned in an ounce of dressing. We've all been served salad like that. You pick the poor wilted greens out of the puddle in the bottom of the bowl. The message is loud and clear: Someone in the kitchen does not care. So why do we read recipe after recipe for drowned salad? There must be people out there spooning it up. My theory is that the pint-of-salad to ounce-of-dressing ratio originated with the manufacturers of bottled dressings. The more of their product you use, the happier they are. Also, I suspect the ratio was conceived with thick dressings such as mayonnaise and Russian dressing in mind. Forget whether or not such dressings have fat, calories, cholesterol—whatever. However they may affect your health, they can only ruin your salad. Some sort of case can be made for putting them on tuna fish or potatoes, but they're an abomination on greens.

I haven't shamed you out of your craving for mayonnaise? Well, at least don't eat the reduced-fat or nonfat commercial varieties or the tofu-based dressings from the health food cookbooks. Try yogurt cheese (page 271) combined with a little olive oil.

If you insist on a totally oil-free salad, just sprinkle it with a little balsamic vinegar or lemon juice and add some freshly ground pepper. It lacks something, but it can still pass for a salad. The something that it lacks is oil. If I had to give up all oil, what I would miss the most is the little in our salad. But nothing will make me resort to bottled dressings.

All commercial salad dressings taste bad, but at least the traditional ones contain the traditional ingredients—oil and vinegar. The "lite" dressings consist mainly of water and vegetable gums—usually augmented with five or ten unpronounceable chemicals. When you buy them you throw away your money, and when you eat them you debase your palate. Just say no.

The difference in kitchen work between serving bottled dressing and a real vinaigrette is the difference between opening one bottle or two. (That is if you omit the garlic, an optional ingredient in everyone's kitchen but mine.) The difference in taste is incalculable. Perhaps you've never made—perhaps never even eaten—a real salad. Now is a good time to start.

AND MUCH, MUCH MORE . . .

I've only scratched the surface of basic low-fat vegetable preparation in this chapter. We'll keep coming back to this exciting subject.

Exciting. Tamar recently purchased a spaghetti squash. It had one of those helpful tags on it. You know, the ones that say SPAGHETTI SQUASH in big letters—just in case you thought you were buying a standing rib roast. Then they go on to tell you the vegetable's history and how to cook it. "This exciting squash . . ." the blurb begins. Hey, I really like vegetables. God knows I eat plenty of them. But if you think spaghetti squash is exciting, you need to get a life.

Stock Answers

Taking Stock

TRADITIONAL **FRENCH FOOD WRITERS** refer to stocks as *fonds de cuisine.* Perhaps foreign words come with exotic shades of meaning, or maybe I'm just a closet Francophile, but *fond* strikes me as somehow deeper than "base" or "foundation." To be *au fond* is to be really, really down at the bottom of something. In cooking, the *fond* is the flavor that underlies all the others. It's the quality that makes you want to keep eating and eating, all the time asking, "What *is* that?"

It happened to me the first time when I was nine and my mother took me to an Italian restaurant. The restaurant was in St. Paul, Minnesota. The year was 1948. I doubt that the sauce on my spaghetti could have been truly remarkable, but it was the first time I was aware of a background flavor: something that lingered in my mouth, growing stronger as the foreground tastes of tomato and meat receded. "Why," I asked my mother, "is this so good?"

I picked through the remains of the sauce on my plate, and my mother was able to help me identify garlic as the major source of my gustatory delight. I also picked out some tiny tasty things that I now know were probably oregano leaves. But I think there was more to it than that. Someone in the kitchen was using odds and ends of meat and chicken to create stock that made that sauce rich in flavor beyond anything my nine-year-old self had dreamed of.

Envy is not one of the Seven Deadly Sins that I really have to watch out for. (Sloth and Gluttony: those are my guys.) However, I do sometimes envy people who cook in restaurants. I covet the huge counters, the wonderful stoves, the slaves (oops, I mean sous chefs) on whom to palm off dreaded veggie prep. But most of all I envy the unlimited access to meat scraps and bones. Just imagine if every time you cooked a pot of rice or barley, every time you wanted to deglaze a pan, every time you needed to thin a sauce or recycle your leftovers into soup, you had all the rich, full-bodied stock you could possibly want.

My son Jake and I occasionally have lunch at a local Dominican restaurant. We always eat the same thing: chicken with black beans and yellow rice. It's always delicious, not because it contains any mysterious gourmet ingredients, but because so much chicken gets cooked there. Everything tastes of rich chicken stock. Whoever's cooking knows how to make the most of her ingredients. But there are a couple of reasons why the opportunistic stocks that have always been a feature of good little neighborhood restaurants may be an endangered species.

In the first place, many foods, from chicken cordon bleu to broccoli, are now available frozen from purveyors that specialize in servicing restaurants. These foods cost restaurateurs more than the raw materials needed to cook from scratch, but they save on labor and deliver consistent quality. Portion control is easy and waste is virtually eliminated. Everyone has eaten in at least one restaurant where nearly all the food goes from the freezer to the microwave. Hardly anyone wants to eat there again. There's nothing really wrong with most of the food. It's just insipid. It satisfies your hunger but not your appetite. Part of the problem, I believe, is the lack of odor. There are no good food smells coming from either the kitchen or your plate. Foods from Ye Olde Restaurante Supplie are like roses from the hothouse—almost no aroma. Naturally, establishments that serve such food have no stockpot simmering on the back of the stove. For all I know, they may not *have* a stove.

The second reason for the decline of the restaurant stockpot is simply that people are eating less meat than they once did. When I look in the open kitchen door of my favorite Italian place in Miami Beach, I can see a row of large cans of chicken stock. Lots of unopened cans—also lots of emptied ones pressed into use to hold utensils. This is a busy kitchen. There's a huge range with all the burners going. Pots and pans, bowls and knives, are all in heavy use. Sous chefs are peeling vegetables. Wonderful smells are being generated. We're not talking microwave here. My first sight of the row of cans caused a frisson of dismay, but on reflection I understood. There are a few meat and chicken dishes on the menu. You can order a veal cutlet or a chicken breast. You can get meat sauce on your pasta or some meatballs to accompany it. But not only do these dishes provide very little material for stock, few people ever seem to eat them. When I look around at adjoining tables I see seafood linguine, *agnolotti pomodoro,* spaghetti *naturale,* penne with vodka and cream sauce, and a sea bass fillet. And these things are not being eaten, I might point out, by yuppie New Yorkers. Many of these Floridians are Cubans, folks among whom meat eating is reputedly alive and well. This is the sort of restaurant where a number of hearty meat dishes would have been served a generation ago, and where opportunistic homemade stock would have formed the backbone of the sauces.

Many fine upscale restaurants, of course, are still producing stocks. The preparation is often a carefully planned part of the routine, and its ingredients are acquired for that specific purpose. As Tamar explains below, every classic cooking text has its own take on the subject, providing precise direction for the home cook and warning of dire consequences for deviance. It can be downright intimidating to even read about making stock. But we think it need not be so.

STOCK: THE CONTROVERSY RAGES

In the world of food, there is universal agreement on very little. On every issue of consequence, there are invariably several points of view. And that's just in my family. But on the importance of stock, there is universal accord. After all, you don't get to be *fonds de cuisine* for nothing.

Auguste Escoffier is generally regarded as the father of classical French cooking, and his *Guide Culinaire,* first published in 1903, is still considered definitive. This (in translation) is how the book opens:

> Before undertaking the description of the different kinds of dishes whose recipes I intend giving in this work, it will be necessary to reveal the groundwork whereon these recipes are built. And, although this has already been done again and again, and is wearisome in the extreme, a textbook on cooking that did not include it would be not only incomplete, but in many cases incomprehensible. . . . Indeed, stock is everything in cooking.

No one, but no one, takes issue with Escoffier on this point. But once you dig deeper into the stock issue and start asking pesky questions like "How do you make it?" you realize (with either dismay or relief, depending on how you feel about being governed by rules) that there's plenty of room for disagreement.

Even the experts disagree. In *Mastering the Art of French Cooking,*

Julia Child uses a combination of meat and bones for brown stock. So does Escoffier. *The New Professional Chef* (textbook for the Culinary Institute of America) calls for bones only. *Larousse Gastronomique* calls for crushed bones. Julia and *Larousse,* in their chicken stock recipes, put in the vegetables and the chicken at the same time. *The New Professional Chef* simmers the chicken for hours, and then adds the vegetables. Herbs are different, cooking times are different, and I won't even get into the salt question.

Yet many of the classics, particularly *The New Professional Chef,* insist that their particular stock recipe be followed to the letter. Why, if there are so many viable ways to make stock, should anyone be so persnickety? Is it just that chefs have strong autocratic tendencies? Many do, but I don't think that's the answer. The answer is consistency. Professional chefs need to turn out the same stock over and over because they use it as a base for soups, sauces, and stews that should taste the same every time. In a restaurant kitchen, reproducibility is important. Customers want the same split pea soup that Ruth Reichl raved about in the *New York Times.* Different stock, different soup. Home cooks have a different agenda, typically that of getting a palatable, nourishing meal on the table. Therefore, they need not be bound by precise procedures and specific ingredients. I find that tremendously liberating.

And so, while the First Rule of Stock for CIA students is that 8 pounds of bones, 6 quarts of water, and 1 pound of mirepoix yield 1 gallon of stock, the First Rule of Stock for home cooks is never throw anything away. Okay, that's not quite accurate. There are some things you definitely should throw away. Greasy paper towels, for example. There are even some food items you should throw away: anything that's rancid or spoiled. Other than that, you should save just about anything. Vegetable trimmings can be turned into stock in under an hour. Chicken leftovers are just crying to have their flavor simmered out of them.

And it's lucky for us that stock making isn't as complicated as classic recipes make it sound; low-fat, veggie-centric cooking needs stock even more than the traditional kind that has recourse to butter and cream and big chunks of meat. If there's a single strategy for palatable healthful cooking, it is the use of flavorful liquids to replace fats in a variety of food preparations. And the quintessential flavorful liquids are stocks. A good-quality stock can mean the difference between a bland, flavorless soup, sauce, or stew and one that is vibrant and satisfying. That same stock can deglaze a hash or stir-fry, enhancing its flavor immeasurably. So let's examine the possibilities, starting with Mom on chicken stock.

Chicken: The Monarch of Stock

As my great-uncle Frank grew old, he sensibly cut back on his farming operation and leased most of his land to his neighbors. By the time I knew him, his cows and horses were gone. When I spent my last summer on the farm—I was twelve, he nearly eighty—even the sheep had been sold. There was a pig, of course. As long as he and Aunt Dag lived on the farm there would be a pig. But mostly, there were the chickens—about three hundred of them. With a touch of irony, he always referred to them as "the stock." The context has changed, but these days I, too, can't look at a chicken without thinking of stock.

A thoroughly modern chicken hardly ever has as much flavor as those Uncle Frank raised in Minnesota half a century ago, but it's still a mighty useful beast. A good chicken stock is the easiest of all stocks to produce, and it's just about the only non-vegan food, besides skim milk and yogurt, that's a staple at my house. (Actually, the liquid I produce by boiling chicken is technically not a stock, but a broth, as it's based on meat rather than bones.) I don't make beef stock, as I find it inconvenient. We eat almost no beef—none that produces debris—and I have no good source for meat scraps or bones. Also, as Tamar points out in her discussion of the subject (page 62), it takes a lot of beef to make a little stock.

A very moderate quantity of chicken, on the other hand, will produce a flavorful broth, and chicken is often very cheap. The backs and the leg quarters, the best parts for making stock, are frequent specials in supermarkets. You can add the bones from any recent chicken (or turkey, since they are interchangeable in stock) you've cooked. You should save raw poultry scraps in your freezer. If you debone chicken breasts yourself, save the bones with the meat that inevitably adheres to them. Save necks. Save giblets other than liver. Feet are great if you can get them and can stand the way they look. Try to acquire the self-discipline to consolidate all these tidbits in one plastic bag rather than in separate little tiny packages. Otherwise cleaning your freezer will resemble an archaeological dig. (Is this the foot of the chicken Columbus brought to the New World? No, that's the next layer down. This chicken foot was the first to be set on Plymouth Rock.)

To make chicken stock all you have to do is put some chicken, some vegetables, and some water in a big pot and cook it for a long time. The recipe below implies it's more precise than that but it's really not. You can cook it covered or uncovered, skim the scum or not skim it, strain the finished stock carefully through cheesecloth or just pour it through a colander to remove the big stuff. Such details only become relevant if you need a clear stock—if you are going to serve what my children used to call "empty soup." I believe that any time you serve clear soup you neglect a wonderful opportunity to stuff yourself and other people with vegetables. Besides, clear soup is a little boring, especially if it's low in salt. Low-sodium foods need contrasting textures. (That's also why I rarely make smooth purées.)

There is, however, one detail that is extremely important to the making of proper, healthful chicken stock. It must be conscientiously defatted. This means you should not plan to use it the same day it's made (although if you need a little stock while the pot is cooking, you can reach in with a bulb baster and extract some from below the fat layer). Give it enough time to chill so that the fat solidifies on the top and can simply be spooned off. Chill your stock in relatively narrow-necked jars to minimize the surface area. It's a lot easier to spoon out a thick glob of fat than to chase a wafer-thin layer spread out over a large surface.

If you've produced a rich, chickeny stock, it will jell when it's chilled. All this means is that you're adding quite a lot of chicken flavor to any dish in which you use this stock. An unjelled stock may still taste pretty good—just longer on vegetable than chicken flavor. On the other hand, if it tastes like water a chicken walked through, throw in anything you've got around that might improve it and simmer it awhile uncovered to reduce it. But even a bland, wimpy stock is better than plain water. It will add some depth to soups and sauces.

Chicken stock will keep four to five days in the refrigerator, and you can restart the clock anytime by returning the stock to a boil—a procedure that will further reduce and improve it. It will keep for months in the freezer. Freeze it in small quantities, as that is most likely the way you will want to retrieve it. Freezing stock in ice cube trays and saving the cubes in a plastic bag is very convenient. When I get it together to do this, which is on extremely rare occasions, I'm always thankful later on.

I hope you'll feel free to work many variations on your chicken stock, but you might want to start with this recipe.

CHICKEN STOCK (A.K.A. BROTH)
Makes about 3 quarts

5 quarts water
5 pounds uncooked chicken parts (everything but the liver—
you can also use cooked chicken and bones if that's
what you have on hand)

2 medium onions, peeled and quartered

2 or 3 carrots, cut into 1-inch pieces

2 large celery stalks, cut into 1-inch pieces

2 or 3 garlic cloves, peeled and quartered

10 to 20 whole peppercorns

5 to 10 whole cloves (stick them in the onions if you like)

5 to 10 large parsley sprigs with stems

*1 tablespoon assorted dried herbs, such as marjoram, thyme, rose-
mary, basil, oregano, or sage, or 5 or 6 sprigs of any of the same
herbs, fresh or frozen*

1. Put the water in a stockpot that holds about 10 quarts. If you have no such pot, of course, this recipe can be halved, quartered, or otherwise adjusted. Write down the amounts your stockpot will hold so you don't have to try to remember the next time. If the largest pot you own holds 2 quarts, you do not have a stockpot. Go out and buy one.
2. Put the chicken in the water and set the pot over medium heat. Prepare the remaining ingredients and add them to the pot while the water is coming to a boil. Let it come to a full boil, skimming the scum occasionally if you wish. Then reduce the heat to low and allow it to simmer undisturbed for 2 to 3 hours.
3. Allow it to cool enough so you can handle it comfortably.
4. Strain your stock through an ordinary strainer, or through cheesecloth if you want to get fancy. Discard the solids (see Notes). Pour the stock into jars and chill until the fat has solidified and can be spooned off. Store in the refrigerator up to 4 days or as long as 6 months in the freezer.

NOTES: You may be reluctant to throw away the chicken that you've boiled to flavor your stock. Eat it if you want to. It may have a little flavor left, especially if it spent its life in a barnyard rather than in a tiny pen on a factory farm. Another approach is to remove the chicken from the stock after an hour or so, cut most of the meat from the bones, then return the bones to the stock to continue cooking. This is about as close as you can come to eating your chicken and having it too.

Chicken stock can deliver an essential meaty flavor without saturated fat and cholesterol. Homemade stock can also be free of—or at least very low in—salt. Even if you have no health reasons to avoid salt, standard commercial chicken stocks are so salty they can easily spoil the flavor of a dish when they're used in substantial amounts. If you're stuck with them in an emergency, dilute them with water or unsalted vegetable stock. Canned stocks that contain fat should be kept in the refrigerator so that any fat is easy to remove when the can is opened. Campbell's Healthy Request chicken broth is about as good as canned stock gets, and that's not very good. But it's fat-free, lower in salt than most canned soups, and it does have a chickeny flavor. By itself, it has a somewhat institutional taste—it will remind you of the soup you were served in the hospital—but it beats plain water in your soup or sauce. The commercial stock option isn't a very good one, and avoiding it is easier than you may have thought. Even if you don't have all day to cook, or access to unlimited chicken scraps, you can make tasty stock in your own kitchen. As Tamar points out, stock making is more a habit than a chore.

There is also opportunistic stock—one of the joys of every post-holiday season. Boil up the bones, scraps of meat, and carcass of your roasted chicken or turkey along with some vegetables. If you roast the ingredients first (see Tamar's Beef Stock recipe, page 63, for specific roasting instructions—they work just as well for chicken), the stock will be especially flavorful. Unless you run a restaurant and are constrained by health department rules, feel free to use scraps left on people's plates in your stock. As long as you boil them, they pose no health hazard.

Beef Eaters

Beef is usually an early casualty of the resolution to eat healthfully. The litany of how to eat better is almost invariably begun with the injunction to cut red meat consumption. Why red meat and not cheesecake or cream sauce or beignets? Because meat has always been thought a staple. Its nutritional shortcomings have been cloaked in a guise of hearty healthfulness, abetted by its insidious partnership with blameless potatoes. Giving up meat is, for many, truly a lifestyle change. Giving up beignets is not, unless you have a very strange lifestyle indeed, like the sisters in *Alice in Wonderland* who lived in a well and ate only treacle.

Cutting down on red meat can be relatively painless because there are so many interesting things you can do with small quantities of it. In fact, meals with just a little meat tend to be inherently more interesting than meals with a lot. A large amount of meat is a steak or a rib roast or a hamburger. Any of these can be delicious, but they are limited. They are what they are. Little pieces of meat, however, can be components of just about anything. And those little pieces can satisfy. It isn't often that I, or anyone else I know who has deliberately cut back on meat, really crave a nice T-bone. (The red meat that does tempt me is lamb, but that's for another chapter, or maybe another book.)

One way to get beef's essence without the saturated fat or calories is with beef stock. A soup or a stew made with beef stock delivers the sensation of a meat dish. It has the beefy smell and the rich mouth feel. If you add small pieces of actual beef to the dish, you end up with something hearty and satisfying enough for the most committed carnivore.

But I have to fess up here. Beef stock is a royal pain. You need lots of bones, which can be difficult to procure. (My butcher makes and sells his own beef stock, so if I want to intercept some bones before they end up in his stockpot, I have to call ahead and ask that they be set aside. I feel a little silly calling to make a bone reservation.) For a stock with real beef flavor, you also need real beef, which is expensive. To get the gelatin out of the bones, you have to cook them a very long time. Compared to chicken stock, where the chicken flavor just leaps out of the carcass and into the soup, beef stock is slow and stubborn.

There are alternatives to making your own. If your butcher, like mine, hoards his bones to make his own stock, that's good news. It means you can buy the stock instead of the bones and save yourself a lot of time and effort. If your butcher doesn't, there are commercial beef broths and bouillon cubes readily available. Most of them are pretty bad, much worse than commercial chicken stocks. *Cook's Illustrated,* one of my favorite magazines, evaluated beef stocks in its January/February 1998 issue, and the results were grim. Only one was "recommended in a pinch": Superior Touch "Better Than Bouillon" Beef Base (Superior Quality Foods, Ontario, Canada).

But if you are inclined to make your own, beef stock isn't complicated. Once you procure the ingredients and set aside the time, the hard part's done. All you have to do is roast the bones, beef, and vegetables, transfer them to a stockpot, cover with water, and simmer for hours.

BEEF STOCK
Makes 2 to 3 quarts

3 large carrots
6 celery stalks
2 medium onions
6 pounds beef bones
2 pounds beef stew meat or beef scraps
5 to 6 quarts water
2 bay leaves
10 to 20 whole peppercorns

1. Chop the vegetables into large chunks. Spread the bones, meat, and vegetables in a large roasting pan. Roast at 350°F until they brown thoroughly, about 45 minutes. Transfer the mixture to a large stockpot.
2. Put the roasting pan over high heat on the stove (most pans will fit over two burners). Add 1 cup water to the pan and deglaze, scraping the browned scraps from the bottom of the pan. Pour the liquid into the stockpot.
3. Cover the ingredients with water, add the bay leaves and peppercorns, and bring to a boil. Lower the heat and simmer, uncovered, for 4 hours. Strain and refrigerate.

NOTES: If you've made chicken stock and try beef for the first time, don't expect your beef stock to be the red meat analog to the rich chickeny broth you're used to. Chicken stock tastes like soup. Beef stock tastes like watered-down beef. But don't be disappointed and don't be fooled—this stock will make an excellent, beefy base for a dish with other spices and ingredients.

The beef that you strain out after your stock is finished is marginally more palatable than chicken that's gone through the same ordeal. I wouldn't want to serve it as a main course, but a little bit of it shredded into a soup or stew adds texture and beefy feel.

Something Smells Fishy

Every summer on Cape Cod we have one great lobster pig-out for our whole family and assorted friends, and when it's over, I throw all the shells in a big pot and make stock. I end up with several quarts, and it tastes wonderful. It forms the base for a fine fish soup the next day, and I freeze the rest to take back to New York with me, where it enhances various fishy dishes for a month or two. But, I admit, that's the only time I make seafood stock. The rest of the year I buy it from my New York fishmonger, who has plenty of shells and fish heads and bones just lying around, and whose premises already smell of fish.

Yes, it's not called "fish *fumet*" for nothing. No matter how fresh your fish is, making fish stock smells up your house. It's not so bad while the stock is cooking, and that process is over in half an hour in any case. But the fish molecules in the air seem to break down just the way they would if they were still attached to the creature, so the odor not only lingers, it gets worse as the hours pass. Perhaps if your kitchen is really well ventilated, this would not occur, but mine isn't, and it does.

On a few occasions long ago, I obtained fish frames from a fishmonger for making stock. Fish frames are skeletons with the heads and tails still attached, like the fish in cartoons after the cat has finished with them. The stock was fine, but I did not enjoy preparing it. Even more disconcerting than the smell were the eyes—there seemed to be hundreds of them—staring up at me reproachfully from the pot. I actually closed my own eyes while I strained the stock.

If you have no real fishmonger where you live, or you can't persuade him to make fish stock, what can you do? I say, use chicken stock. Your soup or sauce won't taste quite the same, but it will be good. You can add some bottled clam juice to your chicken stock for a seafood tang, but use it with a light hand. It's very salty.

As a last resort, if you have ready access to fish scraps, a good kitchen fan, and haven't been entirely disheartened by all my caveats, you might try the recipe below. It's the one with the fish frames that gave me so much pleasure when I made it all those years ago.

FISH FUMET
Makes about 1½ quarts

1 medium onion

1 celery stalk

1 carrot

1 garlic clove

3 pounds bones, heads, frames, and assorted scraps of any low-fat, white-fleshed fish (salmon is okay—a high-fat exception, but avoid bluefish or mackerel, and don't include large pieces of skin. That's another thing to add to Tamar's list of stuff you can throw away: fish skins)

1 bay leaf

½ teaspoon dried thyme, tarragon, or a combination, or 2 or 3 fresh sprigs of each herb

8 to 10 whole peppercorns

3 or 4 large parsley sprigs

2 quarts water

1 cup very dry white wine, such as Fumé Blanc, or (in a wineless emergency) 1 tablespoon lemon juice. (This acidic stuff is reputedly necessary to extract the gelatin from the fish bones during the relatively short cooking process. I have no idea whether this is true, but it certainly makes the stock taste good)

Salt to taste

1. Coarsely chop the onion, celery, carrot, and garlic in the food processor.
2. Combine all the ingredients except the salt in a large pot and bring to a simmer, skimming off the scum if you want to. Simmer gently for 20 to 25 minutes (more time will produce a strong, overcooked taste).
3. Strain immediately, then add salt.

Stock in the Vegetarian Kitchen

DRIVEN TO EXTRACTION

Vegetables were not put on this earth for making stock. There are no classic vegetable stocks. They have been created by vegetarian cooks to avoid boiling up dead animals. If you've struggled to produce good vegetable stock, you know it's not easy. Greens become acrid, cruciferous vegetables like broccoli and cabbage turn sulfurous, and roots seem to contribute only a uniform sweetness. The carnivorous model for enriching flavor—rich, cooked-down stock—has no relevance at all to vegetarian cooking. Reduce a vegetable stock and it's likely to just turn grassy or bitter.

Everything we've said so far in this chapter is completely useless to anyone whose kitchen is an entirely meat-free zone. So how is a vegetarian cook to get that underlying richness in stocks and sauces? Vegetables do have flavorful essences, they just don't like to yield them up. However, there's an appliance that can deliver them to you: it's a juice extractor. Unfortunately, they're expensive and a bit of a mess to use. If you go this route, buy a good one like a Champion (that's what I have) or the Omega.

You won't need hours of prep time. One hourlong session can set you up for an entire week. You won't need careful shopping. Just about any veggie can be juiced to advantage. I've found that thinking ahead to the week of simplified meals I'm going to enjoy after the juicing session can overcome my resistance to dusting off the Champion. You won't need steely resolve. This can actually be fun.

You're going to need lots of little jars—and labels. It's hard to believe that vegetables that look so different can produce juices that look so similar.

Clean your veggies well (peeling is rarely necessary) and cut them into pieces your juicer can digest. Start your juicing session with the blander items and move to the more flavorful. It's a good idea to have on hand plenty of something bland and wet like zucchini or cucumber to separate vegetables with assertive flavors. For example, if you want your onion juice to be entirely distinct from your carrot juice, you can cleanse your juicer's palate with a couple of zucchini spears and you'll have zucchini juice with just a little carrot in it. This strategy helps you avert the ultimate catastrophe: having to clean the juicer more than once. (It can happen, alas. If your juicer does overheat or become clogged, disassemble it sufficiently to remove the worst of the debris and add it to the pulp you're saving for the stockpot. Let the machine cool for a few minutes, then put it back together and continue.)

I've found that most vegetable essences will keep three to five days in the refrigerator, longer if you add a few drops of vinegar, which is fine if you plan to use them in a dish for which the flavor of vinegar is appropriate. They can also be frozen in ice cube trays and stored in plastic bags. (Again, don't forget to label them.) Skim and strain your juices before storing them if appearances are important to you. I never bother. Once you've got a collection of little jars and frozen cubes, you'll be able to use them in preparations where you'd generally be adding stock. Naturally, if you need a lot of liquid, you'll have to dilute them with water (or stock—for an additional flavor punch).

Producing stock can be an effortless part of your juicing session. Start the water boiling while you're cutting up the vegetables and add the trimmings to the pot as you work. Then add the juiced pulp as it accumulates, including what you remove from the juicer parts during cleanup.

Someday you will encounter a recipe that suggests a use for cooked veggie-juice pulp that involves actually eating it. Unless your taste buds were shot off in the war, do yourself a favor and ignore such recipes. Yes, discarding the pulp is a waste of fiber, but I am unalterably opposed to eating anything that doesn't taste good just because it benefits your body. Get your fiber somewhere else. Be satisfied that the two steps—juicing and boiling—have wrung all the flavor and most of the food value from your vegetables. As soon as you've strained your stock (unless you have a compost heap), just open your garbage pail and let those solids go.

QUICK VEGETABLE STOCK
Makes about 6 cups

> 6 cups water
>
> 3 cups fresh vegetable pulp from a session with the juice extractor
>
> 1 teaspoon salt, or to taste
>
> 1 tablespoon white wine vinegar (or more if you've juiced a
>   preponderance of sweet veggies)

1. Bring the water to a boil in a large saucepan and add the pulp. Return to a boil, then lower the heat and simmer for about 15 minutes.
2. Let cool slightly. Strain through a sieve or colander, pressing the solids

to extract as much stock as possible. Discard the solids. Add the salt and vinegar.

3. Refrigerate up to 3 days, longer if you bring it back to a boil every few days. It can also be frozen.

THE LOW-TECH VEGETARIAN KITCHEN

You can make a pretty decent fat-free veggie stock without acquiring a humongous machine to do it. As Alice Waters once said, you can cook anything if you have access to fire. Vegetarian cooks have traditionally been more interested in ideology than flavor, and it's only relatively recently that serious attention has been paid to such matters as making really good vegetable stock. Unfortunately, there's more to it than just boiling up the veggies that happen to be lying around. Deborah Madison, the founder and first chef of Greens Restaurant in San Francisco, has raised the making of these stocks to a high art. Her stock recipes are worth the price of her own *The Greens Cookbook* or of *Dr. Dean Ornish's Program for Reversing Heart Disease,* where they appear in a form adapted to the constraints of Ornish's diet.

Madison recommends cooking a vegetable by itself to get an idea of how it works in a stock. This is too much for me, but if you ever ate the vegetarian soups served at Greens during Madison's tenure, you will appreciate the payoff for this kind of meticulous care. I do manage to follow her advice to be sure my vegetables are clean and in good condition, to cut them small enough to expose maximum surface area, not to overcook, and to strain the stock as soon as it's done. She has taught me to handle lowly stock vegetables much more attentively and respectfully than was formerly my wont. And if I didn't have good old chicken stock, or sometimes just the soaking liquid from dried mushrooms (which has rescued me in many an emergency, see Mushroom to Maneuver on page 209) to fall back on, I'd probably be even more careful.

My own vegetable stocks still tend to be opportunistic, although I try to have essential ingredients like onions, potatoes, carrots, and celery on hand all the time. This is my rough-and-ready stock recipe. It owes a lot to Deborah Madison, but I freely admit she might shudder at such carelessness and imprecision.

VEGETABLE STOCK
With apologies to Deborah Madison.
Makes about 6 cups

1 large onion

2 carrots

1 large or 2 small potatoes

2 celery stalks

*Onion, carrot, celery, and potato trimmings that have accumulated
since you last made stock (see Notes)*

2 or 3 garlic cloves

*1 cup assorted green leaves, such as lettuce trimmings, chard stems,
spinach, and so on*

2 bay leaves

1 small handful fresh parsley or cilantro (see Notes)

Optional: Use all, some, or none. If you have a lot of bulky ones add
more liquid.

1 leek or leek trimmings

1 winter squash or trimmings, including seeds

1 large or 2 small summer squash

1 sweet potato

1 small eggplant or trimmings

1 or 2 small parsnips

1 cup or more green beans or trimmings

Fennel leaves

Pea pods

Corncobs

*Odds and ends of fresh ginger, oregano, rosemary, tarragon, or other
fresh herbs (use caution, as these flavors can be strong)*

*Broccoli stalks, cabbage leaves, asparagus trimmings, and turnips (can
be trouble; use in moderation and add after the stock's been
boiling for about 20 minutes. These are nasty when overcooked.
Even if your stock doesn't taste bad, the smell will discourage
you from ever making it again)*

*2 quarts water, chicken stock, or liquid reserved from cooking
vegetables*

1. Wash fairly thoroughly those vegetables that aren't going to be peeled.
Immerse them in water and swish them around, removing inedible
parts. Cut everything into smallish pieces—nothing much larger than
your thumb. Slicing them in the food processor is crude but effective.
2. Optional: Heat 1 tablespoon olive oil in a large nonstick skillet, wok,
or your stockpot if it's suitable for low-oil sautéing. Add the vegeta-

bles except the herbs and greens and cook, stirring, over medium heat for 10 to 15 minutes. Then add the veggies to the water (or the water to the veggies, as the case may be) and proceed as below. Pre-sautéing is even more effective in releasing flavor if you've coarsely ground your ingredients in a blender or food processor. Either way, it can shorten your stock's simmering time to 20 minutes or so.

3. Put everything but the green leaves and green herbs in a 4-quart pot with the water or stock and bring to a boil. Lower the heat and sim-mer for 15 or 20 minutes. Add the green stuff and continue simmer-ing for 10 or 15 minutes more. Strain immediately. Most of the veggies are best discarded, but the root vegetables—especially pota-toes—can be puréed to give your soup body. Even the others won't taste bad puréed in a soup that's going to be eaten right away. Don't try to save them for another day.

NOTES: Does anyone besides my husband Chuck not know what trimmings are? It's the stuff you've cut off your veggies before you cook them—not the rotten parts, or course—just the parings, tough stalks, out-side leaves, etc., that you removed during dreaded veggie prep. Store the trimmings in a plastic bag (in the freezer if you're keeping them more than a day or two). You can use them in your chicken stock too.

Herb stems are fine for stock. Remember to save them. And if you run a kitchen like mine, you should check the freezer for any herbs you may have stuck in there so they wouldn't rot. I tend to shove anything I don't know what else to do with into the freezer hastily and repent at leisure. For more on freezing herbs, see Barbara's *Grete Herball,* page 163.

Vegetable stock, interestingly, doesn't seem to keep as well as chicken stock. It sours after more than about 3 days in the fridge. Bring it to a boil every other day or so to prevent this. (When you bring it back to the boil, en-rich it with whatever new veggie scraps you've acquired.) Once the stock is part of a soup with something acidic like tomatoes, it holds up better.

Burning Questions: Stock Answers

Now that you've read about stock in all its infinite variety you should be feeling fairly confident. You can use pretty much any kind of leftover, scrap, or by-product your kitchen produces. You can add any herb that strikes your fancy. No precise preparations or time-consuming proce-dures need be involved. Which leads to one inescapable conclusion—this is *easy.* Stock is really more of a habit than a chore, and if you get into the habit, you will be amazed at the number of uses you'll find for it, and how often you'll wish you had more.

We've tried to write the definitive text on stock for the home cook, but you may still have a question or two—probably completely different ones from those we've addressed below.

QUESTION 1. IS SCUM SKIMMING NECESSARY?

Many stock recipes will tell you to stand guard over your stock and diligently skim the scum that comes bubbling up as the pot simmers. How important is that? Not very. The main reason to skim scum is to get a clearer stock. Unless you're making a delicate sauce, clarity is a minor, and mostly cosmetic, concern. If you're standing over the pot and happen to spot some scum, skim! But vigilance is not required.

QUESTION 2. ARE THERE ANY THINGS I SHOULDN'T PUT IN STOCK?

As Mom noted, fish skin shouldn't be put in fish stock. As Mom also noted, some vegetables can turn on you if you cook them too long. Broccoli stalks, cabbage leaves, rutabagas, asparagus trimmings, and turnips should be cooked no longer than about 15 minutes. Cauliflower, Brussels sprouts, and artichokes are best avoided altogether. Onion peels are always a bad idea. Some recipes will tell you to include them because they turn your stock a nice toasty brown. But you have to eat it, not just look at it, so you don't want it to be bitter. Throw your onion peels away. Ditto with your carrot tops and celery leaves.

For chicken and beef stock, anything goes. You might want to trim the visible fat off your beef before you roast it. Unlike chicken fat, beef fat doesn't impart flavor. There's no harm done if you leave it on, though, since you'll remove it anyway when you defat the stock.

QUESTION 3. TO BROWN OR NOT TO BROWN?

Stocks in which the meat and vegetables have been roasted before being immersed have a stronger flavor than those in which they haven't. A classic white stock is made with veal (a very unassertive flavor), and the meat and bones are not roasted first. The point of this stock is to make a base with body that assumes the flavor of whatever is cooked in it.

White stocks are useful if you're making delicate sauces. I don't think I have ever, in my entire cooking career, made anything that could plausibly be categorized as a delicate sauce. While my friends and family will nod knowingly about how ill-suited I am to anything delicate, the real reason I don't make subtle, delicate sauces is that low-fat, high-fiber, vegetable-centric cooking does not lend itself to them.

The classic sauces that are based on white stocks were created to complement meat and game. When we use meat at all we're using it the other way around—in small quantities to complement mixtures of vegetables and grains.

When you're cooking with lots of vegetables, not too much salt, and little added fat, you'll find you have to compensate by intensifying flavors. Don't skimp on the garlic or the ginger or the hot pepper. Or the stock. Because I'm usually looking for assertive flavors, I prefer a stock that begins with roasting. Although a rich chicken stock is certainly flavorful without roasting, you get a little more out of it if you do. To my mind, beef bones must be roasted to make a stock that's of any use at all. The directions for roasting beef stock ingredients (page 63) work for chicken as well.

QUESTION 4. HOW LONG DO I REALLY HAVE TO COOK IT?

Vegetable and fish stocks develop their flavor quickly. You can't cook them more than about 20 to 30 minutes. Some vegetables can go longer, but if you've chopped them into thumb-size or smaller pieces, there's nothing to be gained by extended simmering—you've already gotten all the flavor there is to be had.

Cooking times for chicken and beef stocks are much longer—and not terribly critical. Chicken stock should simmer at least a couple of hours, but you can let it go an additional hour or so if you have the time, as more flavor will leach out of the bones. Beef stock should be cooked for at least 4 hours. It continues to improve even after that, but I'm guessing you have other things to do.

QUESTION 5. ONCE I'VE SKIMMED THE FAT OFF MY STOCK, HOW MANY CALORIES AND FAT GRAMS ARE LEFT?

Good news! Skimmed stock, whether chicken or beef, has only about 10 to 30 calories per cup, and no fat to speak of. Vegetable stock is even lower in calories and also fat-free. Whether your stock comes in at 10 or 30 depends on what ingredients you've used and how much you've reduced it (which is why we don't have calorie counts on the recipes in this chapter).

QUESTION 6. AFTER READING ALL THIS, WHAT CAN I CONCLUDE ABOUT STOCK?

The harsh reality is that beef stock is a pain, fish stock smells up your house, and vegetable stock just isn't very good. Mom's Uncle Frank was right. Chicken is *the* stock.

WHAT'S WITH ALL THE FRENCH?

NOBODY SHOULD HAVE TO MAKE crucial life decisions in seventh grade, but one of those decisions is invariably thrust upon us at that age—which foreign language to study. Seventh graders are ill-equipped to make such an important decision and they invariably go about it in the wrong way. Instead of asking, "Which language will help me better understand the world around me?" or "Which people would I most like to communicate with?" they ask questions like, "Does the French teacher have B.O.?" and "What language are the cheerleaders taking?" It was undoubtedly questions like these that led me to study German. German!

For the most part, I am grateful to my parents for letting me make my own decisions and, thus, my own mistakes. It is largely because of that autonomy that I turned into the confident and thoughtful adult I am on my better days. But just this once, Mom, as a self-confessed Francophile, couldn't you have pointed out that anyone who's serious about food (and I was, even then) needs to know French?

So, when a stock recipe calls for a *bouquet garni* or *sachet d'épices,* I run for my *Larousse* and look it up. And while I concede that French lessons might not have covered those two items, at least I'd know what the words meant and how to pronounce them. But, hey, if you ever need help with a sauerbraten recipe, just give me a call.

Bookay? Sashay? What's going on? If you are as confused as I was by *bouquet garni* and *sachet d'épices,* I can now set you straight. Both are devices to contain aromatics in a simmering stock so they are easy to remove later and won't be skimmed away with the scum. A *bouquet garni* is made up of things like thyme sprigs and bay leaves and parsley stems and is tied with string. A *sachet d'épices* is wrapped up in cheesecloth and so can contain smaller items, like peppercorns, that don't lend themselves to being tied up with string. A classic *sachet d'épices,* according to the CIA's *New Professional Chef,* has thyme, parsley stems, a bay leaf, peppercorns, and garlic.

Now that you know what they are, you can breathe a sigh of

relief that you'll never have to use them. Just toss the ingredients right in the pot. You'll be straining it anyway. All the components of both the *bouquet garni* and the *sachet d'épices* make a fine addition to your stock, and there is no need to be precise about which ones or how much of them you use. Even if you're an inveterate scum skimmer, you can avoid skimming away your herbs and spices by adding them half an hour or so into the cooking process, after most of the scum has been disposed of. If at some later time you wish to turn your stock into soup that you're not going to be straining, you may want to package your herbs and spices for easy removal. Otherwise, no bookay, no sashay.

These cute little packets, however, have become such objects of reverence in the cooking world that Mom once had to talk a magazine editor out of revising one of our vegetable stock recipes to include one. This was totally vegetarian stock, no scum whatsoever was going to be produced. Furthermore, this was a totally vegetarian magazine, in which no stock recipe anytime ever would produce scum. So watch out for recipes that tell you to start fooling around with cheesecloth and string. My mom won't always be there to protect you.

Mire-what? *Mirepoix* is just a fancy name for a mixture of diced onions, carrots, and celery. It was invented by the cook of French nobleman the Duc de Lévis-Mirepoix to enhance the soups, sauces, meat, and game the Duc and his guests consumed. Of course, it was named after the Duc and not the cook. That was one of the facts of life in the eighteenth century. Cook was not the high-status profession it can be today. A cook was a servant and a Duc was, well, a Duc. So the name Mirepoix lives on and the cook's name is forgotten.

I guess those three vegetables are standard because they all have different but assertive flavors, and the combination complements other flavors well. They help provide the "back" you're always looking for in soups and sauces. They're also readily available year-round. There is no law that these vegetables and only these vegetables should be the foundation of stocks, but they are a good start.

While everyone agrees that *mirepoix* contains onions, carrots, and celery (although there are alternate versions that also contain meat and/or other vegetables), there is disagreement (surprise!) about the proportions. The CIA says two parts onion, one part celery, one part carrot. *Larousse* says three parts carrot, two parts onion, one part celery. Julia Child says (essentially) one part each.

So what's the message here? It doesn't matter! Got more celery than carrots? Use it! Like onions? Load up! And you don't have to stop with those three. You shouldn't, in fact. Vegetable stock absolutely requires more than just these three, but even for chicken or meat stock, feel free to add the mushroom stems and the parsnip scraps and anything else you've accumulated. It will be a lot if you're following the First Rule of Stock (which, in case you've forgotten, is never throw anything away). Not only stocks, in fact, but many sauces and stir-frys are best begun by chopping up some celery, carrots, onions, or whatever and sautéing the mixture until it is soft and fragrant. Make *mirepoix* a basic kitchen strategy. Thank the Duc's cook.

Demi-who? *Demi-glace* is the substance you'll always wish you had, but will never actually have. It's really, really reduced stock. The reason you'll never have it is that in order to produce a reasonable quantity (i.e., more than a tablespoon), you have to start with a pot the size of Montana. Montana will produce a Connecticut's worth of good, flavorful stock. Connecticut will then yield a cup or so of *demi-glace. Demi-glace* remains, alas, the preserve of institutional kitchens.

A note to capitalists: This is an open market niche. I have not found *demi-glace* in any of the stores in my neighborhood. And if sophisticated New York City markets don't have it, I imagine it's also hard to find elsewhere. It's a business opportunity for someone with a really big pot.

5.

Grains and Legumes

LET'S FACE IT. GRAINS AND LEGUMES HAVE A PR PROBLEM.
You probably know that they're a big part of a healthful diet. You've been told that by nutrition experts since the dawn of, well, nutrition experts. You can probably guess that we're going to give you some ideas about how to improve your g&l skills in this chapter. And even though there are probably some grains and legumes you're happy and comfortable with, the thought of learning more may not have you sitting on the edge of your chair. Perhaps you're already looking ahead to the chapter on desserts.

I'm the first to acknowledge that beans and grains can be boring. Alone, they seldom inspire rapture or even interest. But that is precisely why it's important that the healthful cook be master of them; in order to be interesting, grains and legumes have to have something done to them. They have to be cooked with.

They are as fundamental as stock, but play a different role. While stocks impart flavor, grains absorb it. In order to transfer flavor, you have to have something to transfer it to. Grains and legumes do have flavor to impart, but they mostly absorb. That's why you might think they're boring, but it's also part of why they're essential.

Besides, if you cut down on meat, you have to find a way to replace both the nutrients and the calories. Vegetables just won't do it. Even though they hold their own on the nutrition front, it's nearly impossible to make vegetables do the caloric work of meat. It takes 10 cups of steamed broccoli to equal the calories of a 7-ounce sirloin. That's good news if you really, really like broccoli, but I think 10 cups of any vegetable is too much. And I'm a vegetable zealot.

Enter grains and legumes. Wheat in the form of bread, pasta, and couscous. Rice, barley, and polenta. Peas, beans, and lentils. These are the basics that give your meals substance and staying power. (They also provide protein, which you're unlikely to get enough of from even the most gluttonous consumption of vegetables.) Judicious and inventive use of grains and legumes can mean not only that your guests never leave your table hungry, but that your meals are varied and interesting.

Some grains and legumes, like rice and peas, are comfortably familiar. Others, like barley and fava beans, are probably less so. Getting comfortable with a wide variety of them is the single best way to expand your overall food repertoire.

To illustrate, let's follow an imaginary tomato sauce for three days. When you think tomato sauce you undoubtedly think pasta, which is what you serve on Day One. But, because you're thinking ahead and you know that tomato sauce is about as versatile as food gets, you make a big batch. On Day Two, you find some nice-looking spinach at the farmers' market. You take it home, steam it, combine it with some of the leftover tomato sauce, and layer it into a baked polenta casserole. On Day Three, you take a trip to the fish market and pick up a few shrimp. You cook up some white beans with an onion and a hot pepper, stew them with the last of the tomato sauce, and serve them with the shrimp. I guarantee you that no one will complain about having tomato sauce three days in a row. They won't even notice. They will be loud in their praise of your grain and legume skills.

And that's using just one grain or legume at a time. Once you start combining them, your options increase geometrically. The good news is that it's easy to improve your g&l skills, because the same basic cooking rule applies to every single one: Boil it until it seems done. This is not to say that there's no nuance in g&l cookery. If there weren't, this chapter could end right here. Some grains (like rice) benefit from cooking in just the amount of water they'll absorb. Others (like pasta) need a big pot of boiling water so they have plenty of room to move around. Some beans take forever to cook, and others cook in under an hour. But the principle is the same—they all cook in hot water.

All this is not to say you have to include every obscure grain, from amaranth to teff, in your rotation. You'll have your favorites; we certainly have ours. (Hey, even my mother doesn't like millet.) But the only way to find your favorites is to expand your g&l horizon, and that means experimenting with foods that are a bit low on culinary cachet.

Stop thinking about food for a moment (a tall order, I know) and think of your wardrobe. You probably have a few favorite things—a suit, a jacket, a dress—that you wear on important occasions because they fit well and they're the right color and they look good on you. You probably also have favorite live-in clothes—a sweater that never itches, the exactly perfect jeans.

Then there are the fundamentals that you wear just about every day but almost never think about. For me, it's black T-shirts (remember I live in Manhattan). I must own five hundred black T-shirts and I wear them all the time. Banana Republic and I are on a first-name basis. (They say Tamar, I say Banana.) My shirts aren't all identical; they're different sizes and styles, and they go with everything. I wear them under the suits and over the jeans. Without them, I'd never get dressed.

And so it is with beans and grains. Don't think of them as the underdogs of the culinary world, but rather as the basics on which many, many good meals are built.

Going with the Grain

The Perils of Refinement. Refinement is good. Refined people know the difference between Manet and Monet, Osetra and Beluga, ascots and cravats. Refined oil makes your car go. Refining is something you do to raw material to make it usable or civilized.

The opposite of refined is crude. Crude is bad. It lacks, well, refinement. Crude is the kind of oil that makes intractable slicks in the ocean, the kind that comes gushing out of wells to make ne'er-do-well (read: unrefined) wildcatters rich. Crude is the kind of remark that construction workers make when anyone who looks vaguely female walks by. Crude is something you want to avoid.

But when it comes to grains, you have to set aside your deeply ingrained affinity for refinement. In the grain world, the opposite of refined isn't crude: It's whole. Whole is good. While I have nothing against refined grains—refinement, after all, is what makes pasta and couscous and baguettes possible—whole grains have more fiber and nutrients.

Because grain anatomy varies, so do refining processes, but most "refined" grains have had the bran and germ, their two outer layers, removed, leaving only the endosperm, or innermost seed layer. "Whole" grains have the bran and germ, and the nutrients and fiber that go with them, more or less intact. The proportion of nutrients lost in refinement varies from grain to grain, but it is usually significant. Most of the B vit-amins, iron, and vitamin E are in the bran and germ, as is almost all the fiber.

White rice and the wheat used in white bread, couscous, and pasta are refined grains. Pearl barley, the kind that's most readily available and user-friendly, has had its outer layers removed, but is still rich in fiber, so we cut it some slack. Cornmeal is available either degerminated or whole; the whole version is preferable for most purposes both in taste and nutrition. (See Horn of Polenta, page 104, for more cornmeal infor-mation.) Brown rice, quinoa, millet, bulgur, and the wheat used in whole-wheat bread are whole grains. So is most oatmeal. So are all kinds of weird grains, like spelt and triticale, that you'll find in the health food store. If most of the grains you eat are refined, it's worthwhile to find some whole grains you like. It's even possible that what's standing be-tween you and whole grains isn't preference, but prejudice.

Whole-Grain Bigotry. This is a test. When you hear the phrase "whole grains," do you think of tie-dyed T-shirts, Earth First! and Birken-stocks? Does it conjure up images of Grateful Dead concerts and second-rate poetry readings? Do you think of whole-grain food as crunchy and unsophisticated? Is it paired with things like fake meat made from soy-beans? Does it come in unpalatably large portions? Is it inadequately salted?

If you answered yes to more than two of these questions, you're a Grain Bigot. Grain Bigots get their carbohydrates from pasta, potatoes, and white bread. It's not that they actively dislike whole grains; most haven't eaten enough of them to have an informed opinion. It's more that they're suspicious not just of the grains, but of the lifestyle that goes with them. Millet, bulgur, and quinoa are for Deadheads, bohemians, and communists. The rest of us like our grains refined and our fiscal policy re-sponsible, thank you very much.

I know a lot about this because I am a recovering Grain Bigot. I have learned that I can embrace fiber-rich foods without falling victim to an al-ternative lifestyle. This is not a revelation that came to me or any other ex–Grain Bigot (Grain ex-Bigot?) overnight. This was a slow process. It began with a sandwich on seven-grain bread. I paid close attention for the next forty-eight hours, monitoring for any untoward consequences such as a sudden urge to buy a 1973 Volkswagen bus or experiment with hallucinogenic drugs. Nothing happened. So I went to my parents' house for dinner one night when I knew Mom was serving quinoa (no Grain Bigot, she!). Again, nothing.

Slowly, I found my bigotry lessening until one day I realized I was a big enough person to take whole grains in stride. Now I eat them regularly. I still can't get behind millet and bulgur, but I've switched to brown rice and McCann's steel-cut oatmeal.

While I may be exaggerating about Grain Bigots, whole grains *are* definitely associated with an Earth Dog sensibility. They have the unfortunate reputation of being foods that are eaten only because they're good for you. This isn't wholly inaccurate. There's no doubt that health is part of the reason many whole grains are eaten, but that's no reason to take a principled stand against them. On the contrary, it's a good reason to try to find some you actually enjoy.

If you are a Grain Bigot, you might want to start with barley. Somehow, barley has managed to escape being tarred with the Earth Dog brush. Perhaps it has been protected by its respectable partnerships with beef and mushrooms, both of which are mainstream, conservative foods. But barley is also the most innocuous of the grains that pack a real fiber punch. It slips unobtrusively into soups and stews. It's almost like pasta, and it's just as easy to cook. You might like it.

BARLEY: THE UNDERGRAIN

I have a theory about barley. I think it's a vastly underrated grain, and if people were only aware of its virtues, it would enjoy an enormous surge of popularity. If you haven't caught on yet to barley's virtues, let me enumerate them for you:

- It's easy to cook.
- It's adaptable.
- It's cheap.
- It's white.
- It doesn't have a characteristic taste that takes over a dish.
- It has a nice, innocuous chewy texture.
- It's low in calories.
- It's nutritious and high in fiber.

In short, barley is great because there's nothing to object to. It can stand in for pasta or rice in almost any dish. And it isn't the kind of food you have to talk yourself into liking. You really will like it. I promise.

As I write this, I'm eating a big bowl of mushroom barley ragout, and I'm willing to bet it would appeal to even the most recalcitrant Grain Bigot you know. It's hearty and flavorful. Nobody'll know it's good for you. (Just don't get it in your disk drive.)

The Jake Test. My brother Jake is even more of a Grain Bigot than I am. How, you may be wondering, did Jake and I get to be Grain Bigots when our mother is so pro-grain? Or, if you have even the most rudimentary knowledge of genetics you probably aren't wondering at all, you simply assume Grain Bigotry is a trait we inherited from our father. Bingo! I think the Grain Bigot gene must be linked to the Big Nose gene. (Both, unfortunately, are clearly dominant.)

I recently had Mom, Dad, and Jake over for beef stew, and when Jake learned it was to be served with barley, he didn't try to hide his skepticism. "I don't know about that," he said. "I like my beef stew with noodles. Egg noodles." (Great guest, my brother.) I asked him to reserve judgment and, sure enough, when he asked for seconds he specified a high barley-to-stew ratio.

If barley passes the Jake Test, surely you can try it on your skeptical friends and relations. Even the ones with big noses.

Cooking Barley: The Basics. The kind of barley most humans (as opposed to pigs and cows and a few health fanatics) eat is pearl barley— that is, barley kernels that have been milled to remove the hulls and most of the outer coating. To cook it, you simply boil it in water. There are two ways to do this—the pasta model and the rice model. In the pasta model, you boil a big pot of water, throw in the barley, and drain it when it's done. In the rice model, you cook the barley in just enough water so you don't have to drain it when it's finished. Oddly, the pasta model seems to take a few minutes longer than the rice model. We've speculated that the covered pot preserves steam and the barley is cooking at a somewhat higher temperature—a mild form of the pressure-cooker effect.

I prefer the pasta model, since precision isn't my long suit. Mom prefers the rice model. Not that precision is *her* long suit, she just finds it more convenient and believes it preserves more nutrients. Take your pick.

Barley: The Pasta Model. Bring 6 to 8 cups of water to a boil. Add 1 cup of pearl barley and return to a boil. Lower the heat to a simmer and cook uncovered until the barley is tender, 35 to 40 minutes. Drain.

Barley: The Rice Model. The name says it all. It cooks just like brown rice, but it needs slightly more liquid. Put 1 cup of barley in a saucepan, add 2 cups of water or stock, and bring to a boil. Then lower the heat, cover the pot, and simmer until the barley tastes cooked and all the liquid is absorbed, 25 to 30 minutes. Check after about 20 minutes. You may have to add a little more liquid. Barley can be very thirsty.

You can also use the pilaf method for cooking your barley. Heat a tea-spoon or two of olive oil in your pot, add the barley, and cook, stirring, for 2 or 3 minutes until the grains are lightly coated with oil and smell just a little toasty. Then add the liquid and proceed as directed above. You can also substitute barley for Arborio rice in any risotto recipe. Again, it may require a little more liquid than the rice, and slightly more time—about 40 minutes, compared to 20 to 30 for risotto.

Reheating Barley. Like cooked pasta and white rice, cooked barley clumps. Unlike cooked pasta and white rice, it's easy to unclump. Just run it under, or soak it in, hot water or, if it's going into soup or stew, just add it to the pot. Because cooked barley is easy to handle, it's often conve-nient to cook more than you'll use that day.

Cooked and reheated grains can be tricky because they absorb more liquid when you reheat them. Cooked pasta and rice can't stand up to this without turning mushy, so they should be reheated very quickly, but barley comes out none the worse for wear. Although the kernels do ab-sorb more liquid and get slightly larger, they retain their chewiness.

Barley Recipes: Variations on a Theme. Some foods, like some words and some people, have such a strong association with a partner-ship that they lose their distinct identity. Pity Ginger Rogers, who was never able to establish herself as anything but Fred Astaire's partner. And when was the last time you heard the word "invidious" without its partner in rhetoric, "distinction"?

And so it goes with barley and its mainstream partner, mushrooms. Mushrooms get paired with lots of other things, but poor barley has only the one partner. Just like Fred and Ginger. When I explained my partner-ship theory to my mother and described Fred Astaire as the mushroom of the dancing world, she suggested that I try it the other way around. Bar-ley is the Ginger Rogers of the culinary world. Yeah, I guess that does sound better.

If you or a person you're feeding is a recovering Grain Bigot, you can use this partnership to your advantage. By all means, partner barley with mushrooms (and their sidekick red wine). You'll find that there are end-less ways to manipulate that basic combination. Here are two suggestions.

LENTIL BARLEY SOUP
Makes four 2-cup servings

2 teaspoons olive oil
2 medium onions, chopped
12 ounces fresh mushrooms, sliced
2 large carrots, sliced
2 tablespoons chopped fresh tarragon, or ½ teaspoon dried
5 cups chicken or beef stock
2 cups dry red wine
One 14-ounce can crushed tomatoes
½ cup lentils
½ cup pearl barley
Salt and freshly ground black pepper to taste

1. Heat the olive oil in a large nonstick pot over medium heat. Add the onions and sauté until translucent. Add the mushrooms, carrots, and tarragon and continue sautéing, stirring frequently, until the mushrooms are wilted, about 15 minutes.
2. Add the stock, wine, tomatoes, lentils, and barley. Bring to a boil, then lower the heat and simmer, uncovered, until the lentils and barley are soft, about 35 minutes. Adjust the liquids until the soup has the consistency you like, adding more stock or wine if it's too thick or cooking it longer if it's too thin. Season with salt and pepper.

340 calories, 3 grams fat, 0 grams saturated fat per serving

MUSHROOM BARLEY RAGOUT
Should make 4 to 6 main-dish servings, although 2 or 3 Haspels have been known to make short work of it.

1 tablespoon olive oil

3 medium onions, chopped

5 garlic cloves, minced

1½ pounds fresh mushrooms, sliced (see Notes)

1 red bell pepper, diced

2 tablespoons chopped fresh sage, or 1 teaspoon dried

½ teaspoon cayenne pepper

2 cups dry red wine

3 cups chicken stock

1 cup water

Splash of Worcestershire sauce

2 bay leaves

1 cup pearl barley

1 to 2 teaspoons sugar (optional)

1 cup frozen baby peas

4 ounces low-fat goat cheese or ricotta (optional; see Notes)

Salt to taste

1. Heat the olive oil in a large nonstick pot over medium heat. Add the onions and garlic and sauté until translucent, about 10 minutes. Add the mushrooms, bell pepper, sage, and cayenne and continue sautéing, stirring frequently, until the mushrooms are wilted, about 15 minutes.
2. Add the wine, stock, 1 cup water, Worcestershire, and bay leaves and bring the mixture to a boil. Add the barley, lower the heat, and simmer uncovered until the barley is tender, about 35 to 40 minutes. As the stew cooks, keep tasting it. If it tastes too winy, add sugar a little bit at a time to cut the acidity. You won't need much.
3. When the barley is fully cooked, add the peas, goat cheese, and salt and cook just enough to melt the cheese into the stew and heat the peas through. Serve.

NOTES: Pay attention to your liquid. It will seem like a lot when you first put it in, but the barley absorbs some and some cooks off. If, as your stew cooks, it gets too dry, add more stock, wine, or water, depending on how it tastes. When finished, it should have (obviously!) a stewlike consistency.

I use run-of-the-mill white mushrooms for this, but you can use shiitakes or creminis if you prefer.

Coach Farm makes a terrific low-fat goat cheese. If you can't get it, omit it or substitute regular goat cheese.

250 calories, 3 grams fat, 0 grams saturated fat per serving of 6

BARBARA KNOWS BARLEY

WHEN I WAS A CHILD, my favorite canned soup was Campbell's oxtail. It wasn't that it tasted so awfully good but it was exotic. It had oxtails in it. You know: oxtails! They're those little white things with the line down the middle. I assumed for years that the only unfamiliar objects in the soup were the eponymous oxtails. At an embarrassingly advanced age—probably ten—I took a mouthful of oxtail soup and experienced an epiphany. I suddenly realized those white things had to be some sort of grain or vegetable. They couldn't possibly be part of an animal, certainly not one as large and hearty as an ox. I fished the can out of the garbage pail, read the list of ingredients, and discovered I'd been eating barley. We live and learn.

You too, although probably not laboring under the illusion that it was meat, may have consumed barley only as a soup ingredient. Almost all the barley grown in this country is used either in brewing or for animal food. The little that finds its way into the kitchen almost always ends up in the soup pot. Check your cookbooks if you doubt me. I've checked twenty and found only five barley recipes—all but one of them for soup. But as Tamar points out, we're high on barley these days. Unlike my daughter, I like all kinds of whole grains (except millet), but barley's neutral flavor makes it work in dishes that wouldn't accommodate brown rice or bulgur. Since Tamar's gone the red wine and mushroom route with all her recipes, I thought I'd do something completely different. This dish would be even better with fresh clams, but most of the canned ones I've tried have had a clamlike taste and decent texture. And they sure are handy.

BARLEY WITH WHITE BEANS AND CLAMS

Makes 2 to 4 main-dish servings

¾ cup uncooked pearl barley

1½ cups water, vegetable or chicken stock, or a combination

1 tablespoon olive oil (use more—or less—if you want to)

4 garlic cloves

4 scallions

½ to 1 small hot pepper (jalapeño, habanero, whatever), seeded, or ¼ teaspoon red pepper flakes

½ small red or green bell pepper

½ cup dry white wine

2 cups cooked cannellini or other white beans (canned are okay, but they should be drained and rinsed)

1 tablespoon dried oregano, or 2 tablespoons fresh

One 10-ounce can whole baby clams

One small bunch fresh basil, washed and destemmed (cilantro or Italian parsley may be substituted)

Salt (taste first as canned clams are very salty) and freshly ground black pepper to taste

1. Place the barley and the water or stock in a saucepan and bring to a boil. Lower the heat, cover the pot, and simmer until the barley is cooked but still chewy, about 30 minutes. (Check after 20 minutes. It may be necessary to add more liquid.)
2. Heat the olive oil in a large nonstick skillet or wok. Put the garlic, scallions, hot pepper if using, and bell pepper in the bowl of a food processor and coarsely chop. Add the vegetables to the skillet and sauté over medium heat until wilted, stirring frequently. Add a small amount of wine if needed to prevent sticking.
3. Add the beans, oregano, and red pepper flakes if using. Continue to sauté, stirring for a minute or two. Add the wine and the liquid from the clams. Bring to a boil and cook for 2 to 3 minutes to reduce the liquid slightly.
4. Meanwhile chop the basil in the food processor (no need to wash the bowl first).

5. Add the clams to the skillet. Stir in the barley a little at a time, continuing to cook, until well mixed. Remove from the heat, stir in the basil, and season with salt and pepper. Let rest 5 minutes before serving.

350 calories, 4 grams fat, 0 grams saturated fat per serving of 4

RICE: THE DEFINITIVE TEXT

As the main source of sustenance for about half the world's population, rice is a very important food. Half the world's population is a lot of people. Estimates of per capita consumption vary, but it's probably safe to say that, in rice-dependent countries, each person eats a pound of rice a day. That's a lot of rice.

As anyone who's seen pictures of Southeast Asia knows, rice is grown in flat, floodable fields called paddies. Most varieties of rice (excluding upland, or mountain, rice) spend their days underwater, as tender rice shoots can't tolerate direct sun for more than a couple of days. The need to keep rice paddies flooded has taxed the ingenuity of rice growers from the time it was first cultivated, about five thousand years ago. In fact, the tools of present-day rice-growing bear a striking resemblance to the irrigation systems of ancient China.

As a child I had a book about rice. Actually, I don't think it was really about rice, but I remember it because it had pictures of rice paddies and people in big straw hats working in them. I most vividly remember the pictures of the water buffalo in the fields. (Admittedly, the pictures that truly resonated were the ones of the children riding on the buffalo's back. The book lost some of its appeal when my parents told me unequivocally that No, I could *not* have my own water buffalo.) To this day, water buffalo help with the rice harvest. Modern agriculture hasn't come up with a more efficient, cost-effective system. Or maybe it has, but no one has the nerve to tell the buffalo.

Although you may have seen lots of different fancy kinds of rice cropping up in your local supermarket, nearly all rice can be categorized as either long-grain (Indian) or short-grain (Japanese). Long-grain rice is drier and tends to separate when cooked; short-grain rice is moist and firm and tends to stick together. Most of the rice Americans buy is long-grain, but short-grain rice is sneaking into American markets in the form of specialty rices for risotto (Arborio and Baldo rice) and paella (Bahia rice).

All rice has a hull that has to be removed before the rice can be eaten. What's left is the kernel and the bran, or brown rice. Brown rice is made into white rice by milling, a process that removes all of the bran and most of the germ layer below it. Milled rice is then polished, to remove the high-fat aleurone layer and consequently improve its shelf life by minimizing the chance for rancidity. Polished rice is generally fortified with some of the nutrients that were removed in processing, applied to the outside of the grain. If you buy polished rice, make sure you don't rinse it, as you'll rinse off all the vitamins your rice processors worked so hard to apply.

Converted rice is white rice that has been parboiled before processing. Before even the hull is removed, the grain is wet, steamed, and dried. This process makes the hull easier to remove and helps the grain retain more nutrients. Converted rice has significantly higher levels of thiamin, riboflavin, and niacin than other white rices.

In the United States, rice takes a backseat to other grains. Most of our starch comes to us in the form of bread and pasta. Rice is something we eat in Chinese restaurants and sometimes cook for ourselves and our families, if we're not intimidated by the prospect of Kitchen Disaster #722, an embarrassing mass of inseparably glutinous rice grains.

Take heart. If half the world's population can cook rice, so can you. A billion Chinese can't be wrong. Here's Mom on the basics.

Perfect Rice, Every Time. No Kidding. There is a foolproof way to cook rice—all rice, any rice. It may not always be the way you choose, but I find myself returning to it again and again. It's a low-oil version of the pilaf method that's a Mediterranean standard. Heat a little olive or canola oil in a saucepan that holds approximately twice the volume of the combined rice and liquid. Use 1 to 2 teaspoons of oil for each cup of rice. Add the rice and sauté, stirring constantly for about two minutes or until the rice grains are coated with oil and smell a bit like popcorn. Add 1½ to 2 cups of water or stock for each cup of rice. (I find that 1⅔ cup is almost always right.) Bring the liquid to a boil, then lower the heat and cover the pot. Most rice will cook in about 20 minutes from this point, although some brown rices will require more time.

Lots of cookbooks will tell you brown rice takes an hour to cook. I've never found any rice that took more than 45 minutes and that's exceptional. I don't know where the cookbook writers are getting theirs. Brown rice may require a little more liquid than white rice, but not much. I think one of the reasons brown rice is so widely despised is that most cooking instructions specify so much liquid and such a long time in the pot that the result is a nasty beige porridge. Try ignoring everything you've ever read before about cooking brown rice, including the directions on the package.

Peek at your rice after 15 minutes. DO NOT STIR. Check for doneness by extracting a kernel or two to taste. Check to see if all the water is absorbed by gently tilting the pot. If it's dry but not done, add a little more liquid and continue cooking. If it's done but still wet, drain it in a colander, then return it to the pot and cook for a minute or two, stirring until it's dry enough.

High-quality rice is fairly forgiving. It tastes good either a bit crunchy or quite soft. You're all right as long as it's not hard or wet or gummy, and if you cook it my way, it won't be. You can fluff it up a bit with a fork before you serve it if you want, but I find I can dump it right into a bowl or onto a platter and the grains separate beautifully.

Some cooks prefer the free-boiling method for cooking rice. That just means boiling it in quite a bit of water until it's done and then draining it and steaming it briefly in a colander. Unfortunately, free-boiling leaves a lot of the nutrients and flavor in the water. If you do it this way, don't use more than about four parts water to one part rice, and by all means save the cooking liquid for soups, sauces, baking, etc. This is rice water, a major source of nutrition for close to half the world's population. If you throw it away, you deserve to be tortured by guilt. (And don't send me your rice water in the mail with a note telling me I can send it on to Ethiopia.) The advantage of free-boiling, of course, is that it requires no oil. But my way only adds about ten fat calories to every ½ cup of rice, and it provides the base for a lot of excellent variations.

Before you add the rice to the oil you can sauté garlic, onions, green and red bell peppers, orzo pasta—almost anything that can cook along with the rice and augment its flavor—to create a pilaf. Just don't add anything that's going to end up limp and boiled tasting after 15 to 20 minutes in the pot. Tamar's lists in Adding Veggies to Risotto, page 92, are just as applicable to plain old rice. If you have just a little of one of the quick-cooking vegetables, you don't even need to cook it separately. You can put it on top of the rice to steam during the last few minutes of cooking, after most of the liquid is gone.

Rice is one of the least complicated, most versatile foods you'll ever cook. Even risotto, commonly believed to involve an intimidating mystique, Tamar has found simpler than she would have thought possible.

CONQUERING RISOTTO: DON'T PANIC, IT'S ONLY RICE

I have a cookbook called *An Invitation to Italian Cooking,* which was naturally the first place I looked when I wanted to know how you *really* cook risotto. After it warned me, rather sternly, to choose Arborio or Vialone rice and to cook it in a pan that was big enough for the rice and the stock, this is what it had to say:

The spoon for stirring must be a wooden one. The heat must be moderate and constant. The stock that is to be added to the rice must be kept simmering to avoid interruption of the cooking process. . . . Add only as much hot stock at a time as the rice calls for—that is, not too wet and drowning the rice, but enough to see the grains gradually absorbing the liquid as they cook. . . . Continue to stir and add the stock until the rice appears to be cooked.

Sheesh! No wonder risotto has a reputation for being difficult.

So, the first time I ever made risotto, I did what I always do with a recipe that seems too exacting. I ignored it. And guess what? The sky didn't fall, the wrath of the food gods didn't descend upon me, and the risotto was delicious.

On further investigation, I discovered that other cookbooks took my view of the subject. In fact, some advised cooking risotto just as you would cook regular rice, by covering it and leaving it alone. Others suggested a compromise: Cook the risotto uncovered, add the stock in several stages, and stir occasionally.

For the last word on risotto, I thought I'd try all three methods (although I reduced the amount of oil in the traditional version) and report on the results.

METHOD 1

THE TRADITIONAL ITALIAN METHOD
Makes 2 to 4 servings

4 cups stock, preferably chicken
1 teaspoon olive oil
1 cup Arborio rice
¼ teaspoon salt, or to taste

1. Heat the stock to a simmer and keep it hot on the stove as you cook the rice. This ensures that the cooking process isn't interrupted by adding cold stock.
2. Heat the olive oil in a heavy nonstick skillet over medium heat. Add the rice and stir until it is coated and heated through. Add 1 cup of the simmering stock and stir until the liquid is absorbed by the rice. Add the remaining stock ½ cup at a time, stirring constantly and waiting until it is absorbed before adding the next ½ cup.

3. The risotto is done when the grains are cooked through and have a creamy consistency. This usually takes 20 to 30 minutes. Season with the salt and serve.

260 calories, 1 gram fat, 0 grams saturated fat per serving of 4

METHOD 2

THE COOK-IT-LIKE-RICE METHOD
Makes 2 to 4 servings

1 teaspoon olive oil
1 cup Arborio rice
¼ teaspoon salt, or to taste
1⅔ cups stock, preferably chicken

1. Heat the olive oil in a small nonstick saucepan with a close-fitting lid. Add the rice and salt and stir until the rice is heated through and coated with the oil. Add the stock and bring to a boil. Lower the heat to a simmer, put the lid on, and cook for about 17 minutes.

180 calories, 1 gram fat, 0 grams saturated fat per serving of 4

METHOD 3

THE COMPROMISE
Makes 2 to 4 servings

1 teaspoon olive oil
1 cup Arborio rice
3½ cups stock
¼ teaspoon salt, or to taste

1. Heat the olive oil in a heavy nonstick skillet over medium heat. Add the rice and stir until it is coated and heated through. Add half the stock and simmer, stirring occasionally, until the stock is absorbed, 5 to 10 minutes. Add the remaining stock 1 cup at a time, waiting until it is absorbed before adding the next cup. Stir occasionally throughout the process. Season with the salt and serve.

190 calories, 1 gram fat, 0 grams saturated fat per serving of 4

The Results. All three were excellent. It's true that the traditional method yielded risotto that was better than the others (it had a nice creaminess, while each grain maintained its texture), but the other two were just fine. If you didn't have the three risottos side by side, you might have a hard time distinguishing among them.

Adding Veggies to Risotto. Vegetable additions to risotto fall into two categories: those you add at the beginning of the cooking process and those you add at the end. Those added at the beginning are the ones that stand up to long cooking times and add their flavor to the rice. Those added at the end are the more delicate, quick-cooking veggies that would be reduced to green mush if they were subjected to the 20 minutes or so of cooking risotto requires.

Those to Be Added at the Beginning. Once you've heated the olive oil, add the vegetables and cook until they've wilted. Then add the rice and cook as directed.

Examples of veggies to add at the beginning:

- Onions
- Garlic
- Mushrooms
- Leeks

Those to Be Added at the End. Steam, blanch, or sauté these vegetables separately, timing them so they're done just as the risotto finishes cooking. Add the cooked vegetables to the cooked risotto, stir to combine, and serve.

Examples of veggies to add at the end:

- Spinach
- Asparagus
- Broccoli
- Peppers
- Peas
- Green beans

Adding Other Stuff. I would suggest adding fresh herbs at the end, but dried herbs and spices, especially the latter, are best added at the beginning. Another good (and traditional) last-minute addition to any risotto that doesn't contain seafood is freshly grated Parmesan cheese. As little as 1 tablespoon per serving can be a significant enhancement.

Cooking Liquids. Most risotto recipes call for stock and some for a combination of stock and wine. You can, however, use just about any flavored liquid to cook your risotto. Use the liquid from canned tomatoes, the water you soaked dried mushrooms in, clam juice, or even leftover soup.

Jump Right In. So what do you conclude when you cook something three different ways and it's just fine in each case? Well, I conclude that risotto is one of the easiest, most forgiving foods to cook. It really doesn't matter much how you do it. Just pick your vegetables and herbs and forge ahead, confident that it's incredibly difficult to screw it up. After all, this isn't nuclear physics. It's just rice.

Mom's leek and mushroom recipe is for a more-or-less traditional risotto, but it can obviously be adapted to one of the heretical methods above.

LEEK AND MUSHROOM RISOTTO
Makes 2 to 4 main-dish servings

1 ounce dried mushrooms

3 cups water or stock, slightly warmed

2 or 3 large leeks

3 or 4 garlic cloves

1 medium onion

½ teaspoon olive oil

1 cup Arborio rice

½ cup dry white wine

¼ teaspoon dried tarragon, or
     1 teaspoon chopped fresh

1 small bunch Italian parsley

Salt to taste

1 or 2 tablespoons plain nonfat yogurt, yogurt cheese (page 271),
     or low-fat goat cheese (optional)

1. Soak the dried mushrooms in the water or stock for an hour. Strain the broth. Check the mushrooms to see that they are free of sand and remove their stems and any tough portions. Put the stems in the food processor fitted with the chopping blade.
2. Slice the leeks lengthwise in half and clean them carefully. Add some of the green outer leaves of the leeks to the mushroom broth. (Not too

many. You want to augment the broth's flavor, but you don't want a lot of long, tough pieces of leek getting in your way when you're cooking the risotto.) Add the tender parts of the leeks to the food processor. Bring the broth to a gentle simmer in a small saucepan.

3. Peel the garlic cloves. Peel and quarter the onion. Put them in the food processor with the mushroom stems and leeks and chop to a coarse purée.

4. Heat the oil in a heavy saucepan over medium heat. Add the vegetable purée and sauté until it is soft and has lost its raw odor. Add the rice and sauté for 2 to 3 minutes, stirring to coat it well. Add the wine and cook, stirring gently, until it has been absorbed.

5. Add the simmering broth about ½ cup at a time, stirring gently and frequently, until the rice is cooked to your satisfaction and is moist but not soupy. This will take approximately 20 minutes.

6. About 10 minutes into the cooking process, add the soaked mushrooms and the dried tarragon if using.

7. Remove the tough stems from the parsley and place it in the food processor along with the fresh tarragon if using. Process to a coarse purée.

8. Remove the risotto from the heat, add the parsley, salt, and the yogurt or cheese (if using) and mix thoroughly. Turn out onto a serving platter and serve with a green salad and/or a steamed green vegetable.

240 calories, 0 grams fat, 0 grams saturated fat per serving of 4

LUNDBERG RICE

RICE QUALITY CAN VARY, so I try to find Lundberg rices. The Lundbergs grow and package at least five different rices that I know about, all delicious and distinctive in flavor. They are widely available—at least in New York and San Francisco. They can also be ordered from Walnut Acres (page 304).

I once wrote to the Lundbergs but learned that they have no mail-order division. They did, however, send me several issues of a wonderful newsletter that told me more about rice and organic farming than I ever wanted to know. It had a regular feature called "Out Standing in the Field," illustrated with a picture of the Lundberg brothers hip deep in rice plants under a sunny sky.

The first time I saw this I chortled audibly and attracted my husband's attention. "Oh," he remarked when I shared the source of my pleasure with him, "a Norwegian joke." It's really not fair. I laugh at Jewish jokes. We Norwegians cherish our jokes. We have so few of them. But whatever you may think of Lundberg humor, the rice is unbeatable.

QUINOA: A CHALLENGE TO GRAIN BIGOTRY

I have a love-hate relationship with health food stores. On the one hand, I am offended by the hype: the mindless touting of anything "natural" and "organic," the aggressive marketing of worthless herbs and supplements. On the other hand, I know that, without health food stores, foods I've been enjoying for years would have been unavailable to me—things like unusual dried legumes and freshly ground peanut butter. Not to mention quinoa.

Here's the quinoa report: Quinoa (pronounced KEEN-wah—Tamar thinks it sounds like a Japanese management concept) is a grain native to Bolivia, Chile, and Peru, where it has long been cultivated by natives of the Andean plateau. Quinoa, corn, and potatoes were the three staple foods of the Incan civilization. (These foods can combine excellently in your kitchen too. Quinoa, sliced potatoes, and corn kernels—all precooked—can be heated together in a nonstick skillet and topped with some parsley or cilantro to make a fine main dish. But I digress.) Quinoa means "Mother Grain" in the Incan language, and this plant was so important to the Incan diet that the king planted the first row of quinoa each year with a solid gold spade, at least that's what it says on the quinoa box. Independent of information disseminated by the packagers, I can assure you that quinoa is a source of high-quality protein. It contains much more lysine than other grains—almost as much as dreaded soybeans—and can be a valuable addition to a plant-based diet.

I admit that I was initially a little reluctant to try quinoa. I'm not much for food mystique, so "The Supergrain of the Ancient Incas" ballyhoo put me off. On the other hand, it was something people ate and I hadn't eaten any yet, so eventually my curiosity got the better of me. A number of other such experimental forays—into sea vegetables, for example—have led nowhere. But I found quinoa had possibilities and I went back for more. I've been cooking it fairly regularly for about fifteen years.

Quinoa tastes good. Its flavor is not especially assertive, but it's light and pleasant. Pleasant, that is, provided the saponin coating is thoroughly removed. These clever little grains have evolved with a bitter covering that makes them unpalatable in their natural state, enabling them to fall to the ground and reproduce themselves undisturbed. Most packagers of quinoa do a pretty good job of washing off the saponin, but giving it another rinse at home is a good idea. I have occasionally forgone this step when I've placed a raw grain on my tongue and been unable to extract any bitterness. This seems to be a reliable test. I should warn you, though, that a few times I've had quinoa that tasted slightly bitter even after thorough washing. If this happens to you, try another package, or perhaps another brand. Use up your inferior quinoa in spicy soups.

You can use quinoa just as you would rice or barley or couscous. Make a quinoa pilaf or just serve it under vegetables or seafood. It cooks in less time than brown rice, so if your public is hungry and time is of the essence, a pot of quinoa can bail you out. It will be done by the time you've stir-fried whatever you're stir-frying.

Quinoa is the best grain I've found for cold salads. It doesn't get sticky and clump up, and a little of its cooking liquid can replace some of the oil in the dressing. It has just enough flavor and textural interest not to be lost among the other ingredients, and its color, a sort of goldy beige, is attractive. A number of people to whom "health food" is an oxymoron have eaten such salads at my table without complaint. I've provided a few suggestions for quinoa salad in the recipe below, but just about anything goes.

These days quinoa is often sold in supermarkets as well as health food stores, and most likely you can get both whole-grain quinoa and quinoa flakes. The latter make a decent quick-cooking cereal, albeit rather expensive.

QUINOA SALAD
Makes 3 main-dish or 6 side-dish servings

For the salad
1 cup raw quinoa
2½ cups water
1 cup thinly sliced carrots
1 cup coarsely chopped fennel bulb or celery
½ cup coarsely chopped red bell pepper
3 scallions, chopped

For the vinaigrette
1 tablespoon lemon juice

¼ cup quinoa cooking liquid, olive oil, or a combination

1 to 4 garlic cloves, minced or pressed

*1 teaspoon dried herbs, such as thyme, oregano, rosemary, or a
combination, or 1 tablespoon fresh*

Salt to taste

1 cup minced fresh parsley or cilantro

1. Rinse the quinoa thoroughly and drain. Combine with the water in a small saucepan and bring to a boil. (This amount of water provides for leftover cooking liquid. If you want your quinoa to absorb all the water, use only 2 cups.) Lower the heat to a simmer, cover, and cook for about 12 minutes. (Some quinoa takes a few minutes longer.) The cooked grains should be slightly translucent, and the crescent-shaped germ should be visible.
2. Let the quinoa cool to tepid, then add the vegetables. Combine the ingredients for the vinaigrette, being sure to immerse the cut or pressed garlic in the liquid before it can oxidize. (Alternatively, use roasted garlic, which is more forgiving, but you'll need at least twice as much.)
3. Combine the vinaigrette with the salad ingredients and add the parsley or cilantro. Let stand at least a few minutes before serving. If the salad must wait much more than an hour, refrigerate it, but I think it tastes best at room temperature.

150 calories, 4 grams fat, 0 grams saturated fat per side-dish serving

We've covered two common grains and one slightly weird one. We could go on and on, but at least you and the major grains have been introduced. Let's talk about a grain food we all know and love.

NOODLING ALONG

If you're happily scarfing up the standard American diet, pasta may well be the only main dish you consume on a regular basis that we discuss in this book. As you move away from a meat-centered regimen, most likely you will continue to rely on it as a base for a number of favorite meals. I certainly do. Pasta is familiar gastronomic ground to most of us. Every wheat-eating culture seems to have developed some variation of the noodle, and the Italian version has conquered the world. Later in this book we'll talk about a number of things to combine with your pasta. But first, for the pasta novice, a few notes on the noodle itself.

Cooking pasta properly is not as tricky as you may have been led to believe. For years I tried to cook the standard American brands of dried pasta—made from a combination of durum and semolina flours—so as to achieve the proper al dente bite and no gummy coating. After many years of trial and error, I was usually successful. Just about the time I mastered the technique, imported Italian all-semolina pastas became widely available in the New York area and changed my life forever. No longer was it necessary to remove the pasta from the heat at precisely the crucial moment and rinse it with water of precisely the proper temperature.

Not that you can leave your pasta boiling unattended while you write the Great American Novel. But it won't go from raw to mushy in 30 seconds. Lots of all-semolina pastas are available, several of which are now made in this country. If you want to buy American, Ronzoni and Master's Choice (the A&P house brand) are both excellent, reasonably priced, come in a variety of shapes, and are packed in boxes that protect the strands from breakage. (I can't get exercised about whether or not my pasta's broken, but I guess it bothers some people.) The better-known boxed Italian brands are expensive, but most markets seem to carry at least one cheap obscure brand of imported all-semolina pasta in cellophane bags. I think it tastes just as good as the pricey kind.

Now that I don't use butter, cream, or large quantities of olive oil in my pasta sauces, I almost always opt for dried rather than fresh pasta. Unless it's very fresh and cooked very carefully, fresh pasta is too soft to marry well with low-fat sauces. This is especially true of fresh pastas that don't contain egg yolk. If you make your own pasta and you're good at it, or if you can buy it freshly cut from the pasta maker on the corner, fine. Otherwise, I strongly recommend sticking to the dried varieties.

Pasta may be the ideal vehicle food. It can serve as a bed for almost any combination of vegetables. It also makes an excellent foundation for a cold salad. It's easy to keep around the house and it cooks quickly. Besides, you like it and so do your kids. You probably eat it pretty often. However, some nutrition gurus will tell you to eat only whole-grain pasta because it's more nutritious. Well, it is. That's indisputable. When you eat lots of all-semolina pasta, you're cheating yourself of the fiber and some of the nutrients you'd get from whole-wheat pasta or from other whole grains. But if you want a pasta that blends well with any sauce or topping, all-semolina is the way to go. It doesn't take a Grain Bigot to perceive that whole-wheat pasta has a distinctive texture and flavor that overwhelms all but the most assertive sauces. So try to branch out in other directions. If you can't hack whole-wheat pasta (I can, but just barely), maybe you can strike up an enduring relationship with brown rice, or barley, or even quinoa. Variety, as well as being the watchword of every nutritionist, really is the spice of life.

If You Can Boil Water . . . To cook dried pasta, boil a lot of water, at least 2, but preferably 3, quarts for every ½ pound. Add the pasta, stirring gently with a fork to separate strands or pieces. Stir every 2 or 3 minutes as the pasta cooks, just enough to make sure that none sticks to the bottom and sides of the pot. (The more water you use, the less frequently you need to stir.) When the pasta begins to seem limp rather than stiff, taste a strand or piece and repeat every couple of minutes until you're satisfied that it's cooked.

Pour the cooked pasta into a colander to drain. Don't rinse it, but it's not a bad idea to add a little of some slightly viscous liquid at this point (while it's draining in the colander). Chicken, fish, or vegetable stock will do, as will evaporated skim milk, or the cooking liquid from beans, or a little of the sauce you're cooking, or the water you've put into the tomato can to wash out the remains—you get the idea. Some of this liquid will drain off with the cooking water, but it will get the marriage of pasta and sauce off to a good start.

I do sometimes use whole-wheat pasta. Cook it as directed above; it takes a minute or two longer. It's all right with a really assertive red sauce, but if it's lightly sauced, it cries for oil in a louder voice than semolina pasta. As for so-called vegetable pastas—spinach, beet, whatever—use them if you like the color or the taste, but don't expect anything special from them in the line of nutrients. They don't contain enough of the vegetable to make any nutritional difference.

Another pasta variation we enjoy is soba noodles. They are made of a combination of buckwheat and wheat flours and cook fairly quickly. They are flavorful and contain more fiber than semolina pasta. Unfortunately, they also contain salt, often a substantial amount. As a result, we don't eat them very often and then only with lots and lots of vegetables. They make a tasty base for stir-fry, but not for the salt sensitive.

Saucing the Pasta. It's fine to just move your cooked pasta promptly to the finished sauce, but most low-fat pasta preparations are improved if the pasta cooks for a minute or two in the sauce before serving. I drain most of my pasta (not too conscientiously if my sauce is thick) while it is still quite firm (I can still see an uncooked core when I bite into it) and add it to the sauce in its pot. I combine it with the sauce and cook it over low heat for about 2 minutes. Off heat, I add a lot of chopped parsley, basil, or cilantro to the pot and stir or toss gently to incorporate. Finally, I turn it out on a serving platter and top it with a bit more of the herb and some freshly ground pepper.

If you use this method for fresh pasta, cook it very briefly in boiling water—not more than a minute after the water returns to a boil—before you add it to the sauce. It's delicate, and when overcooked it's a disaster. Don't forget that it will continue to cook in the sauce after you've removed it from the heat. By all means, however, finish your whole-wheat pasta this way. In fact, I would go so far as to say that you should definitely use this technique if you want your whole-wheat pasta to be worth eating.

Lots of you out there may be eating pasta that is not really sauced but merely tossed with a lot of oil and garlic and topped with some vegetables. I used to do that a lot in olden times. You can still prepare pastas in more or less that style.

Start by cooking 4 to 6 ounces of fresh pasta. Meanwhile, sauté 2 to 4 cloves of minced or sliced garlic in 1 or 2 teaspoons of olive oil in either a nonstick pot or one with good food-release properties such as Calphalon. Keep the heat fairly low and watch carefully. As soon as the garlic is soft and has absorbed most of the oil, raise the heat slightly and add about a tablespoon of vinegar, wine, or stock. Stir to deglaze the pot. Immediately add ½ to 1 cup dry white wine or stock. In my opinion, chicken stock works best. Boil to reduce to approximately half its original volume. Add some red pepper flakes if you like them. Add the cooked pasta to the pot (for this technique it should be well drained) along with whatever else you want to include: steamed, sautéed, or roasted vegetables, and/or some precooked shellfish. Hold a little stock or some evaporated skim milk in reserve to add in case the pasta seems too dry. Incorporate lots of one or more of the big three herbs—parsley, cilantro, basil—reserving a little to sprinkle on top. Serve at once.

I think the above method adapts well to either all-semolina or fresh homemade-style pasta. You can prepare whole-wheat pasta this way if you want to but don't invite me to dinner.

There'll be more on pasta in Chapter 6, where we discuss sauces. But before we move on to cornmeal we should mention that there's yet another way to add variety to your pasta repertoire. Couscous, the Moroccan version of pasta, is just about the handiest grain food there is.

COUSCOUS: ONE OF THE BASIC FOOD GROUPS

Twenty years ago I don't think I was even sure what couscous was. I just had a vague idea it was some sort of Middle Eastern dish with a cute name. When I began to read the work of Paula Wolfert and became somewhat better informed, I conflated it with the classic Moroccan stews that bear its name and in which, along with meat, fish, or vegetables, it plays a role. But couscous is really just another kind of semolina pasta. The only unique thing about it, besides its extremely small size, is that each grain is coated with all-purpose flour to prevent sticking. The stews are called "couscous" just the way you call linguine "linguine" no matter what you combine it with.

Few people who weren't into Middle Eastern food ever ate couscous until quite recently. Now, however, it's available in most neighborhood supermarkets. (In unenlightened localities you may still have to seek it out in a health food store or specialty market.) This change is not the result of a surge of interest in the foods of Morocco, but rather of a growing interest in grain dishes as mainstays of healthful eating. And, of course, there's also the fact that preparing couscous really can be as easy as boiling water.

Couscous the Hard Way. That's not the traditional Moroccan way, however. For really authentic couscous, you start by spreading medium-grain semolina on a large, flat platter. Moisten it with cold water and rub it, gradually adding all-purpose flour as you work, until it looks like couscous to you. An experienced Moroccan cook then tosses the grains from one basket to another in such a way that the ones that are too small remain in the first basket. Then she steams the couscous, uncovered, in her couscoussière (a tall pot into which fits a smaller, rounded receptacle with holes in the bottom) for 15 minutes and spreads it in a flat dish to dry. Now she's got the equivalent of what you buy in the box at the supermarket. Don't try this at home or, if you do, don't blame me when you're left with nothing but a sticky mess and children who keep asking why they can't play with flour too. But perhaps you can make couscous happen this way. I'm told that millions do.

The remaining steps in making traditional couscous aren't really all that arduous. You need a couscoussière or a large pot with a steamer insert. You moisten the couscous, *the kind that comes in the box* (using 1 cup of water for each cup of couscous), spread it out in a large flat pan, and allow it to sit for about 15 minutes. Then work it by hand, breaking up any lumps with your fingers. Perhaps at this point you'll have a meat or veggie mixture cooking in the bottom of your couscoussière (if not, just bring some water to a boil).

Fit the steamer into the pot, sealing the seam between the two parts with a moistened length of cheesecloth (or any other thin cloth, or aluminum foil) so that no steam escapes. Spoon the couscous into the top section and steam, uncovered, for about 15 minutes. Dump the couscous back in the flat pan, allow it to cool a few minutes, sprinkle it with a little cold water (about ¼ cup for each cup of couscous), and again work it with your fingers to break up lumps. Let it dry for up to an hour.

A little before serving time, work the couscous by hand one last time. By now you almost certainly have something cooking in the bottom of the pot, so just insert the steamer again, seal as before, add the couscous, and steam, uncovered, for 15 minutes.

I would never have paid attention to such complications except that several years ago I ate couscous in a Middle Eastern restaurant in Montreal that was a revelation. I learned that the way to produce this wonderfully light, virtually ethereal stuff was by following the steps above. But if you think it's just too much trouble, there is an easier way to get nearly as good a result.

Couscous: A Kinder, Gentler Method. Begin by preheating your oven to 350°F. Then place your couscous in an ovenproof dish with a tight-fitting lid. Add 1 cup of water or stock (at room temperature) for each cup of couscous and stir to mix. Soak for at least 20 minutes, uncovered, then use your fingers to break up any lumps. Cover the baking dish, using aluminum foil if necessary to make a tight seal. Bake for 20 minutes, fluff with a fork, and do with it what you will.

After the soaking step, your couscous will look rather dry and you'll be tempted to add more liquid before you put it in the oven. Try to resist the impulse. If your dish is tightly covered, you'll get lighter, fluffier couscous with the liquid kept to a minimum. Only if you're using a liquid that contains a certain amount of solid material, like the V-8 juice in the recipe below, will you need to add a little extra. Trust me on this.

We're indebted to Frances McCullough and Barbara Witt (*Great Food Without Fuss,* Henry Holt, 1992) for this method of cooking couscous. While it's more time-consuming than the mode usually recommended on the package, it's really no more work for the cook, and the results are vastly superior.

Couscous to the Rescue. My pantry is never without a supply of couscous, and much of it is used in an ad hoc, impromptu fashion. Couscous is very, very small, so it cooks very, very quickly, and its ingenious coating makes it resistant to terminal clumping. (If you've ever drained your pasta and then been distracted by a crying child or an interesting phone call, you know what I mean. You come back to one huge, colander-shaped noodle.) When you need a starch in a hurry, you can just bring some water or stock to a boil, add the couscous, and let it stand for 5 minutes. Your results won't match the traditional or the McCullough/Witt method described above, but, fluffed with a fork and served with a flavorful sauce or stew, this instant couscous will be perfectly satisfactory—a whole lot better than Minute Rice.

Couscous has other uses the directions on the box don't tell you about. Do you avoid oatmeal because you find the quick-cooking kind cloying and sticky? Next time, use one part couscous for every two or three parts oatmeal. I find Quaker Multigrain Oatmeal, one of the most nutritious and fibrous hot cereals but rather a trial to eat by itself, highly palatable when combined with couscous.

Something wrong with your soup? Too thin? Grainy, overlegumed texture? Add a little couscous. Let the soup simmer a few minutes, and then, if your problem persists, add a little more. You can serve it almost immediately after the last addition. By the time you get the soup to the table, the couscous should be cooked. (Anyway, it'll continue to cook in the bowls, so your family will decide that the little hard things they detected in the first couple mouthfuls must have been imagined.)

Is couscous nutritious? Not especially. It has the faults and virtues of all processed grain foods. It's a complex carbohydrate and it's very low in fat: That's good. It lacks the fiber and lots of the nutrients you find in whole grains: That's not so good. Whole-wheat couscous can be found in some health food stores, but it cooks and tastes so much like regular couscous that I doubt it really contains all that much whole wheat.

Couscous certainly isn't bad for you, and nearly everyone likes it. It can cook in just 5 minutes and is endlessly versatile. It can be a major weapon in averting culinary failure. Never run out of it.

SPICY COUSCOUS WITH LEEKS, CHICKPEAS, AND PEPPERS
Makes 2 or 3 main-dish servings or 6 side-dish servings

1 cup couscous
¾ cup V-8 or tomato juice (see Notes)
½ cup water
3 medium or 2 large leeks, or 6 to 8 scallions
1 to 2 tablespoons olive oil
1 cup cooked chickpeas, drained and rinsed if canned
¼ to ½ teaspoon red pepper flakes (optional: V-8 juice may deliver
    enough spice for some tastes)
Salt to taste (be careful if you're using salty juice)
1 medium to large red bell pepper, sliced
¼ cup chopped cilantro or Italian parsley

1. Preheat the oven to 350°F.
2. Place the couscous in an ovenproof dish with a tight-fitting lid. Pour

the juice and ½ cup water over the couscous and stir to mix. Allow the mixture to stand, uncovered, for at least 15 minutes. Cover the dish (use aluminum foil if the lid is not really tight) and bake for 20 minutes. Meanwhile, clean the leeks and cut them into ¼-inch slices. Heat the olive oil in a nonstick skillet with a cover. Add the leeks and sauté briefly over medium heat. Add the chickpeas, red pepper flakes, and salt if using. Lower the heat and cover the skillet. (If you're using just a little olive oil, stir in about 1 tablespoon water or juice at this point to prevent sticking.) Cook until the leeks are quite soft, about 5 minutes. Uncover, raise the heat slightly, add the bell pepper, and sauté for 2 to 3 minutes.

3. Combine the vegetables and couscous in a large bowl, adding the cilantro or parsley. (Or spread the vegetables over the couscous in the dish in which it was cooked.)

NOTES: Hard-core veggie eaters enjoy this as a main dish. For others it makes an excellent accompaniment to fish or shellfish.

Be aware that V-8 and most commercial tomato juices are high in sodium. If that's a concern for you, either look for a juice that's low in salt or substitute good old chicken stock.

220 calories, 4 grams fat, 0 grams saturated fat per side-dish serving

HORN OF POLENTA

Next time you're in an upscale restaurant eating your grilled polenta with exotic mushrooms and sun-dried tomatoes, stop and listen very carefully. Underneath the clatter of cutlery and the chatter of happy diners, you'll hear another sound. It's the ghosts of a whole lot of Italian and Irish peasants from the nineteenth century. Look closely and you'll see them lining the walls. They're thin and dressed in rags and they're pointing at your plate. The sound you hear is their laughter. They're slapping each other on the back, doubling up in uncontrollable mirth. Don't let them disturb you; be glad they could come back for the joke.

Until very recently cornmeal was the food of the poor. Cornmeal mush was something you ate when it was all that stood between you and starvation. During the great potato blight of 1846 Sir Robert Peel imported cornmeal into Ireland from America. Repelled by its yellow color, and without a clue as to its proper preparation, the Irish dubbed it "Peel's Brimstone." There were rumors that it poisoned those who ate it, and when it was fed to poorhouse inmates, they rioted. Ultimately, the quality of the meal that reached the countryside was improved, and the peasants learned the art of making cornmeal mush. "Peel's Brimstone" saved a lot of lives in Ireland, but the people never took it to their hearts.

In Italy, however, especially in Tuscany where a malaria epidemic in the late nineteenth century resulted in famine and the virtual disappearance of wheat for a time, cornmeal quickly became a staple food. It was easy for the Italians to embrace this new grain. *Pulmentum*, mush made from grain, had been eaten in Rome from its founding, most likely enjoyed by Romulus himself. In the early days it was made from spelt or millet; barley and wheat came later. It was the peasant's daily fare as well as the field ration of the Roman soldier. Every soldier received daily about two pounds of grain, which he roasted on a hot stone over his campfire and crushed. He could put it into his haversack, and it was available to boil into gruel—either to be eaten on the spot, or allowed to harden into a sort of unleavened pancake.

So, unlike the Irish, the Italians were ready for corn. There is no grain that is so well adapted to the *pulmentum* system. Its major shortcoming in baking—the lack of gluten—becomes a virtue when it comes to making porridge. Cornmeal isn't sticky. Corn eating caught on in Italy about 1650, earlier than anywhere else in Europe. Gradually it became the first choice for porridge among the poor, especially in Lombardy and Tuscany. And while cornmeal was still eaten in the New World, where it had originated, American cooks tended to mix it with wheat flour and enrich it with a lot of eggs and butter.

But basic polenta—cornmeal mush in various guises—is back. How to explain its journey from rags to riches, from peasant hovel to restaurant of the moment? Partly, of course, it has benefited from grains' general rise in status. They form the base of the new nutritional pyramid. What used to be plain old starch is complex carbohydrates now. Besides, we've become more adventurous in our eating. We keep investigating the world's great cuisines in search of new tastes and textures. And polenta is just new enough. It offers the familiar taste and texture of good old cornmeal in a slightly unusual guise. You can have a gastronomic adventure without going very far afield, sort of like the kid who runs away from home but doesn't want to cross the street.

All you need to prepare polenta at home is cornmeal, a pot, and a sturdy spoon (preferably a wooden one) for stirring. We like stone-ground cornmeal, made from corn that hasn't been degerminated (it's excellent for the Cornmeal Griddlecakes, page 108), but the blander supermarket variety works fine in most recipes, especially those with a number of other ingredients. Some people prefer it, in fact. If you like stone-ground whole cornmeal, you say it has a chewy consistency. If you don't, you say it contains little hard things that get between your teeth. If you use whole cornmeal, store it in the freezer. The corn germ contains a lot of polyunsaturated oil, so whole cornmeal will go rancid if left to its own devices. Or make a lot of polenta and use your cornmeal up fast.

Cooking polenta is an undemanding, albeit somewhat time-consuming activity. The fact that it's easy to make enough for more than one meal takes some of the pain out of the preparation. (In fact, it's the cornerstone of the Tuscan *incatenata* that serves as the model for the concept of pantry momentum we'll discuss in Chapter 7.) You do need to add the cornmeal to the liquid gradually, stirring all the while, or you can get irreversible clumping. You can control the flow better if you let the meal trickle between your fingers rather than pouring from a container. Some recipes recommend whisking the meal into the liquid, but we've always found the trusty wooden spoon to work well. Don't worry if a few lumps form. Break up the large ones by pressing them against the side of the pot with the back of your stirring spoon. If one or two remain, they will be undetectable in the finished dish. That's another one of the joys of a gluten-free grain. Lumps don't develop a life of their own the way they do, for example, in sauces thickened with flour. Your little bag of cornmeal contains a world of possibilities. It's a cornucopia!

BASIC POLENTA
Makes 4 to 6 servings

> 5 cups water
> 1 teaspoon salt, or to taste
> 1½ cups cornmeal

1. Bring the water to a boil in a nonstick pot. Add the salt. Sprinkle in the cornmeal gradually, stirring constantly with a wooden spoon. When all the cornmeal has been added, reduce the heat to low. Cook, stirring frequently, until the spoon can stand upright and the mixture pulls away from the sides of the pan, about 30 minutes. Serve hot.
2. If you are making polenta to slice, transfer it to a large pan or baking sheet and smooth to a uniform height, ½ to 1 inch.
3. Chill several hours or until firm enough to slice.

150 calories, 2 grams fat, 0 grams saturated fat per serving of 6

GRILLED POLENTA WITH HERBS
Makes 4 to 6 servings

1 recipe Basic Polenta (page 106)
1 teaspoon fresh or dried rosemary
½ teaspoon dried thyme leaves
Olive oil for basting

1. While the polenta is still soft, stir in the herbs. Spread the polenta approximately ¾ inch thick in a pan and chill until firm, at least 2 hours. Cut into slices about 3 x 2 inches.
2. Brush both sides of the slices with olive oil and grill, about 2 inches from hot coals, until browned, about 3 or 4 minutes per side. Try not to move the pieces around. Grill marks are desirable.

N O T E :   As an alternative to grilling, the polenta slices may be heated in a nonstick skillet until heated through and lightly browned.

160 calories, 3 grams fat, 0 grams saturated fat per serving of 6

FOUR-LAYER POLENTA CASSEROLE
Makes 2 to 4 main-dish servings

1 medium eggplant, cut crosswise into ½-inch slices
2 teaspoons extra-virgin olive oil
½ cup sun-dried tomatoes, chopped
4 garlic cloves, minced or pressed
1 medium onion, chopped
1 teaspoon dried rosemary
⅛ teaspoon cayenne pepper, or more to taste (be careful)
Salt to taste
12 ounces fresh spinach, washed and stemmed
½ recipe Basic Polenta (page 106)

1. Preheat the oven to 350°F.
2. Brush the eggplant slices with 1 teaspoon of the olive oil, arrange in a single layer on a baking sheet, and roast about 30 minutes, or until soft (see Notes). Keep the oven on.
3. Meanwhile, soak the sun-dried tomatoes in warm water about 10 minutes to soften. Drain.

4. Heat the remaining 1 teaspoon olive oil in a large nonstick skillet. Add the garlic and onion; cook over medium heat until the onion is translucent, about 10 minutes. Add the tomatoes and seasonings; cook 2 or 3 minutes more. Add the spinach in batches until it has all cooked down.

5. Spread a third of the polenta in the bottom of a 9 x 9-inch baking dish. Cover with roasted eggplant slices. Spread the vegetable mixture on top of the eggplant and top with the remaining polenta.

6. Bake for 30 minutes. Let cool slightly before slicing so that pieces will hold their shape.

N O T E S :   You have undoubtedly seen recipes that call for salting eggplant in order to drain it of bitter juices. I don't bother, and I've never had a bitterness problem. I have, however, had a saltiness problem the few times I've tried the salting technique.

This dish can be assembled ahead of time through step 5, even the day before.

210 calories, 4 grams fat, 1 gram saturated fat per serving of 4

CORNMEAL GRIDDLECAKES
Makes 18 to 24 small pancakes

1¼ cups cornmeal, stone-ground if you can get it
1 teaspoon baking soda
1½ cups buttermilk
1 large egg, or 2 large egg whites
Salt to taste

1. Combine all the ingredients (preferably in a pitcher or a bowl with a spout) and stir until the batter is fairly smooth and as thick as very heavy cream. (John Thorne, author of *Simple Cooking,* makes cakes like these and stirs with a finger, undoubtedly the ideal tool as it allows you to feel for and break up lumps. However, I prefer a fork. As I am the original hands-on cook, this preference baffles me. Perhaps it's because I make these griddlecakes early in the day—my Hour of Squeamishness—that I am oddly reluctant to immerse my hand in cold cornmeal mush.) Allow the batter to stand for at least 15 minutes.

2. Heat a nonstick griddle until a drop of water skates across. Then, if you're not entirely confident in its nonstick properties, brush on a little oil. Dot the griddle with the batter. The cakes are best if they are

very thin and no more than 2 to 3 inches in diameter. They take longer to cook than other pancakes; don't turn them until the edges look quite dry and the entire top seems solid.

3. Serve with honey, maple syrup, fruit—whatever you like. These make excellent finger food. Just dip them in your sweetener. I've also enjoyed leftovers as savory snacks with salsa. But we rarely have leftovers.

40 calories, 1 gram fat, 0 grams saturated fat per serving of 24

Legumes: From Mystery to Mastery

I was standing in line at the only market in my neighborhood that sells Goya brand large white lima beans, holding five bags of them, when I heard a voice behind me. "What," it asked incredulously, "are you going to do with those?" I turned to confront a woman about my own age, dressed like me in blue jeans and sneakers, the standard Upper West Side freelancer's uniform. A number of possible responses occurred to me, one of the least offensive being, "What are *you* going to do with those pork chops?" However, civility and the wish to be instructive carried the day, and I described some of the uses for the beans that are a staple of our household.

"But how do you cook them?" she asked, still dubious that someone who looked so much like her and the people she knew could be preparing and eating something so bizarre. "You just put them in very hot water," I replied, "and leave them there a very long time."

That's all there is to it. Really. These little guys are dried out and it's your job to make them nice and plump and soft. Everything else I'm going to tell you is glossarial.

What could be more convenient than a food you just have to rehydrate? Starting a pot of dried beans takes approximately 5 minutes, and even if you eat them every day you can carry a month's supply home in one small bag. That may not seem like a big deal to someone who doesn't live where she has to schlep everything she eats back from the market and up three flights of stairs. I, however, as Schlepper-in-Chief of our household, have learned to appreciate foods you put the water *into* after you bring them home as opposed to those, like spinach for example, that you take the water *out* of. Water is heavy stuff. The pound of dried beans I bring home can be the foundation of a main dish that feeds six or eight people; the pound of spinach will make a side dish for two.

You do have to think ahead, though. When it's well into the afternoon and you're already getting hungry, unless your beans are very small and you're fairly sure they're from this season's crop, you should plan to eat them tomorrow, not today.

If you want to cook your beans fairly quickly tomorrow, by all means soak them today. Cover them with cold water and put them in the refrigerator overnight. Alternatively, you can do a quick presoak: Put your beans in cold water, bring the pot just to a boil, cover, and let them cool in the water for at least an hour. All but the largest and most intransigent beans will cook in an hour or two after either treatment.

When you're ready to cook the beans, drain them, cover them with fresh cold water about 2 inches above the top of the beans, bring them to a simmer, cover the pot, and keep them barely simmering until they taste done.

Unfortunately, shortening the cooking time is all presoaking accomplishes. Whatever you may have heard to the contrary, it will make no appreciable difference in your beans' ability to create flatulence. The only thing that will do that is eating a lot of beans regularly. Your gut's tolerance will increase.

I rarely presoak beans. I favor long, slow cooking. An excellent method involves the resurrection of an appliance that just may be reposing in a far corner of your pantry. Remember crockpots? (Really? And you're still alive and cooking?) They enjoyed a brief vogue in the seventies, but since they are rather cumbersome and are useless for any preparation that includes a browning stage, most of them have long since been relegated to culinary limbo along with fondue pots and electric knives. If you were too small to reach the stove in the seventies or were so improvident as to discard your crockpot, look around. Manufacturers seem to be making them again. I know they can be purchased from the Vermont Country Store (page 303).

A crockpot certainly isn't a necessity, however. You can put your beans in any large, heavy pot (I find that my clay pot is ideal), set it in a 200°F to 250°F oven, and leave it for 6 to 8 hours. Use about one part beans to four parts water, perhaps a cup or two more if you're going to be out of the house for more than 6 hours. In the crockpot I use about 3½ parts water to 1 part beans and set the heat to just below the simmer.

Whatever receptacle I'm using to cook beans, I add a coarsely chopped onion, 3 or 4 garlic cloves, a chopped jalapeño or other hot pepper (dried chipotle peppers impart a wonderful smoky flavor), and sometimes a chopped carrot or some celery to enrich the broth. If I have a lot of chicken stock and am feeling prodigal, I use some in place of some of the water. Add salt if you want. Bean cooking mythology says that it toughens the skins, but recent experiments have demonstrated that this isn't the case. The Tuscans, who understand bean cookery, say your pot should always threaten but never bubble. If you can achieve that effect—and it's not difficult in a crockpot or a slow oven—it's certainly the way to get the creamiest texture and the fewest split skins.

From time to time you will encounter, usually in a vegetarian cookbook, a chart that purports to tell you how long different varieties of beans should be cooked. Fuhgedaboutit! Just remember that, as you might expect, small beans take less time than large beans, and fresh ones less time than old ones. It's impossible to predict with any degree of accuracy how long your beans will take to cook unless you cooked some from the same bag yesterday. Wait until they start to smell beany and then snag a sample. Only tasting will tell you when they're done.

If you're as casual as I am in your approach to life, and you make beans frequently, you're occasionally going to open your pot and find that they have cooked to the point of disintegration. Perhaps you were planning a gorgeous bean salad to impress your rich aunt Rosalie, in which case this is a bummer. However, overcooked beans are not like overcooked broccoli, fit only for the garbage pail. The flavor will still be excellent, there are plenty of uses for bean purées, and Aunt Rosalie might prefer a roast chicken anyway, with maybe a nice potato kugel.

A major perquisite of home-cooked beans is the broth. Your broth will be thick. In fact, after you've refrigerated it in jars, you may have to spoon it out when you want it. (The thicker stuff will settle at the bottom.) It's wonderful for thickening soups and sauces and for adding just a bit of moisture to salads and pastas. (Always taste it first, however. Occasionally it acquires a granular texture that makes it unsuitable for anything but soup or tomato sauce.) Ideally, bean broth has a viscous quality that, if you use it in small quantities, will fool your mouth into believing it's oil.

Beans can cook quietly all night while you sleep or all day while you work. They smell and taste wonderful. They freeze well and it's a good idea to make enough so you'll have some for that purpose. I freeze mine in plastic yogurt containers, which I regret to say I am often too lazy and arrogant (I'll never forget what's in there!) to label properly. But when I find them again, it's always a wonderful surprise.

Whatever sort of bean you choose to cook, you'll find the effort minimal and the results well worth it. You'll have a basic ingredient for chili, refried beans, bean salads, soup, and instant grain/legume combos. What's more, you'll find that a few beans or chickpeas can add substance to green salads, potato salads, stir-frys, and some pasta dishes.

Try stewing your beans with eggplant, tomato, and capers. (Chickpeas work particularly well for this kind of dish, since they have the virtue of holding up well to a second cooking. Even after an hour in the stew pot, your precooked chickpeas won't be mushy.) Beans can also give meatless curries textural variation and a substantial feel.

For a different take on beans, purée them and use them as an ingredient in sauces, soups, and dips. Puréed white beans and roasted garlic make an excellent spread. Add some black pepper or some lemon juice to change the flavor. Or, if you're in the mood to splurge, a little Parmesan cheese.

However, there are alternatives to home-cooked beans.

The Instant Bean

> At our house we open cans.
> We have to open many cans.
> And that is why we have a Zans.
> A Zans for cans is very good.
> Have you a Zans for cans? You should.
>
> —DR. SEUSS

There are four things wrong with canned beans. First of all, the broth is inedible. A related problem is that they are too salty. That's really why you can't use the broth—it has a nasty briny taste. Canned beans should be drained and rinsed. The third reason to hate them is that they're often overcooked—slightly mushy. And the fourth reason is that they cost a lot more than home-cooked beans, although beans in any form are so cheap that this is probably not a significant issue for most of us.

There is, of course, one good reason to love canned beans and we all know what it is. They are wondrously convenient. If you want to stock your pantry with canned legumes, it is best to choose the slow-cooking ones. I find that canned chickpeas (garbanzos), kidney beans, and fava beans are the most acceptable. The more delicate white beans get much too soft. I admit that I haven't made an exhaustive survey of canned beans. If you want to use them extensively, try several different varieties and brands.

Although I cook my own beans regularly, I find that having a few cans on hand gives me the option of serving more than one bean at a meal. A bean salad, for example, really needs at least two kinds of beans. (Black beans and small white beans or kidney beans and chickpeas are two of my favorite combinations, but anything goes. Add some chopped scallions and herbs and a tablespoon of vinegar for every cup of beans. A chopped fresh tomato is a nice addition when they're in season. Moisten with a little olive oil or broth from home-cooked beans and allow to marinate half an hour or so before serving, stirring occasionally.) Chickpeas from a can make a grain/legume combo seem less like a plate of rice or barley and more like a main dish. Some canned beans can help extend a soup that's wearing thin.

Were I cooking only for myself, or for a family that consumed legumes sparingly, I might never cook any legumes but lentils and split peas—the rest would come from cans. So, if you're in that position, stock your shelves and get yourself a Zans. (The Zans, by the way, is a wonderful Dr. Seuss animal—a particularly large one. It will take up all the space in your kitchen and you'll need to stand on a ladder to open your cans.)

My favorite legume, however, is one that cooks so quickly you don't even have to think about putting your Zans to work. Only recently have I realized that the Lovable Lentil has engendered considerable controversy.

LENTILS: LOATHING AND LUST

They're funny little critters, but people will eat the damnedest things if they think it's good for them.

—JEFF BOYD, IDAHO LENTIL FARMER

Boyd's remark probably expresses a certain wry affection for the lentil. Many of its critics are less equivocal. In 1475 Platina called lentils "the worst of all vegetables." But Boyd, Platina, and my son Jake can't come close to matching the lentil hate expressed by George Gissing in *The Private Papers of Henry Ryecroft*. It's Gissing's last work, published in 1903, and purports to be the thoughts of a writer who has received a legacy and retired to the country. Most of it has a rather mellow valedictory tone, but lentils arouse the fictional Ryecroft to heights of malediction.

I hate with a bitter hatred the names of lentils and haricots—those pretentious cheats of the appetite, those tabulated humbugs, those certificated aridities calling themselves human food. An ounce of either, we are told, is equivalent to—how many pounds?—of the best rump-steak. There are not many ounces of common sense in the brain of him who proves it, or of him who believes it. In some countries, this stuff is eaten by choice; in England only dire need can compel to its consumption. Lentils and haricots are not merely insipid; frequent use of them causes something like nausea. Preach and tabulate as you will, the English palate—which is the supreme judge—rejects this farinaceous makeshift. Even as it rejects vegetables without the natural concomitant of meat; as it rejects oatmeal-porridge and griddle-cakes for a mid-day meal; as it rejects lemonade and ginger-ale offered as substitutes for honest beer.

What is the intellectual and moral state of that man who really believes that chemical analysis can be an equivalent for natural gusto?—I will get more nourishment out of an inch of right Cambridge sausage; aye, out of a couple of ounces of honest tripe; than can be yielded me by half a hundred weight of the best lentils ever grown.

To judge by the statistics, many Americans agree with Henry Ryecroft. The average annual lentil consumption in this country is .15 pounds per person, the equivalent of a small hamburger. Some of us, however, are eating far more than our share.

Loving the Lentil

It seems to me that we are somewhat unjust towards a vegetable which, though it may not be worth a birthright, merits the consideration of the gourmet. It is called vulgar. . . . Nevertheless the true gourmet revels in it . . . at every moment of the meal, from lentil soup to lentil salad.

—ROBERT COURTINE, FORMER GASTRONOMIC EDITOR OF *LE MONDE*

Well, thank you, Robert. Your encomium may lack the passion of George Gissing's diatribe, but we lentil lovers need all the help we can get.

If someone offered you a chance to wrestle with angels, endure famine, and take on truly awesome patriarchal responsibilities *or* tuck into a large bowl of lentil stew, which would *you* choose? I can't help thinking Esau got the best of the bargain.

I came to lentil lust late in life. My childhood, like those of most Americans, was entirely lentil free. But when Chuck and I got married, and my mother-in-law passed along her recipes for his favorite dishes, one of them was for lentil soup. It was a stew, really—the spoon was supposed to stand upright in the bowl. In addition to lentils, it contained a large quantity of boiled beef, something else I had never eaten.

I quickly discovered that I detested boiled beef, but I loved lentils. I liked the slight chewiness and the distinctive, vaguely meaty taste that seemed to be complemented by almost any mix of seasonings. Every time I made the soup it contained less beef and more lentils, and Chuck didn't seem to notice. We ate a lot of that soup in those far-off days. But when our children got old enough to join us at the table, they cast a jaundiced eye on lentil soup. The verdict was that it was brown and yucky and it felt funny in your mouth. (Jake believes that to this day. Barley may pass Tamar's Jake Test, but lentils assuredly do not.) So, in the interest of harmonious family dinners, my lentil soup became history.

As meat, cheese, and eggs disappeared from our dining table, however, and our children went their separate ways, lentils reentered my cooking repertoire. They show up here so often that Jake is always careful about committing himself to staying for dinner. "Are there lentils in that?" he asks, looking suspiciously into a pot.

Besides tasting good, an admittedly subjective evaluation, lentils have a multitude of objective virtues. They are virtually fat free and high in protein, fiber, and folic acid. They are really cheap—usually less than a dollar a pound, which is about 2 quarts of cooked lentils. They keep indefinitely. They're also versatile. You may be most familiar with them in their soup incarnation (the Lentil Barley Soup on page 83 is a more-or-less classic lentil soup, but with barley standing in for half the lentils), but that's not all they're good for. I use them in soups, stir-frys, and pasta sauces. They can be stewed with eggplant and crushed tomatoes, perhaps with some cumin and coriander. Or oregano and flat-leaf parsley. Lentils can also be used cold in salads with tomatoes, chickpeas or other beans, cooked potatoes, or roasted peppers.

Unlike many legumes, lentils don't need soaking and cook in less than half an hour. I don't even rinse them before cooking, although everyone I read tells me I should and perhaps I'll be sorry someday. I just dump them into a pot and add cold water (in approximately a three-to-one ratio or to about an inch above the lentils). I add a piece of dried chile pepper or some dried herbs if I feel like it. It's my impression that the texture is better—less grainy—if I don't let my lentils boil hard, just keep them on a slow simmer, but I haven't conducted a study. I may be extrapolating from my knowledge of beans, for which it's definitely true.

Lentils and brown rice are an excellent combination and can be cooked together quite satisfactorily. I use equal parts lentils and rice, add water or stock in a two-to-one ratio, bring the pot to a boil, then cover the pot, lower the heat, and cook about half an hour or until both lentils and rice are soft enough to eat. This works best with standard brown lentils and rather wimpy brown rice like River Brand.

Small red and yellow lentils from the Indian grocery need even less cooking time than the standard brown kind, but they should be watched carefully. One minute they're hard little pellets and the next minute they're mush. Overcooked lentils, like beans, can be puréed and make a fine soup ingredient. However, if your meal plan calls for lentil salad, mushy lentils can bum you out.

Recently I discovered that I can satisfy my lentil cravings and help save the American family farm at the same time. Nearly all the lentils grown in this country are produced on three thousand family farms in an area on the Washington-Idaho border called the Palouse. Most of them are exported, but they are being priced out of the market by Canadian lentils. Americans have got to eat more lentils—*American* lentils.

There's an especially flavorful, uniquely American, small lentil called the Pardina. I have two pounds of them that I ordered from Meacham Mills in Lewiston, Idaho (page 302). I also have two pounds of each of the seven other varieties Meacham sells. When I called to place my order, I specified a pound of each, but then the nice woman told me the total was five dollars and change. It seemed such a miserably skimpy sum that I decided I'd better double the order. It's so easy to buy stuff on the telephone. Only after I'd hung up did I fully realize that I was about to become the proud owner of *sixteen pounds of lentils.* (What with shipping costs, the package set me back about twenty-five dollars.) When they came, there was no storage space to accommodate them. But having them delighted me. I enjoyed visiting them in the hall where they lived in their shipping box. I fingered the bags and repeated the names— Red Chief, Petite Green French, Eston. We ate a lot of lentil meals for a long time. Jake ate elsewhere.

Just as there are few uniquely American legumes other than the Pardina lentil, there are few uniquely American legume preparations. One, though, is inextricably linked with New England. I went to college in New England and was frequently served Boston baked beans, the quality of which did not encourage me to ever attempt the dish myself. Tamar, however, had no such prejudice.

FROM THE HOME OF THE BEAN AND THE COD

Where legumes have made inroads into the American diet, it's usually by way of exotic, faraway places. Lentils in Indian food, white beans in Tuscan, pinto beans in Mexican. There is, however, one notable exception. Baked beans are one of America's food icons, up there with apple pie, hot dogs, and ice cream. Baked beans conjure up images of potluck suppers and backyard barbecues. For most people, that is. For me they conjure up images of baby-sitters.

When I was growing up, we ate very few things that came in cans or boxes. Frozen blintzes, the only childhood food I remember actively disliking, occasionally made their way to our table. So did frozen pizza, a food I remember actively liking very much. Now and then we had canned soup, and the only thing I remember about that is trying to spell my name with Campbell's alphabet soup. There were never enough As.

These were the foods my parents sometimes turned to when they were going out for the evening and leaving my two brothers and me with some luckless baby-sitter. (My father's parting words were always the same: "In bed at nine-thirty. Not beginning to commence to think about trying to start to go to bed. IN BED at nine-thirty.") Instead of the blintzes or the pizza we sometimes had Campbell's baked beans, usually accompanied by hot dogs. They were the only kind of baked beans I ever had, and they therefore set my personal standard for what baked beans should be.

I wouldn't trust a memory of my childhood food sense to judge whether Campbell's baked beans were actually good. I certainly remember liking them, but I liked almost everything (except those damn blintzes). My mother, however, assures me that they were perfectly fine, certainly better than the ones she remembers from college. They probably still are, but I haven't had them in twenty years.

And so, when I set out to make baked beans, the taste I had in mind to duplicate was Campbell's—the gold standard. If you ever set out to precisely duplicate the taste of a packaged food you're fond of, I have one piece of advice: Don't do it. Just go out and buy the package. I tried to do this once before, and I should have learned my lesson.

I tried it with Near East Rice Pilaf, of which I am inordinately fond. I grew up with Near East Rice Pilaf and I eat it as an adult, but not without misgivings. I am, after all, a cook. I should be able to cook this. I've tried. I've tried, and I can't. I read the ingredients on the package and went out and purchased them. I tried them in different proportions. I must have made rice pilaf a dozen times, and each time it was good, but it was never Near East Rice Pilaf. I failed.

I confessed my failure to my mother, and she laughed. Now, my mother doesn't usually laugh at my failures. She generally makes annoyingly constructive suggestions. Once her mirth subsided, she explained. She had tried to do exactly the same thing, with exactly the same product and exactly the same results. (Mom and I are frequently surprised at how often we come to the same culinary conclusions independently.)

So I should have known better than to try to duplicate Campbell's beans, but I didn't. I tried and, predictably, failed. The beans were good, though. So, if you want Campbell's baked beans, don't use this recipe—go out and buy a can. If, however, you want a pot of slightly spicy, not-too-sweet baked beans, give these a shot.

BAKED BEANS
Makes 6 to 8 servings

2 teaspoons olive oil

1 dried chipotle pepper

2 medium onions, chopped

1 pound dried navy beans

4 ounces smoked ham, cut into small cubes

¼ cup molasses

2 tablespoons honey

1 tablespoon vinegar

1 teaspoon Worcestershire sauce

2 teaspoons salt, or to taste

1. Heat the olive oil in a large Dutch oven or ovenproof stockpot. Remove the seeds from the pepper and cut it into 8 or 10 pieces. Add the onions and pepper to the oil and sauté over medium heat until the onions are nicely browned.
2. Add the dried beans and enough water to cover by at least 2 inches. Bring the mixture to a boil, lower the heat, and simmer, uncovered, until the beans are soft, 1 to 2 hours. (Even though the beans will bake for several hours, they should be completely cooked before you put them in the oven—there isn't enough liquid for them to soften during baking.) If necessary, add water to keep the water level about ½ inch above the beans. Toward the end of the cooking time, let more of the water cook off so that it is at about the same level as the beans.
3. Preheat the oven to 275°F.
4. Add the remaining ingredients to the beans and stir gently. Cover the pot and bake the beans until the liquid has thickened, 4 to 5 hours. If at the end of the baking time there is too much liquid, simmer the beans, uncovered, over low heat until enough liquid has evaporated.

250 calories, 3 grams fat, 1 gram saturated fat per serving of 8

Grain and Legume Combinations: The Dynamic Duo

You've doubtless seen vegetarian cookbooks that tell you to eat a lot of grains and beans in combination in order to obtain complete protein. This is not going to be yet another dreary discourse on protein complementarity. All recent data indicate that it is almost impossible for an adult who isn't pregnant, lactating, or recovering from a serious illness to get enough to eat and not get enough protein. Furthermore, although it's true that most grains and beans (quinoa and soybeans are exceptions) do not contain all the essential amino acids, that's not a problem either. You need not complete your protein in the same dish, or even at the same meal.

The reason that grain/legume combinations are fundamental to the meals Tamar and I serve is that they're easy to cook, versatile, filling, low in fat, and they taste good. The texture of beans can be rather cloying on its own, but the slight chewiness of the grains provides just the right contrast. Together they are delicious. But if you don't like legumes, don't eat them. You can get plenty of protein, even if you don't eat meat or fish, without ever biting into a bean or a lentil. I maintain, however, that if you give these foods a chance you are very likely to find some combinations that appeal to you.

Always cook more of any grain/bean combo than you'll eat in any one meal. There is no end to their uses, both freshly cooked and at a later time. Here are just a few suggestions, some of which are enlarged upon elsewhere in this book:

- Base for stir-fry
- Main-dish accompaniment to steamed vegetables and salad
- As a salad combined with warm or cold vegetables and lots of some fresh herb, dressed with vinaigrette
- Heated in stock to make a soup or added to an existing soup
- Refried with leftover roasted vegetables

On page 120 I've listed some of the grains and dried legumes that I've found suitable for cooking together. I've found that the combinations almost always work. However, I suggest you not make them when you're in a big hurry. It's possible to get hold of the occasional grain or legume—beans are especially open to suspicion—that takes forever to cook. Presoaking suspect beans (just cover with cold water and let stand 6 to 12 hours in the refrigerator) can help ensure good results. You can get an awful sinking feeling when your 45 minutes are up and your rice is perfect but your adzuki beans resemble tiny pebbles. The only solution is to just keep cooking, adding more liquid if necessary. Brown rice remains acceptable even when it's been cooked quite a long time. Sooner or later those beans will soften. Mix and match the grains and legumes in any combination that appeals to you.

Grains	Legumes
• Brown rice	• Brown lentils
• Barley	• Small white beans (pea size)
• Millet	or adzuki beans, presoaked
• Wild rice	• Split peas
	• Black-eyed peas

THE COMBO
Makes 4 to 6 servings

1 cup each grain and dried legume from the list above
  (see Notes)
1 medium onion, chopped
2 to 4 garlic cloves, minced or pressed
1 jalapeño or other hot pepper, coarsely chopped
  (optional)
1 bay leaf
4 to 5 cups water or stock
Large bunch of freshly chopped parsley or cilantro
Salt to taste

1. Place all ingredients except the parsley or cilantro and salt in a large pot (about 4-quart capacity). Bring to a boil, cover, lower the heat, and simmer for about 45 minutes. Taste to make sure the grain and legume are fully cooked. If not, add more water if necessary, raise the heat slightly, and cook for 5 to 10 minutes more with the lid removed. Ideally both grain and legume will be completely cooked and the liquid will be almost all absorbed.
2. Optional: Let the covered pot stand off the heat for about 10 minutes. This step gives the flavors some time to develop and is an especially good idea if your legume is a bean, as the skins are less likely to split.
3. If there is unabsorbed liquid left in the pot, either pour the contents into a colander or serve from the pot with a slotted spoon. (Be sure to save the liquid to use another time.) Combine whatever portion you're serving with some of the chopped fresh parsley or cilantro and add the salt.

NOTES: I loathe millet and only include it because it's a nutritious grain and cooks up nicely with legumes. (By "nicely" I don't mean it tastes good, I mean it achieves its full potential. It tastes like millet.) I don't mind it in soup with lots of other stuff or in multigrain bread. This will be the only reference to millet you'll find in this book, but some people like it.

It's perfectly okay to change the proportions of legume to grain and to use more than one of each. Wild rice combines especially well with any grain on the list (even millet if you insist).

310 to 380 calories, 1 to 2 grams fat, 0 grams saturated fat per serving of 6

Variation 1: My favorite combo—perhaps my favorite food (see Tamar's response, J'accuse, page 122)—is brown rice and lentils with dried mushrooms. It is made according to the above instructions except that I begin by soaking 1 ounce dried porcini or shiitake mushrooms in 4 cups warm water for 1 hour. I then use the mushroom broth (with the mushrooms) as the liquid in which to cook the rice and lentils. (Pour it through a strainer as dried mushrooms can harbor sand and other debris.) I like to add a lot of chopped cilantro just before serving. This mushroom variation also works well with a barley/split pea combo.

Variation 2: You can also make a wet combo, a.k.a. soup. A wet combo requires about twice as much liquid as a dry one. The flavor of the liquid becomes a significant issue in this case, as you'll be tasting it independently of the solids. Tomatoes count as liquid. (Also see the soup section in Chapter 6.)

Variation 3: Another favorite in our house is the instant combo, although it's a bit of a cheat because you have to use two pots. Cook red, yellow, or green lentils in boiling water or stock. This only takes about 10 minutes for the red or yellow, 20 or so for the green. Watch them closely as they can go from hard to mushy in about 3 seconds. In another pot cook one of the quick grains—bulgur or quinoa—according to the directions on the box, except omit oil if it's called for. That, too, will take only 10 to 15 minutes. Drain the lentils, reserving the liquid, and mix them gently with the grain. These quick-cooking grains can also be combined with cooked beans or even with canned beans or chickpeas. (A wet instant combo requires only one pot. We describe one in our discussion of stone soup on page 142.)

J'ACCUSE

EATING HEALTHFULLY ISN'T AS EASY, or as much fun, as eating unhealthfully. Even if you are a master at finding and making the most of all the right foods, the unfortunate but inevitable bottom line is that you have to give up some things you enjoy. But the degree of struggle this entails varies. For some, those whose dreams are inhabited by cream soups and rich desserts, it's difficult indeed. For others, however, it's easier because they are naturally inclined to enjoy foods that are good for them. These people are very annoying. My mother is one of these people. I don't hold it against her because, after all, she can't help it, but I resent it nevertheless. Or at least I thought I resented it. On further reflection, I've concluded that what I really resent is that I didn't inherit this trait. (I blithely assume it's genetic and therefore outside my control.)

So, when Mom and I sit down to a meal of, say, quinoa salad, she digs in with relish and I with tepid enthusiasm and visions of french fries. All this because I didn't inherit the Quinoa Gene, or the Lentil Gene, or even the Brown Rice Gene.

My mother specializes in enviable traits that are, unfortunately, recessive. While I never blame her for my own shortcomings, I do wish some of her characteristics were made of genetically sturdier stuff. Then I might have an ear for poetry, an intuitive understanding of human foibles, and a total indifference to fast cars. Instead, I have the Sausage Gene.

(Please don't get the idea that I have inherited only problematic genes from my father. He is a man of many fine qualities, and I would like to think that, by some combination of genetics and environment, I picked up a few of them. It is from him, for example, that I get my joke-telling skills, which are undeniably superior to those of my mother. She has an excuse, though. She is Norwegian.)

I try to be at peace with the fact that my mother is fonder of many healthful foods than I am. I have had years to get used to it. I bristled, however, when I read her dubious claim that her favorite food is brown rice, lentils, and dried mushrooms. I called her up and said, "Mom, I know you to be a discriminating eater and an inveterate truth teller, BUT NOBODY'S FAVORITE FOOD IS BROWN RICE, LENTILS, AND DRIED MUSHROOMS!"

Because we are both adults, this conversation quickly gradu-
ated from the "am too, are not" stage to a more sophisticated (or
at least less ridiculous) discussion of what constitutes a favorite
food. My mother's definition, on which she based her question-
able claim, is that your favorite food is the one you'd pick if you
had to eat just one food for the rest of your life—the Desert Island
approach. I contend that this takes all the fun out of the question,
since instead of thinking about she-crab soup and braised lamb,
you're thinking about how miserable it would be to live on a
desert island eating only one food.

My idea of a favorite food is the one you would choose to ma-
terialize in front of you right now. While I think this definition is
more in the spirit of favorite foods, it does have one drawback: It's
almost impossible to decide. At any given moment, I'm hard
pressed to choose the one thing I'd like to be eating. There are so
many fine choices, and they depend on my mood, the time of
day, the temperature, and any number of other variables. So,
when you ask me what my favorite food is, I'm stymied.

So I admit, grudgingly, that the Desert Island question has the
merit of being answerable. You can't respond with the whim of
the moment, you have to think it through. Carefully. After all, this
is the rest of your life we're talking about. And if those are the
constraints of the question, I'm even willing to believe that my
mother's favorite food is brown rice, lentils, and dried mushrooms. Me? I'm pretty sure I'd pick pasta and tomato sauce. With
sausages.

G&L Skills Put to the Test. My parents and I have an informal
agreement. When they return from a trip, assuming they're home in time
for dinner, I cook for them. And vice versa. When I traveled a lot, I benefited immensely from this arrangement. Now that I barely travel at all, I
find myself more frequently on the feeding end of the deal. Particularly in
the winter, when my parents commute to their Miami Beach outpost, they
come eat with me regularly. (Don't feel too sorry for me, since our other
informal agreement is that I, as the daughter, get to call Mom, as the
mother, any day and invite myself to dinner.)

The last time my parents came to dinner, I planned a fish soup. I had
some stock and the remains of a can of crushed tomatoes in the refrigerator. I picked up some monkfish, shrimp, and scallops, along with a fennel
bulb and fresh rosemary, and was sanguine in my preparedness for

guests. Then the phone rang. It was my friend Katie, who was overdue to be introduced to my parents, so I invited her over. Then my little brother Jake called, asking me if I knew what time the 'rents were due home. (He stays in their house while they're gone, makes a big mess, and times his Herculean cleanup to the minute.) I told him when they were expected, and I couldn't very well not invite him too. Okay, so I'd have five for dinner instead of three. I could handle that.

Then the phone rang again, and it was my friend Laura, who had been on her way home from New York to San Francisco. She made it as far as Kennedy Airport, where she was informed that San Francisco was rained out, and she'd best extend her stay in the city. What's one more? Then the phone rang one more time, and it was the Moscow Circus. Just kidding.

So it was six for dinner. This put my improvisational skills to the test. I surveyed my materials. I was going to have to extend my soup dramatically if it was going to feed twice as many people as I had intended. Grains and legumes to the rescue! I had some leftover white beans from last night's pasta, and those combined with a cup or so of brown rice would turn my fish soup into a satisfying, interesting main dish for six. And so they did.

EMERGENCY FISH SOUP
Makes 6 main-dish servings

3 medium onions

1 small fennel bulb

1 tablespoon olive oil

1 jalapeño or other hot pepper

6 garlic cloves

1 teaspoon chopped fresh rosemary

4 to 5 cups fish or chicken stock

2 cups dry white wine

One 14-ounce can crushed tomatoes

2 teaspoons Worcestershire sauce

¾ cup brown rice

1 pound monkfish, cut into bite-size pieces

¾ pound shrimp, peeled and deveined

¾ pound scallops

2 cups cooked white beans

Salt to taste

1. Put the slicing blade in the food processor and slice the onions and fennel. Heat the olive oil in a large pot. Add the onions and fennel to the oil. Change to the chopping blade and chop the jalapeño (including the seeds) and the garlic cloves. Add the garlic, jalapeño, and rosemary to the pot and sauté over medium heat until everything is thoroughly wilted, at least 20 minutes.

2. Add the stock, wine, tomatoes, and Worcestershire. Bring the mixture to a boil, lower the heat, and simmer until it cooks down to a soup-like consistency, about 20 minutes. Add the brown rice, cover, and simmer until the rice is almost done, about 30 minutes.

3. Add the monkfish and simmer until the pieces are no longer opaque in the center, 5 to 10 minutes. Add the shrimp, scallops, beans, and salt; simmer just until the seafood is cooked through, no more than 5 minutes. Remove from the heat and serve at once.

450 calories, 5 grams fat, 1 gram saturated fat per serving

G&I skills are to cooking what scales are to piano playing, what compulsories are to figure skating, what conjugating verbs is to mastering a foreign language. Ignore them at your peril! The good news is that, however essential they are, they're just beans and grains. You boil them until they're done. You'll be happy you did.

6.

Sauces and Soups

Sauce by Numbers

YESTERDAY I WENT TO LUNCH at my favorite neighborhood Chinese place. While I was waiting for my shrimp dumplings and chow fun, I had time to check out what the people at the next table were eating. There were four women; they had opted against family style and each had her own dish. Three of the women had ordered classic Chinese restaurant grease-fests, dishes like beef with black bean sauce and sweet and sour pork. They were digging in with gusto. The fourth woman had a plate of steamed vegetables and brown rice. She didn't look happy. Virtuous, but definitely not happy.

Steamed vegetables is one of the reasons healthful food gets a bad rap. As fond as I am of vegetables, I think plain steamed veggies are not very appetizing. Naked and exposed, they're just not equipped to carry the whole weight of a meal. They need help. They cry out for . . . SAUCE!

Sauce can be intimidating, especially those classic French sauces. Auguste Escoffier, the father of intimidating French cuisine, had very definite ideas about what a sauce should and shouldn't be:

Warm sauces are of two kinds: the leading sauces, also called "mother sauces," and the small sauces, which are usually derived from the first-named.... Experience, which plays such an important part in culinary work, is nowhere so necessary as in the preparation of sauces, for not only must the latter flatter the palate, but they must also vary in savor, consistency and viscosity, in accordance with the dishes they accompany. By this means, in a well-ordered dinner, each dish differs from the preceding ones and from those that follow.

Furthermore, sauces must, through the perfection of their preparation, obey the general laws of a rational hygienic, wherefore they should be served and combined in such a way as to allow for easy digestion by the frequently disordered stomachs of their consumers.

Jeez, Auguste! No wonder sauces scare people. All of a sudden those steamed vegetables don't sound so bad.

There are, however, many, many things that qualify as sauces, and they aren't all difficult. Some of the classical French ones are indeed intimidating—they're precise and labor intensive—but this isn't the kind of sauce I'm talking about. I use the term loosely. When I say sauce, I mean anything you put on pasta or rice or barley or couscous to make it a meal. My sauces don't involve complex recipes and delicate emulsions. They involve vegetables and seafood and stock. They are imprecise in the extreme.

These are not the sauces of an anxious guy in a toque but rather the sauces of the practitioners of what food writer Laurie Colwin called *la cuisine de la "slobbe" raffinée,* the cooking of the refined slob. Colwin wrote that she first resorted to refined slob cuisine after the birth of her daughter, when speed and convenience were her top priority. I don't have a small child to justify my caring about speed and convenience but care about them I do. It's a good bet that at least two-thirds of the meals I make are a simple variation of the sauce-grain-salad theme.

I think even these more prosaic sauces can instill fear. You're taking a bunch of ingredients, liquids and solids, and combining them in such a way that the end product has a taste and texture that none of the original components had: neither a liquid nor a solid. It is mysterious.

But it isn't difficult. Many very different sauces have a lot in common, and I think it's possible to extract some universal (or almost universal) truths about sauce ingredients and cooking procedures that will make sauces simpler to understand and improvisation a little easier.

FIRST, THE INGREDIENTS

Although the list of possible sauce ingredients is infinite, it's possible to categorize those ingredients to make sauce logic easier to grasp. I tend to think of sauces as having six components. Not all sauces have all six components, but almost all sauce ingredients can be classified according to the scheme:

Foundations. These are the long-cooking, flavor-imparting ingredients you start with, like onions and garlic. You cook them for a while in a little olive oil (an integral part of the foundation) and gradually add the other ingredients. The kinds of vegetables suitable for this are the ones that can stand up to long cooking and impart flavor to the finished sauce. Onions and their relatives from the house of *Allium* play this role well and are an essential part of almost every sauce I make. Mushrooms can (and many exotic mushrooms should) be cooked for a long time, and also do well as a foundation. Chile peppers will infuse your sauces with their spiciness best if you add them at the very beginning of the process.

- Onions
- Garlic
- Shallots
- Leeks
- Mushrooms
- Chile peppers

Vegetables. Vegetables are the main constituents of most sauces I make. Some veggies, like broccoli or bell peppers, can be added right after you've cooked your foundation. Others, like spinach, cook almost instantly and need to be added at the end. Your choice of vegetables goes a long way toward defining your sauce—they give it substance, flavor, and bulk.

I also include beans in this category. Even though you may not think of them as vegetables, they are the same kind of sauce-building ingredient. The disadvantage of beans is that they usually have to be cooked ahead of time (unless you use the canned kind, of course, or, like Mom, you're a big lentil fan). But beans can help thicken your sauce, as can the liquid that you cooked them in. (For more on beans, check out Chapter 5, Grains and Legumes.)

- Eggplant
- Spinach, chard, kale, mustard greens
- Green beans
- Broccoli
- Potatoes
- Sun-dried tomatoes

- Bell peppers (red, green, yellow)
- Asparagus
- Peas
- Beans of all kinds: black, white, pinto, kidney, chickpeas

Meat, Poultry, and Seafood. You can include limited quantities of these without compromising the healthfulness of your sauce. Shellfish is my particular favorite. It's easy to throw into the sauce at the very end and it adds very few calories but a lot of flavor and texture. Meat and poultry usually need to be either cooked separately or added earlier.

- Chicken
- Turkey
- Fish
- Shellfish
- Beef
- Game
- Ham

Liquids. Liquids give your sauce a flavor base, as well as a saucelike consistency. Some, like vinegar and clam juice, have very pronounced flavors and should be used carefully. Others, like stock and bean liquid, add body and flavor without assertive flavors. Wine and beer fall somewhere in the middle.

- Stock
- Wine
- Clam juice
- Low-fat or nonfat milk or evaporated milk
- Bean liquid (also a thickener)
- Vegetable juice
- Leftover soup
- Mushroom hydrating liquid
- Beer
- Vinegar
- Water, if you don't have anything else

Herbs, Spices, and Condiments. This category doesn't include just seasonings like basil and thyme and pepper but also prepared condiments like mustard and anchovy paste.

- Fresh herbs
- Dried herbs and spices

- Mustard
- Worcestershire sauce
- Anchovy paste
- Tabasco and other pepper sauces
- Horseradish

Thickeners. These are the means to increase the viscosity of your sauce. If most of your ingredients are vegetables and liquids like stock and wine, you may need to thicken the mixture to make it more of a sauce and less of a soup.

There are two kinds of thickeners: actual ingredients like flour or bean liquid, and techniques like reducing and puréeing. Note that cornstarch (as well as arrowroot and other conventional thickeners) *doesn't* appear on this list. There's a simple reason for that—I hate it. I think cornstarch-thickened sauces have an awful artificial consistency and a nasty translucent look. I don't use it.

Ingredients:

- Roux (combination of flour and oil or butter)
- Browned flour
- Bean liquid
- Crushed tomatoes
- Low-fat soft cheese

Techniques:

- Reducing (boiling or simmering to evaporate liquid)
- Cooking pasta, rice, barley, etc., in the sauce
- Puréeing part of the sauce

Many of these ingredients do double duty. Bean liquid is both a liquid and a thickener. All the liquids are also flavoring agents. Tomatoes could count as a thickener or a vegetable. You may take issue with some of the ingredients in some of the categories. If bell peppers seem more like a foundation than a vegetable to you, by all means use them that way. The point of inventing a sauce taxonomy is to give cooks unaccustomed to improvisation a framework for inventing dinner.

SECOND, THE PROCEDURE

Once you've decided on your ingredients, there are really only two important questions in assembling your sauce: How to cook your ingredients, wet or dry, and how (and whether) to thicken your sauce.

Wet or Dry? Once you sauté your foundation vegetables and start wondering in what order to add the rest of your ingredients, that's the decision you have to make—cook wet or cook dry? What's the difference? If you add vegetables and meat after you add your liquid, you're essentially boiling them. That works fine for some ingredients—spinach, potatoes, shrimp. Sometimes, however, wet cooking isn't the best idea.

When you cook something in liquid, you limit the cooking temperature to 212°F, the boiling point of water. A dry skillet with a little olive oil in it gets much hotter than that, and therefore lets you brown foods. Because of the higher heat, sautéing can often release food's flavors in a way that boiling cannot. If you're adding chicken, meat, or crunchy vegetables like peppers and broccoli to your sauce, you're better off adding them before you add your liquid. You don't have to cook them completely by sautéing—it works well to start them that way and let them finish cooking in liquid.

Once you get a feel for dry versus wet cooking, sauce assembly is easy. It's just a matter of deciding when to put things in the pot.

Thickening. Probably the simplest way to make your liquid more saucelike is to add a thickening agent, but there are several other ways to do it. Often you'll find using one of these methods thickens your sauce sufficiently. Sometimes, though, you may want to use them in combination either with each other or a thickening agent.

Reducing. As a sauce cooks, liquid evaporates and the sauce reduces, that is, decreases in quantity and thickens. A reduction is simply a sauce that has been reduced. This is an easy, although sometimes time-consuming, way to thicken a sauce and concentrate its flavors.

Adding purée. Near the end of the cooking time, purée a portion of the sauce in a blender or food processor and return it to the pot. This works particularly well if you're using beans or potatoes.

Cooking starch in sauce. If you're planning to serve your sauce with rice or barley, you can cook the grain right in the sauce. This has two effects: First, the grain absorbs a lot of the liquid and, second, some of the starch from the grain is released into the sauce and thickens it. If you use this technique, make sure you start with a lot of liquid, and keep an eye on it as it cooks to make sure it doesn't dry out. If you're serving your sauce with pasta, you probably shouldn't cook the pasta right in the sauce. Instead, boil it separately until it's almost cooked, and let it cook its last minute or two in the sauce.

Once you've mastered wet versus dry and thickening, the rest is easy:

Sauté the Foundation. This is also a good time to add dried herbs and spices. They'll be subjected to higher heat than if you add them after you add liquid, and will release more of their flavor. You'll also avoid the raw spice taste.

Add Vegetables and Liquid. This is where the wet cooking versus dry cooking decision comes in. This step is the heart of sauce making, and there aren't any rules. In deciding whether to add liquid before vegetables or vice versa, you need to take vegetable cooking time and overall cooking time into account. Some quick-cooking vegetables (or vegetables that have been precooked, like frozen peas) should be added at the very end. Other, more substantial veggies, like broccoli or asparagus, should be given a chance to cook before the bulk of the liquid is added.

Add Meat, Poultry, or Seafood. The meat and poultry I add to sauces is almost always in small pieces, so unless I'm making a sauce that cooks very quickly I either sauté it separately or sauté it with the foundation and then remove it from the pan. The reason for this is that pieces of chicken, turkey, or beef boiled in liquid can get tough. It's better to sauté them separately so that they brown nicely and add them to the sauce at the last minute.

Seafood is different. I add shrimp, scallops, and pieces of fish directly to the sauce a few minutes before I serve it. It only takes a minute or two for most seafood to cook through, so don't let it stew too long. Remember that it will continue to cook after the sauce is removed from the heat.

Herbs, Spices, and Condiments. These can be added at any time, but keep one thing in mind—dried spices need to cook properly to impart their flavor, and they don't do that well in liquid because it doesn't get hot enough. If you do add dried spices after adding liquid, try to keep them simmering at least 10 to 15 minutes—long enough to take the edge off their rawness. Dried herbs are more forgiving than dried spices. I prefer to add them at the foundation stage, but it's perfectly okay to add them to liquid. They rehydrate and release a lot of their flavor. Fresh herbs are very flexible. The less time they cook, the fresher they taste, but the less they contribute to the rest of the sauce. I frequently add half my fresh herbs at the beginning and the other half at the end, to get two kinds of tastes out of one ingredient.

Thickening. This is usually the last step, when you're making final decisions about your sauce's consistency. Although there's no rule that says you can't add thickening agents at the beginning, I usually save them for the end because I'm never sure how much I'm going to need. A sauce that I think is identical to one I made last week may turn out with a very different consistency. If you do add a thickening agent like roux or browned flour at the beginning of the process, you can easily adjust the consistency at the end by adding either more thickener or more liquid.

ROUX THE DAY

If you read Cajun cookbooks, you know that, to real Cajuns, roux is a very serious business. There is blond roux and brown roux and woe unto you if you don't understand the difference! If you're interested in true-to-life reproductions of authentic Cajun and Creole dishes, you do indeed have to pay attention to your roux, and almost any Cajun or Creole cookbook can help you. Paul Prudhomme is my source of choice.

If, however, you're looking for an easy, effective way to thicken a sauce, all you need to know about roux can be summed up in one sentence: Roux is a mixture of equal parts flour and fat, cooked until it begins to brown. If you're keeping fat to a minimum, it's possible to stretch the proportions a little, but not beyond two parts flour to one part fat.

The point of doing this is twofold. First, combining the flour with fat prevents clumping. Second, because flour doesn't cook well in liquid, cooking it with fat beforehand avoids that nasty raw flour taste. (Traditionally, there's a third reason: The color of the roux determines the color of the sauce. But if, like me, you use small quantities of roux and large quantities of other ingredients, you'll find that the color of your roux gets lost in the shuffle.)

To make a basic roux, simply put your flour and fat (I usually use olive oil) in a small nonstick saucepan over medium heat. Mix the two ingredients thoroughly, and stir the mixture as it cooks. When it begins to change color, the flour is cooked and you can add the roux to your sauce.

Not Too Rouxful. A while back Tamar and I visited New Orleans and were inspired to reproduce some of the foods we ate there. We learned that it's possible to brown flour and use it to replace the roux in traditional Cajun recipes. The results won't be quite so dark, rich, and mysterious as you'd get with real Cajun roux, but they'll taste very good and be much, much more healthful. Even more to the point, you and I would probably never make a real Cajun roux. To do it right requires at least half an hour of constant stirring and, furthermore, the process is messy and tricky. A dark, rich roux can turn into a nasty black coating on your saucepan in a heartbeat.

Not that producing roux flour is any day at the beach either. Heat a large heavy skillet over high heat, add 2 cups (or more, if your skillet's big enough to spread it fairly thin—the stuff keeps) of all-purpose flour, and cook, stirring constantly with a wire whisk or a wooden spoon, for about 25 minutes, or until the flour turns the color of light brown sugar. If it begins to darken too fast, stir off heat until it cools slightly and return it to the heat at a lower setting. Continue stirring after you've removed it from the heat until it's completely cooled.

The above method comes from Enola Prudhomme's *Low-Calorie Cajun Cooking*. Interestingly, according to her brother Paul (see his slimmed-down recipes in *Fork in the Road*), this can be done in 6 minutes rather than 25. Not only does it take me the entire 25, but a fair amount of smoke is generated in my poorly ventilated kitchen, so I certainly couldn't work at a higher temperature. I envision Paul Prudhomme's sous chef, no doubt an enormous young man with biceps the size of my thighs, desperately whisking flour over an enormous flame on a restaurant stove twice as big as my kitchen, with a huge exhaust fan working at high speed. "Faster, faster," shrieks Paul. The young man collapses in a wet heap, but the flour is nicely browned: 6 minutes.

Both Enola and Paul recommend sifting the flour once it's browned, but we found that wasn't necessary. Once we started to produce this flour we were delighted to find that it could also replace the roux in non-Cajun sauces and gravies. Just stir it into a small amount of liquid and add it to your sauce or stew. It doesn't need to be cooked in fat, because it's already cooked. However, there's no harm in sautéing it in a little oil for a slightly richer result. Browned flour keeps indefinitely in the refrigerator.

Incidentally, I can't leave this topic without telling you about a mistake I managed to avoid. The only good pots in my Florida kitchen are the Circulon brand with the grooves. I had my flour all measured out and was about to heat up my skillet when I took a good look at it and realized that the flour would settle in and become unremovable scorched groove-filler. I'm old enough so that there are a few things I don't have to try to know they won't work. If you make roux flour, use a pot with a smooth cooking surface.

BASIC TOMATO SAUCE
Makes 3 or 4 main-dish servings

   1 teaspoon olive oil
   1 medium onion, chopped

6 garlic cloves, pressed
One 28-ounce can crushed tomatoes
1 to 2 tablespoons dried oregano
½ cup loosely packed fresh basil leaves
Salt and freshly ground black pepper to taste

1. Heat the olive oil in a nonstick saucepan and add the onion and garlic. Sauté over medium heat for about 10 minutes.
2. Add the tomatoes and oregano; simmer for about 30 minutes, stirring occasionally, until some of the liquid from the tomatoes cooks off.
3. Chop the basil coarsely and add it to the sauce. Add the salt and pepper. Cook for about 5 minutes more.

90 calories, 1 gram fat, 0 grams saturated fat per serving of 4

BASIC CLAM SAUCE
Makes 2 or 3 main-dish servings

1 teaspoon olive oil
1 medium onion, chopped
4 garlic cloves, crushed
¼ teaspoon cayenne pepper
2 small cans chopped clams
⅓ cup evaporated skim milk
¼ cup chopped Italian parsley

1. Heat the olive oil in a nonstick saucepan and add the onion, garlic, and cayenne. Sauté over medium heat for about 10 minutes.
2. Add the clams with their liquid and the evaporated skim milk and bring to a simmer. Simmer until the sauce reduces and thickens slightly, about 10 minutes. Stir in the parsley. Serve over pasta.

130 calories, 1 gram fat, 0 grams saturated fat per serving of 3

BASIC MUSHROOM SAUCE
Makes 2 or 3 main-dish servings

1 teaspoon olive oil

1 pound assorted sliced mushrooms (oyster, shiitake, white,
*   or whatever else you like)*

1 medium onion, chopped

1 red bell pepper, chopped

¾ cup dry red wine

2 teaspoons Worcestershire sauce

1 tablespoon Dijon-style mustard

1. Heat the olive oil in a nonstick saucepan and add the mushrooms, onion, and bell pepper. Cook over medium heat until they wilt, 15 to 20 minutes. If they stick, add a little of the red wine.
2. Add the red wine, Worcestershire, and mustard. Cook until the sauce reduces, about 10 minutes. Serve over pasta, rice, or barley.

100 calories, 2 grams fat, 0 grams saturated fat per serving of 3

RED SAUCE

Red sauce has had a lean time of it among gourmets for the last decade or so. As Molly O'Neill commented in a *New York Times* article (9/11/91) on the subject: "By the late 1970s, 'cooked' in terms of a tomato, meant 'not fresh.' " So good old tomato sauce became a casualty of nouvelle cuisine with its philosophy that nearly all food should be, if not raw, barely cooked.

Like most home cooks, I kept right on making red sauce regardless of culinary fashion. It's much too tasty and versatile to be relegated to the dustbin of gastronomic history. Cook it enough so that the tomato's astringency is suppressed and you'll achieve the mellow taste that is so difficult to come by in low-fat mostly vegetarian meals. And an intensely flavored tomato sauce requires neither oil nor salt.

Red sauce is making a comeback in the fashionable food world. According to the headline of O'Neill's article, "It's No Longer Better Dead Than Red." Not that I cared. Not that you should care. I'm with Romana Raffetto, a New York City grocer quoted in the same article: "Styles come and go. Red sauce remains."

Perhaps the most controversy in any discussion of red sauce is generated by the question of what kind of tomatoes you should use to make it.

I just use whatever tomatoes taste best at the time. That usually means vine-ripened beefsteak tomatoes in the summer, Italian plum tomatoes in the spring and late fall, and, in the dead of winter, canned tomatoes (as in Tamar's Basic Tomato Sauce, page 134). The roasted tomato sauce below should be made only when there are good fresh tomatoes in the market.

This recipe may look moderately complicated, but it's really just another example of Tamar's sauce logic. First you sauté stuff; then you add liquid. All that's different is that the ingredients of this sauce spend some time in the oven first. Since this extra step makes the preparation somewhat time-consuming, when I make roasted tomato sauce, I make a lot.

ROASTED RED SAUCE
Makes about 3 quarts

10 pounds fresh ripe, juicy tomatoes, such as beefsteak,
*   Italian plum, or whatever tastes best*
4 large onions
1 large garlic head
1 or 2 large celery stalks
1 carrot
1 jalapeño or other hot pepper
1 tablespoon olive oil
1 bunch fresh oregano, or 1 tablespoon dried (optional; see Notes)
1 teaspoon brown sugar
Salt to taste
2 to 3 tablespoons tomato paste (optional)

1. Preheat the oven to 200°F to 300°F. Oven heat depends on how closely you want to watch your vegetables as they roast.
2. Cut any black spots from the tomatoes, peel and quarter the onions, and, without separating the cloves, remove some of the papery outer peel from the garlic.
3. Place the tomatoes, onions, and garlic in shallow pans in the oven and roast slowly until the garlic is soft, the onions look wilted, and the tomato skins have cracked and are just slightly charred. If your oven is fairly hot this will take only about an hour; at a low temperature it will take 3 to 4 hours and you need not supervise closely. If the oven is set under about 250°F, you'll have to raise the heat for half an hour or so at the end if you want to achieve a roasted flavor.

4. Remove the garlic and onions and reserve. Let the tomatoes cool in their roasting pans unless there's a lot of burned juice on the bottom, in which case dump them into a large bowl or two. When the tomatoes are cool enough to handle, drain them in a colander, saving the juice (see Notes). Pull off the skins (they should be very loose) and trim or pinch off the stems. (For me, this is a finger procedure.)

5. In the food processor, coarsely purée the celery, carrot, jalapeño pepper, and the roasted onions. Heat the olive oil in a nonstick pot that will hold at least 4 quarts and sauté the purée over medium heat until the vegetables are soft. If sticking occurs, add a little of the reserved tomato juice.

6. Meanwhile separate the garlic cloves, squeezing the roasted garlic out of the peel, and add it to the vegetables in the pot. If you're using fresh oregano, tie the bunch up in a white string so you can remove it easily later. Oregano stems are nasty little sticks.

7. Add the tomatoes, sugar, salt, and oregano to the pot and cook slowly, uncovered, stirring from time to time to prevent sticking and to break up the tomatoes. (For a smoother sauce, chop the tomatoes in the food processor before adding them.) Cooking time will depend on how much juice was left in your tomatoes and how thick you want your purée to become. I usually cook the sauce about 2 hours.

8. Optional: After an hour or so of cooking, if the mixture seems thin and astringent, add 1 or 2 tablespoons of canned tomato paste. Stir in well and continue to cook at least another half hour.

9. Remove the fresh oregano, let the sauce cool, and ladle it into jars or freezer containers. It will keep a couple of weeks in the refrigerator, several months in the freezer.

NOTES: Because fresh herbs generally should not be cooked much and because I like this to be an all-purpose sauce, I add most herbs and spices to the portion I'm using for a particular meal. For a marinara sauce to serve over pasta, I'd probably add fresh basil and Italian parsley. For a sauce to be mixed with beans for chili, I'd add cilantro and more hot pepper. I make an exception for oregano, as its flavor improves with cooking, but if you don't much like the taste of oregano, cut back or omit it.

The juice you poured off your tomatoes has multiple uses. Unless you have an immediate need for it, freeze it in small quantities. It's excellent for soup, for the deglazing technique I described when I discussed stir-frying, and for thinning the red sauce. There are many uses for which the above sauce is too thick and rich. In a pasta primavera, for example, it overwhelms the flavor of the vegetables. When you reheat the sauce for some such purpose, dilute it with tomato juice, chicken or vegetable stock, bean broth—any or all of the above—until the flavor and consistency satisfy you.

....

480 calories, 9 grams fat, 1 gram saturated fat per quart

....

All Wet: Soup Strategies

> People say you have to have sex in every picture because it reflects real life. But I say, people also have soup. I never heard anybody in a movie say, "I'm looking for a nice plate of soup."
>
> —JACKIE MASON, ON HOLLYWOOD'S OBSESSION WITH EXPLICIT SEX

I'd like to ask Jackie Mason which he would choose if he had to do without one or the other. As for me: I'm thinking, I'm thinking! Low fat/high veggie would be an awful drag without soup. Lunch might never be served at my house again.

Tamar's sauce logic (page 127) also applies to soup. The difference is that you don't have to agonize about the delicate balance between the wet and dry. Soup is supposed to be wet. Just about any savory substance can find a home in soup. Unlike sauces, many hearty soups (The Mother of All Soups, page 140, is an example) don't really require a sautéing step. For others, especially those containing mushrooms, like the Lentil Barley Soup on page 83, it's a necessity. In all cases, taking the time to sauté some of the foundation vegetables before adding the liquids enhances flavor, but you may not always want to bother.

A good basic grain/legume/vegetable soup is part of the repertoire of many good home cooks. Every one of these soups is a wet version of one or another of the grain/legume combos we discussed in Chapter 5. If you've already got a soup you like, by all means stick with it. It can be a mainstay of a healthful diet. If not, try the Mother of All Soups. Use what you learn in succeeding chapters to work variations on it. It's a terrific vehicle for sneaking all sorts of unfamiliar foods into your family's dinner.

If you're using chicken stock, since it must be cooled and defatted, you'll probably want to make soup preparation a two-day process. That may sound like a lot of bother, but your total prep time—stock and soup—even if you skim the stock as it cooks, will be less than a hour. The rest of the cooking process won't require your attention. Both stock and soup freeze well. See that you make enough to generate ample leftovers.

THE MOTHER OF ALL SOUPS
Makes about 4 quarts

6 cups chicken or vegetable stock

4 cups water

1½ cups brown lentils

1½ cups brown rice

4 carrots

1 large celery stalk

1 large onion

3 large garlic cloves

One 28-ounce can whole tomatoes

1 teaspoon dried oregano, or 1 tablespoon fresh

1 teaspoon dried thyme, or 1 tablespoon fresh

1 or 2 bay leaves, crumbled

1 bunch Italian parsley or cilantro or mixed
    fresh herbs

2 tablespoons wine vinegar or cider vinegar

Salt and freshly ground black pepper to taste

1. In a pot that will hold at least 5 quarts, combine the stock, water, lentils, and rice and set over medium heat.
2. While your pot is coming to a boil, cut up the carrots, celery, onion, and garlic, using the slicing blade of your food processor. Add them to the soup pot.
3. Pour off the juice from the can of tomatoes into the soup pot and feed the solids through the slicing blade of the food processor. Add them to the pot. Add the dried oregano and thyme here if using and the bay leaves.
4. When the soup comes to a boil, lower the heat, cover the pan, and simmer the soup, stirring occasionally, for 45 to 55 minutes or until the lentils and rice are tender. If the soup seems too thick, add some stock or water, then return the pot to a simmer.
5. Switch to the chopping blade in your food processor (no need to clean the work bowl) and coarsely chop the parsley or cilantro. Stir it into the soup along with any other fresh herbs, the vinegar, salt, and pepper.

580 calories, 3 grams fat, 0 grams saturated fat per quart

The Mother of All Soups, with the addition of some good bread and a green salad, makes a satisfying and complete meal from the standpoint of both the eater and the nutritionist. At the heart of this soup is my favorite among those grain/legume combinations that are essential to vegetarian cookery. Brown rice and lentils are made for each other. They both cook in about 45 minutes, their flavors and nutritional components complement each other, other flavors combine well with them, and they're virtually indestructible. You can soak them, overcook them, reheat them over and over, and they'll still have most of their characteristic flavor and texture.

You're not restricted to rice and lentils though. The Mother of All Soups is susceptible to a number of variations. Use barley and split peas instead of rice and lentils. Any of the grains and legumes suggested for g&l combos (page 120) are good in soup. Alter the vegetable components. Sautéed mushrooms, okra, potatoes, peppers—any vegetable that won't be ruined by extended cooking—can find a home in this soup. Soup is probably the most obvious and simplest component of the *incatenata* we'll define in Chapter 7. No great care is required in its reheating. In soup thoroughly melded flavors are usually desirable rather than objectionable. Even here, though, as we'll discuss later, flavor melding can get out of hand.

Let's assume that, having made a meal out of the Mother of All Soups or some similar concoction, it's a day or two later and you are ready to lunch on some of the leftovers. Put into a saucepan only about as much of the remaining Mother Soup as you think you can eat in a single sitting. While the pan is heating over low heat, case the refrigerator for odds and ends.

There's almost no food we discuss in this book outside of the dessert chapter that's out of place in soup. Roasted vegetable remains are especially fine. Cut them into bite-size pieces and add them. And there is life for leftover salad in the soup pot. It can be pretty desiccated; just check to see there's nothing growing on it and taste to be sure it hasn't picked up an off taste. (If it doesn't look all that great, run it through the blender.) In fact, if you're adding a lot of some sweet vegetable like roasted carrots, the pickled taste of old salad will balance them. If you have no old salad, you may want to add a few chopped-up dried tomatoes or some bottled salsa. Add herbs and spices if your soup seems bland. Make your additions gradually, tasting as you go.

Other good additions are frozen vegetables such as peas or corn. (Plain, of course. You don't buy the ones with the awful sauces.) Just pop them out of the bag or box into the soup pot. Any leftover cooked grain or legume is also wonderful. By now you may have added so much stuff that your soup's too thick. Thin it with any of the flavorful liquids Tamar lists in the sauce section (page 129) or, if worst comes to worst, water. Incidentally, if you had all this stuff around, I hope you didn't heat up too much of the original soup. You've probably doubled its volume by now. If you've got a green herb like parsley or cilantro, chop it and add it at the last minute. It will give your second-generation soup a sprightly look and taste.

SOUP: BEYOND THE SECOND GENERATION

Don't throw away leftover second-generation soup. I prefer not to put it back with the original Mother Soup but to use it to start a third wave, augmenting it with more of the mother batch along with yet more odds and ends when I'm ready to reheat it.

I hope I'm making this clear. The point is to keep on hand some of the Mother Soup in its pristine state as long as the cycle lasts. Then if you make a flavor error—too much hot pepper, curry, rosemary, etc.—in one of the later stages, you can dilute it with a bit of the original rather than being stuck with a ruined potful. It also keeps the original soup from being reheated into an overcooked mush with unrecognizable ingredients. You always have some relatively fresh-tasting brew to add to your later variations.

The soup cycles could theoretically go on forever. Your great-grandchildren could celebrate the 10,000th cycle with a special party. But I rather doubt that anyone would want to come. I certainly wouldn't (never mind that I'd be about 130 years old). I like to have a fighting chance of identifying what's in my soup, and I don't want it to be a seventy-five-year-old fava bean. So I deal in smallish batches that are likely to be consumed in one meal, preserving the Mother Soup for later batches. If you find yourself growing tired of the Mother Soup, you can always freeze whatever's left. It will most likely taste good again in a month or so. Leftovers from later cycles are best frozen in single portions for future lunches. Line a bowl with a plastic bag, fill with soup, and freeze. Then you can remove the bag from the bowl for freezer storage and later unmold the soup into the same bowl to thaw in the microwave.

SOUP FROM A STONE

There's a great old folk tale about an itinerant beggar who finds himself in a village of uncommonly stingy peasants. He tries every house, but no one will give him a morsel of food. At the last house, he asks for the loan of a large cooking pot. His request arouses the curiosity of the housewife, who knows he has nothing to cook. "Oh," he tells her, "I just want to make some stone soup."

The woman, who believes she has mastered every strategy for household economy ever devised, naturally sneers at the idea. He is so convincing, however, that she eventually lends him the pot. He builds a fire in a nearby field, puts several large stones in the pot, and fills it with water. As the pot boils, he enlarges on the virtues of stone soup. "Of course," he tells the villagers who have gathered to watch, "it would be even better if I had a bit of beef." A man tears off and returns with a nice piece of brisket, which is consigned to the pot. "Stone soup is wonderful," says the beggar, "but a few onions can make it ambrosial." The onions are brought. You get the idea. He obtains carrots, potatoes, turnips, salt—everything he needs to make a fine soup. And he and all the villagers dine on it, all the time exclaiming: "Soup from a stone! Fancy that!"

During lean times, according to Dan Rather in his memoir (appropriately entitled *I Remember*), his grandmother actually made stone soup. She selected a large stone, cleaned it carefully, and set it to boil in a large pot of water. Then she added lots of grass, preferably gone to seed, a few carrots and onions, and some Tabasco sauce. Why the stone? I suppose to distract everyone's mind from the absence of some of the more traditionally preferred ingredients. So get a real stone if you want. It's cheaper than a quart of heavy cream and a lot easier on your arteries.

Stone or no stone, there may be days when you want soup and your larder and refrigerator seem as unforthcoming as the peasants in the story. Suppose, at some improvident moment, you find yourself left with a mere smidgen of leftover soup or, worse, none at all. Do not despair.

If you have a little soup, heat it, adding odds and ends as above. If you're short on odds and ends, a can of tomatoes is a big help. So are canned beans or chickpeas. In a separate pot, boil 2 or 3 cups of water for each person you wish to serve. When the water is boiling add approximately ½ cup of dried pasta (bite size or smaller; if you have only spaghetti break it up first) and ¼ cup red or yellow lentils per serving. Boil 8 to 12 minutes or until the pasta and lentils are cooked. (Couscous is the ideal stone soup pasta, but it should be added after the lentils have been cooking for about 5 minutes.) You are using less water than is generally recommended for cooking pasta so be sure to stir occasionally. Add the pasta and lentils to the soup pot with enough of the cooking water to create a souplike consistency. Stir to mix, and simmer a minute or two. Incidentally, you can use larger green or brown lentils but you must start them well before the pasta. The green take about 20 minutes, the brown about 40.

Suppose, heaven forfend, you are *out of soup,* and there's no stock of any sort in the house. Take any vegetables you can find—raw or cooked, even canned will do—and grate or chop them in the food processor. You want a somewhat coarse purée. (If you have the time and inclination, sauté this purée briefly in a little olive oil before putting it into the soup pot. Try to have at least a cup of veggies per serving of soup.) Don't forget to check the freezer and, once again, your supply of canned goods.

Boil the pasta and lentils as above but turn off the heat while they are still slightly firm. Pour off and reserve most of the liquid. Immediately add the vegetables to the pot with the pasta and lentils. Add enough of the reserved cooking liquid to achieve soup consistency and return the mixture to the boil. As it cooks, add herbs and spices, tasting as you go, until it tastes like soup to you. Even if you don't usually cook with salt, this is an occasion when a little can help you a lot. If all goes well, the vegetables will be cooked by the time the pot boils and the pasta and lentils will be neither hard nor overcooked. Let everything simmer for 5 or 10 additional minutes and serve. This is a fine main-course soup that can be ready within half an hour of your entering the kitchen.

Note that the stone soup technique can be adapted to almost any set of ingredients that may be hanging out in your pantry, refrigerator, or freezer. As long as you have a supply of the foods I recommend in Chapter 7, page 160—at least two or three of them—you have a potential soup. Add a green salad and perhaps a whole-grain bread and you've got dinner. Soup from a stone! Fancy that!

CONFESSIONS OF A CHOWDERHEAD

I have many weaknesses. Among the most egregious (that I can admit to publicly) are a tendency toward sloth, a high tolerance for dirt, and a habit of reading thrillers. All of these manifest themselves in obvious ways. A 10 A.M. phone call will wake me up as often as not. I probably don't wash my sheets as frequently as I should. I fritter away my time reading books with no literary or educational value. (I justify this by figuring I'm entitled to spend all the time I don't spend cleaning reading fluff, but since maintaining this illusion is important to me, I stop short of doing the math.)

I also have food weaknesses. Cheese. Ice cream. Spicy Italian sausage. And cream soups. I have an inordinate fondness for cream soups. Vichyssoise, she-crab soup, and lobster bisque must have been invented by diabolical geniuses determined to sabotage the weight-control efforts of people everywhere. And their low-rent cousins (the soups' cousins, not the geniuses'), chowders, are equally insidious. Chowders turn wholesome, nutritionally correct foods like clams and potatoes and corn into dangerous artery-cloggers. Bummer.

Making low-fat chowders is a thankless job. If they're not thickened with flour or cornstarch, they tend to be thin and insubstantial. If they are starch-thickened, they tend to be starchy. You can't win. But my fondness for chowder is such that I was motivated to give a low-fat version the old college try. After a few unsuccessful attempts, and one unrecoverable disaster, I found that puréed potatoes make a reasonable thickening agent, and that buttermilk can lend an almost full-fat feel.

Cooking potatoes (or other root vegetables) and then puréeing them to add body to a soup or sauce is a time-tested technique. You'll find other recipes in this book, and many other books, that make use of it. It's easy to do and difficult to screw up. Adding buttermilk to a hot soup, however, is not so straightforward. If you heat it too quickly, or to too high a temperature, it may curdle, and you, like me, will have an unrecoverable disaster on your hands. And some soups are trickier than others. In Mom's Root Soup, on page 186, the buttermilk doesn't seem to be a problem. In this soup, however, it displays an unfortunate curdling tendency, and I would recommend not adding buttermilk to the hot version. If, however, you're planning to (or I can convince you to) serve the soup cold, buttermilk is a great idea. Even though it has little or no fat, it has a lovely thick texture that will help make up for the lack of cream in your soup.

The chowder below works pretty well even without the buttermilk, so if you're in the mood for a hot soup, just make it as is. But try the leftovers cold with buttermilk, and you'll see what I mean. You won't mistake it for vichyssoise, but you may be surprised at how creamy and satisfying it is.

CORN CHOWDER
Makes 4 servings

2 teaspoons olive oil

4 garlic cloves, minced

½ jalapeño or other hot pepper, minced

2 onions, chopped

½ cup chopped cilantro

5 or 6 small red potatoes, enough to make 2 cups when cut into bite-size pieces

4 cups nonfat or low-fat milk

One 10-ounce package frozen corn, or kernels from 3 ears

Salt and freshly ground black pepper to taste

1. In a pot large enough to hold all ingredients comfortably, heat the olive oil over medium heat. Add the garlic, jalapeño, and onions and sauté until the onions wilt, about 10 minutes. Add half the cilantro and sauté another minute or two.

2. Add the potatoes and milk and bring to a boil. Reduce the heat, cover, and simmer until the potatoes are tender, about 20 minutes.

3. Using a slotted spoon, transfer the potatoes from the soup to the blender or food processor. Don't worry if you miss a few. (In fact, if you prefer your chowder with potato chunks, by all means leave some behind.) Add a little of the soup's liquid to the potatoes, and purée to a smooth paste. Return the puréed potatoes to the pot.

4. Bring the soup back to a simmer, add the corn, and continue simmering for 5 minutes more, until the corn is tender. Add the salt and pepper and remaining cilantro.

N O T E : For the cold variation of this soup, chill it and then add a cup of buttermilk. The buttermilk gives the texture a little more heft and adds a nice tang. Be warned, however, that if you add buttermilk to the hot version, it may curdle and you will have a big mess on your hands.

300 calories, 4 grams fat, 2 grams saturated fat per serving

CHILLING OUT IN THE SOUP BOWL

Cold soups are hot! It was hardly possible to open a food publication last summer without encountering an effusive article about how cold soups are just right for hot weather. The article was always accompanied by a bunch of recipes—most of them designed to keep the cook in the kitchen. Some featured ingredients like Bing cherries, which have to be cooked and put through a food mill. Some instructed you to peel and seed vast numbers of tomatoes. Here are a couple simple and tasty recipes that have worked well for us on hot days.

Many cold-soup mavens instruct you to let the soup chill for several hours after blending to let the flavors meld. I, however, believe that this compromises the extremely fresh taste you're looking for when you're using uncooked ingredients. Generally, I've been happiest with my cold soups when I've served them right away. I like to be able to distinguish the separate flavors. Of course, if you serve your soup fresh out of the blender, you've got to have everything extremely cold. Chill your serving bowls well. You can even put your ingredients in the freezer for a while—just don't let watery vegetables freeze. Cucumbersicles are not delicious.

As for fruit soups, I've never been able to see the point of them. They're not really an appropriate appetizer, nor are they a real dessert. I always think they're something you should save to drink for breakfast. But they're harmless enough, and we do say a few words about them in the dairy chapter (page 265).

YOGURT CUCUMBER SOUP
Makes 2 servings

> 1 large, seedless cucumber, or 2 regular cucumbers,
>   peeled and seeds removed
> 2 scallions
> ¼ to ½ cup fresh mint leaves
> 2 cups nonfat plain yogurt
> Juice of 1 lime
> ½ teaspoon ground cumin
> Salt to taste
> Chopped nuts or scallion tops for garnish (optional)

1. Combine all ingredients except the garnish in a blender or food processor and blend until you've achieved the consistency you like. Chill thoroughly. Stir well and taste before serving. You may need more mint leaves, lime, or perhaps some salt. Sprinkle with nuts or scallion tops if desired.

250 calories, 0 grams fat, 0 grams saturated fat per serving

TAMAR'S GAZPACHO
This is strictly a soup for summer when local tomatoes are in season.
Makes 4 to 6 servings

5 large ripe tomatoes

1 cucumber, peeled

1 medium onion, peeled

1 green bell pepper

4 garlic cloves

1 bunch cilantro, stemmed

1 tablespoon red wine vinegar

Juice of 2 limes

Approximately 4 cups tomato or V-8 juice (see Note)

Salt (optional) and freshly ground black pepper to taste

1. Chop the vegetables coarsely and purée in a food processor with the garlic and cilantro. Unless your food processor is industrial size, you'll probably have to do this in shifts. Stir in the vinegar and lime juice, then add the tomato juice until the consistency is the way you like it. Season with the salt if using and pepper. Serve chilled.

N O T E : V-8 juice is one of those prepared foods that I'm a little embarrassed about liking, but I'm fond enough of this gazpacho to swallow my pride and pass along the recipe. If you're worried about sodium, however, V-8 juice is a bad choice. Even some tomato juices are very salty, so make sure to check the labels.

150 calories, 0 grams fat, 0 grams saturated fat per serving of 6

We've only scratched the surface of soup making in this section. What I hope we've conveyed is that soup can be made from almost anything and is always an option to be considered when you want a quick meal. Elsewhere in this book there are a few soup recipes for which you actually have to plan ahead and maybe even shop for the ingredients: Potage Bonne Femme (page 207), Root Soup (page 186), Borscht (page 191), and Roasted Pepper Soup (page 180).

7.

The Dreaded Broccoli Kitchen

Pantry Momentum

PANTRY MOMENTUM IS WHAT YOU GET when you cook every day, or most days. It's the combination of leftovers, ingredients, and ideas that means you can walk into your kitchen, survey the terrain, think for a moment, and start cooking. No recipes, no lists, no special shopping trips. It's just you and food, one on one.

It means that you have a routine, that cooking is as taken for granted an activity as anything else you do every day. Like, say, eating. It means you can stop at the farmers' market or the grocery store or the fish place and buy whatever looks good, knowing you'll be able to combine it with whatever you've already got to produce something interesting when you get home. This kind of ad hoc, creative approach means you have to think about food a lot of the time, but for me this poses no problem.

My mother has major-league pantry momentum. She can get home at 6:00 and invent dinner in the time it takes her to walk up the three flights to her apartment. She's got the means: great inventory and a palate to be reckoned with, and motive—a husband coming home in an hour. Voilà! Dinner.

Half of pantry momentum is pantry, and you need a well-stocked one. If you have a physical pantry—a separate room specially designed for food, with shelves and cabinets and drawers—I envy you. I recently took a tour of my friend Valerie's new apartment, still in the final stages of renovation. She's a serious cook and has taken pains that the kitchen should be everything a kitchen could be. She has an industrial range, a Sub-Zero refrigerator, and lots of work surfaces. She also has a room right off the kitchen that could store enough food to see them through Armageddon. It was only after the tour, when I mentioned how impressed I was that she had both ample kitchen storage space *and* a pantry, that she told me it was the maid's room. Shows you how my mind works.

Mom and I are used to working in small kitchens with limited storage, and we both make the necessary compromises to accommodate food. My parents' apartment has one and a half bathrooms, and there's a small linen closet in the half bath. What little Mom and Dad have that can be dignified with the title of "linen" coexists happily in that closet with containers of dried beans, cans of tomatoes, and boxes of pasta. I grew up with more respect for food than food storage conventions, so this seems perfectly reasonable to me. It does, however, make for some curious exchanges that occasionally startle dinner guests. "Where are the peppercorns?" my father asks as he prepares to refill the grinder. "In the bathroom, next to the pillowcases," replies Mom.

I don't have a closet in my bathroom, but I find other ways to cope. Tall, skinny shelves, for example. There isn't much spare floor space in my kitchen, but there is a little patch to the left of the door, about 6 x 9 inches, that could house shelves all the way to the ceiling. Theoretically, at any rate. Just try going into Hold Everything and asking for shelves that are eight feet tall with a 6 x 9-inch footprint.

The more space you have, the more stuff you can store. The more stuff you can store, the more choices you have when dinnertime rolls around. (For advice on the most important items to have on hand, see Staple Foods: The Big Ten on page 160.)

In case you are thinking of "pantry" in its literal sense, let me be clear that we mean more than just those shelves that house your jars, boxes, and bottles. When we say pantry, we mean all the food in your house. This includes, of course, the contents of your refrigerator, freezer, wine cellar, and even linen closet, if that's where you happen to keep your sardines. And your garden, if you are lucky enough to have a yard and the skill to cultivate it. (I have neither—the only thing I can cultivate is friendships with gardeners, whose surplus tomatoes I hope to appropriate.)

Pantry momentum requires a good supply of kitchen staples, whether from garden or supermarket, refrigerator or cabinet. This means you have to be a contingency shopper. Instead of planning a menu, making a list, and shopping for those specific items, you shop for what's in season, what looks good, what might combine well with yesterday's leftovers, and what you're in the mood for.

Well-honed shopping skills are required, particularly with regard to perishable ingredients. Since you're not shopping with a particular meal in mind, you have to cover enough gastronomic contingencies that you don't cramp your own style, but not so many that your produce turns to mulch before you get to it. It's a little like inventory control in factories and warehouses. You try to predict what you're going to use and buy just enough. In its ideal state, it's a FIFO system. First in, first out. Yeah right. My kitchen's more like a Just-in-Time system. Much too often, I use things right before they go bad—just in time.

Which is not to say that I'm against planning a meal. Far from it. When I have guests, particularly guests I want to impress, like the Pope, Paul Newman, or the President, I plan. It's not just dinner, it's an event, and it calls for event cooking. A menu, a list, a special shopping trip. While pantry momentum may help with meals like this (dinner's always easier if you've got chicken stock on hand, for example), it's not meant to be the last meal-preparation strategy you'll ever need.

The other half of pantry momentum is, of course, momentum. Every time you cook you should be thinking about generating recyclable leftovers. It's a bit like sourdough starter, where you deliberately set aside a chunk for the next batch.

For example, suppose you've cooked up a pot of black beans. The first day you might serve them with rice and mushrooms. Your next dinner could consist of a pasta salad with some of the beans added (and even some of the rice/mushroom combo, if there's any left). And, of course, you've not only got beans, but bean broth. Your third day's dinner might be a soup with beans and their broth, rice, pasta, and mushrooms—all from your cache of leftovers.

But you never use things up in quite such an orderly fashion. Pantry momentum is not without side effects, chief among them being a refrigerator full of mysterious jars and plastic tubs. When you're salting away your leftovers in their little containers, keep in mind that you might be creating chaos. Labels and leftovers make good fridgefellows. (But if Failure to Label is your worst kitchen infraction, you're doing very well. It's easy for me to extol the virtues of labels, but the truth is I don't think I've labeled leftovers more than twice in my life.)

If you cook every day or almost every day, the concept of pantry momentum probably strikes a responsive chord. You know that dinner doesn't usually start with a cook and a book. It starts with a cook and the leftovers from yesterday and whatever looked good at the market and the asparagus that's about to wilt in the crisper. Since you'll never find a recipe with exactly those ingredients, you have to rely on your judgment and experience to come up with something on your own.

If you're more of an event cook, and unused to cooking regularly, the idea of improvising and experimenting may be a bit daunting. Don't panic! All the cookbooks you know and love will be a great source of ideas, and we hope to give you some more here. Start small by working variations on recipes you're familiar with. Before long you'll be cooking confidently without a net. And remember that this isn't brain surgery. If you screw up, no one's going to die on the table; the worst-case scenario is take-out Chinese.

Pantry momentum can also be the mother of invention. Many's the time I've envisioned a meal and started cooking only to discover that I didn't have some crucial element. Just the other day I began a pasta sauce with garlic, chicken, and mushrooms without realizing I had no suitable liquid to turn it into a proper sauce. No white wine, no chicken stock, no sherry, no bean liquid. But way in the back of the refrigerator, behind the half-empty jar of salsa and the leftover lentils, was one lone beer. Aha! I added beer to the chicken, stirred in a little dry mustard, and it was great. Not quite what I had in mind, but you'll find that happens a lot.

Every now and then you'll find yourself with a half-made meal, stymied. Nothing in the refrigerator will get you out of the corner you've painted yourself into, and you will wish for a deus ex machina to drop in and rescue your dinner. When that happens, do what I do. Call your mother.

Incatenata: Avoiding the "L" Word

Despite the rigors of veggie prep and some relatively long cooking times, you'll find that low-fat, veggie-centered food is good for more than your health. There are a few tricks to be mastered to make this stuff taste really good, but the basic cooking is a snap. Grains and beans are the ultimate convenience foods, with vegetables like potatoes, onions, and carrots not far behind. They keep well and their cooking times are flexible.

Nouvelle cuisine has conditioned us to believe there is only one right way to cook anything—just beyond raw. Anything more is overdone. Not true. Rice, for example, is good either a bit chewy or quite soft. So are most dried legumes. A carrot that has been stewed for a long time, or roasted slowly, has quite a different—and arguably better—flavor than one that has been blanched just enough to soften it slightly. Even green beans that have been cooked until they are soft develop a more interesting beany taste than the crisp ones, although like all green things they must not be allowed to become gray and mushy. All this means that you need not exercise preternatural care in timing the original cooking, and that these foods can be reheated with little if any loss of flavor. On the other hand, most fish, egg dishes, and foods containing butter or cream do not store well and don't taste or look very good when they reappear. They are leftovers. Your experience has taught you that they are undesirable, and they usually are.

A basic *Dreaded Broccoli* strategy is the deliberate generation and judicious use of leftovers. I think of pantry momentum as the process of generation. Its result is the *incatenata*—the chain of meals—pantry momentum in the pot and on the plate. I am indebted to Pino Luongo, creator of New York's Le Madri restaurant and author of *A Tuscan in the Kitchen,* for this wonderful Italian word describing an old Tuscan concept.

According to Luongo, *incatenata* "stands for the chain of meals that Tuscan women could get out of one simple, poor dish." He describes *la polenta incatenata,* made by the women of ancient Tuscany when there was little food available but cornmeal and a few vegetables. The first meal would be a broth of beans, potatoes, onions, and cabbage thickened with cornmeal. By the second meal the broth would have become firm (*rappressa,* as the Tuscans say) and could be sliced and fried. The following day it might be reheated in a garlic tomato sauce.

Now you too can eat like an impecunious Tuscan peasant. If money is a problem for you, your *incatenata* can be cheap and tasty very much in the way that Luongo describes. However, if what you add to your polenta on the second or third day is a whole lot of exotic mushrooms, you can easily spend as much as you would on filet mignon. The sort of food we're touting in this book is, at its most elaborate, nothing but a very expensive third-world diet.

Tuscan women knew how to save kitchen labor. You make a whole lot of polenta and nobody bothers you again until it's all gone. When they ask you for something different, you can curse them with ancient Tuscan curses—there isn't anything different. We don't have that excuse. There's lots of variety down at the supermarket, so we can have several dishes going at the same time. It's just as well. Besides the pleasure it provides, a large variety of food is the best ensurer of good nutrition.

Our chain of meals is several interwoven strands. The pots and bowls and containers in your refrigerator and freezer are like money in the bank. They are there ready for you to combine to make an interesting, fresh-tasting meal in less time than it would take to send out for pizza.

INCATENATA: HOT VERSION

There are three basic reheating techniques you will use over and over again as you recycle the leftover food in your household. The first might be called pan-grilling and is appropriate when you want to preserve the integrity of your original ingredients. In fact, you can produce a meal that is a virtual clone of the first.

The second technique is the one to use when you want to produce a mélange of ingredients—something resembling hash. As you probably know, there's usually quite a lot of fat involved in hash making. However, using precooked ingredients and very small amounts of liquid, you can prepare a hash—or a related dish like refried beans—with almost no added fat.

The third technique is reheating other ingredients in plenty of liquid—sauce or soup. This technique should be applied very cautiously. Its injudicious use is the cause of a lot of the world's bad recycled food, but it definitely has its place. (We discussed it in some detail in Chapter 6.)

1. THE PAN-GRILLING TECHNIQUE.

Perhaps you've made a lot of stir-fry. You and your significant other have eaten until you can't stuff in another bean sprout, and it looks as though there's more than when you started. Your stir-fry can live again tomorrow, or the next day, or the day after—even the day after that. (Actually, I've reheated stir-fry that was as much as a week old.) It gets to look a bit unattractive, but the vinegar and the acidity of some of the vegetables preserve it pretty well if there's no animal protein to go bad.

Before you put your leftover stir-fry away, drain it well and save any liquid in another container. Then, on a day when you can stand to look at it again, heat a large nonstick skillet. Make it quite hot. The idea is to reheat everything as quickly as possible without steaming it, so you want the largest, flattest surface available. Examine your stir-fry. You may want to discard some of the limpest greens. Check the refrigerator for cooked vegetables to augment the meal. Frozen ones will do in a pinch; just add them right out of the bag or box. Cooked beans or chickpeas make a nice addition too.

Pour everything into the hot skillet, spreading it over the surface, and stir. It will be hot in a couple of minutes. (Because the food has already been cooked, and some liquid and fat adheres to it, it won't stick.) If you prefer your stir-fry moist, add the leftover liquid or a little stock at the last minute, cooking only a few seconds to heat it. I hope you also have leftover rice or noodles, or some of any grain combo. If so, heat it with the stir-fry or, using the same technique, in a separate skillet. This method preserves the character of your stir-fry much better than steaming and produces the world's quickest hot meal, leaving the microwave in the dust.

This is the best way to reheat any dish when you want to preserve the integrity of the ingredients. It also works well when you want to augment the original preparation with some freshly sautéed vegetables. In that case, begin by heating the skillet only to moderate heat, sauté several minced cloves of garlic, along with some chopped scallions or shallots, in a teaspoon or two of oil. Add your mushrooms, zucchini, broccoli florets, or any other quick-cooking vegetables, and cook for just 2 or 3 minutes. (They should be slightly underdone when you add your precooked ingredients. This is particularly important for broccoli, which is unpleasant when overcooked.) Then raise the heat and add the leftovers. Just be sure not to crowd the pan. Cook as above.

The important thing to remember is that things shouldn't pile up in the pan. You want a thin layer. When in doubt, use two skillets. It's hard to follow that advice, of course, if you don't own two large nonstick skillets. A cook who is feeding more than one person would do well to acquire at least one very large skillet. I have a 13-inch one that I use constantly.

My approach to nonstick cookware has always been to buy the inexpensive kind on the theory that the surface ultimately becomes damaged no matter how much it costs or how carefully you pamper it. These cheap pans also have the advantage of being light in weight—a real virtue in a large skillet full of food. However, I have recently acquired a Circulon pan that shows signs of being very durable, so perhaps some of the expensive new surfaces are good price-performers.

The pan-grilling technique can give you a reasonable facsimile of a fried potato. Boil small potatoes—firm low-starch ones, not mealy baking potatoes—until they are barely cooked, still slightly hard. Slice them about ¼ inch thick. Prepare the skillet by heating a teaspoon or two of olive or canola oil or spraying with an oil spray. Add the potatoes and cook them over fairly high heat until brown, about 10 minutes, stirring frequently. If you have a roasted onion or two in your refrigerator, chop it up and add it during the last 5 minutes of cooking. A sprinkling of paprika (added in the last minute or so of cooking) will enhance the color and, if it's good Hungarian paprika, the flavor. Sprinkle with salt and freshly ground black pepper before serving.

2. THE HASH TECHNIQUE.

The pan-grilling method described above is a high-heat, dry-cooking method. This second technique, on the other hand, resembles conventional frying except that it uses liquid as a substitute for nearly all the fat. The trick is to use enough liquid to prevent sticking but not enough to steam the food.

It's a technique well worth mastering. It can produce that rarity—a really savory low-fat vegetarian meal. I've been struggling for years with the problems posed by fat limitations: too dry, too wet, too acidic, no taste. I'm about to share one of my favorite solutions with you. There is something about the crustiness foods develop with this kind of pseudo-frying that tricks you into believing you are eating actual fried food.

I can't say enough good things about the dinner that you can make out of leftover root vegetables. It is delicious and takes 20 minutes to prepare. It is nutrient-dense and low in fat. In the following suggestion for preparation (it seems pretentious to call anything so simple a recipe), I have added some cooked legumes—something that you should have around the house all the time. This makes for a taste variation on the dinner you produced when you baked or cooked a whole lot of vegetables using one of the methods we discussed in Chapter 3.

REFRIED VEGETABLES
Makes 2 large servings

1 to 2 teaspoons olive or canola oil

About 4 cups precooked root vegetables, such as potatoes, sweet potatoes, carrots, and turnips (half of them should have a fairly high sugar content—e.g., carrots, sweet potatoes; the sugar caramelizes and contributes to the hash effect)

1 to 2 cups cooked legumes, such as white or red beans or lentils

½ teaspoon red pepper flakes (optional)

1 to 2 cups liquid, such as stock, bean broth, beer, even a very dry white wine (a combination of liquids, though I don't recommend wine with beer, is desirable; 1 or 2 tablespoons of your liquid can be vinegar if your vegetables are quite sweet)

Salt and freshly ground black pepper to taste

1. Heat the oil a large nonstick skillet over medium-high heat. Add the leftover veggies, cutting the firm things like potatoes to approximately bite size. Sweet potatoes will break up as they fry. Add the beans and the red pepper flakes, if using. Keep the pan quite hot; when sticking occurs, add a tablespoon or so of liquid, stirring until it evaporates. After each addition of liquid has disappeared, press the vegetables down into the skillet and let them cook until they begin to stick again (about 3 minutes). When you have something resembling hash (this will take about 15 minutes), add the salt and black pepper and serve over couscous, quinoa, rice, barley, or pasta on a serving platter.

2. Optional, but highly desirable: Add about 1 cup of liquid (preferably bean broth) to the empty skillet and boil it rapidly for 2 to 3 minutes, scraping with a plastic utensil to loosen stuck pieces of vegetable. Reduce to about ½ cup and pour over the vegetables. This produces an excellent gravy that, if your hash includes sweet potato, is also a very lovely color.

NOTE: The calorie and fat content depends on your choice of ingredients, but don't worry, it's good for you.

This is the basic technique to use when you want the flavors of your leftover ingredients to merge. It requires considerable deglazing, as opposed to the pan-grilling method, which requires little or no deglazing. It also takes about 15 minutes, as opposed to 3 to 5 for pan-grilling. You might like to think of them not as two separate methods but as the two poles of a continuum. The amount of liquid you use and the number of times you add it will determine how hashlike the finished dish will be. You will note that both these techniques are related to our pseudo-sautéing method for cooking fresh ingredients. (See, for example, Dare We Call It Sautéing?, page 39.) Understanding these two ways of managing the *incatenata* will enable you to use the remains of former meals to maximum advantage.

3. REHEATING IN LIQUID.
This is a warning. One of the things that has traditionally made leftovers undesirable is the propensity of a lot of cooks to reheat leftover solids in leftover liquids. Often, sad to say, these poor, unoffending foods are actually boiled.

First of all, remember to store the solid foods you intend to use in your *incatenata* separately from the liquids. You don't want all your ingredients to end up tasting exactly the same. You may want to combine them again, but it should be done just before serving. Solids should be heated using either the pan-grilling or the hash-making method. The liquid should either be heated in a separate pot or poured over the solids at the last minute and heated very quickly. Naturally, it can also be used in the deglazing process. The ratatouille below is an example of what I mean—a particularly interesting one because you'd think it would be the sort of thing that would turn out well if you just sautéed the garlic and onion, dumped everything into a bowl, and stuck it in the microwave. But you'd be wrong.

RATATOUILLE INCATENATA
Makes about 4 cups

> *3 or 4 garlic cloves*
>
> *1 large onion*
>
> *1 teaspoon olive oil*
>
> *1 cup chicken or vegetable stock*
>
> *1 medium roasted eggplant (page 47)*
>
> *1 medium roasted zucchini (roast it with the eggplant, but it will require only about 15 minutes)*
>
> *1 medium roasted red pepper (page 179)*
>
> *1 cup tomato sauce or canned crushed tomatoes*
>
> *Salt to taste*

1. Chop the garlic and onion fairly coarsely or run them through the food processor using the slicing blade. Heat the olive oil in a large nonstick skillet, add the garlic and onion, and cook until soft, stirring to coat well. Add small amounts of stock if necessary to prevent sticking.

2. Chop the eggplant and zucchini into bite-size chunks and the pepper into coarse strips. Add these to the skillet. Cook, stirring frequently but gently, until the vegetables are just heated through, adding stock when necessary.

3. Meanwhile, heat the tomato sauce or tomatoes in a small saucepan, thinning with the unused portion of the stock.

4. Combine the sauce with the vegetables, add salt, and serve at once over pasta or as a side dish.

100 calories, 1 gram fat, 0 grams saturated fat per cup

You get the idea. This dish illustrates a principle applicable to any number of combinations of liquids and precooked solids. Minimal contact between them preserves the separate flavors best. If you're in a hurry, just heat the tomato sauce quickly on top of the sautéed vegetables. I do think, though, that the finished dish is better if the sauce is added at the last possible moment. Eggplant and zucchini are highly absorbent and sacrifice their own identities to the tomato without the slightest struggle. They're the Jewish mothers of the vegetable world.

COLD INCATENATA

When you remove most traditionally cooked leftovers from the refrigerator, you have to deal with congealed fat. No way do you want to eat them without reheating. Low-fat foods don't create this problem. Your stir-fry (with the exception of its leaves) or the firmer parts of your veggie roast will look much the same when you resurrect them as in their original incarnation.

A basic vinaigrette—one that is slightly more complex than the one you use on your green salad—can turn any combination of previously cooked vegetables, legumes, and grains (provided all the ingredients are more or less solid and dry to begin with) into a main-dish or side-dish salad. The following is a good all-purpose dressing. It's fine for green salad too, but don't use it on more than one dish in any one meal or too many days in a row or you'll soon tire of it. It will keep at least a week in the refrigerator.

VINAIGRETTE INCATENATA
Makes about ⅔ cup

  3 garlic cloves
  1 shallot or scallion
  1 small bunch Italian parsley, cilantro, basil, or a combination
  ¼ cup red or white wine vinegar
  2 tablespoons wine, preferably matching the vinegar
  2 tablespoons olive oil
  1 tablespoon Dijon-style or Pommery mustard
  Salt to taste

1. Remove the inedible portions of the garlic, shallot, and herb. Place all ingredients in a blender or food processor and process until fairly smooth. Taste for seasoning and adjust proportions slightly if necessary. If it seems too acidic, a little salt can help.
2. Pour this over your resurrected food in the approximate proportion of 1 or 2 tablespoons to every 2 cups.

30 calories, 2 grams fat, 0 grams saturated fat per tablespoon

Below are some combinations that have been reincarnated successfully under this vinaigrette at my table:

- Steamed broccoli and chickpeas
- Potatoes (any firm ones will do) and pinto beans
- String beans and kidney beans
- Bulgur and carrots
- Any of the above mixed with a can of water-packed tuna

Roasted peppers and chopped raw red onion are good additions to any one of these cold dishes.

Staple Foods: The Big Ten

Strategies, techniques, and recipes are all very well, but to implement them you need to have some idea how to start. Below is a list of the basic foods that make pantry momentum possible at my house. If you have them, and acquire whatever fresh vegetables appeal to you when you're shopping, you'll be able to improvise healthful, tasty meals without becoming a kitchen slave. They are almost sure to be available at your supermarket. However, if you've been hanging around in the wrong aisles, you may have to ask where some of them are.

The following items are the ones I try never to run out of. They are my Big Ten Dinner Staples:

- Pasta in favorite shapes (all semolina, and if you like it, whole wheat)
- Rice (preferably brown)
- Barley
- Dried beans (at least two or three kinds)
- Lentils
- Chickpeas (dried, canned, or both)
- Potatoes
- Carrots
- Onions
- Garlic

All these things are nutritious and versatile. (All right, maybe onions and garlic aren't all *that* nutritious, but no Norwegian cook can manage without them, and they do have putative health benefits.) These staples can be combined with each other and with fresh vegetables in nearly endless variations. They are also extremely cheap. Enough of these basic foods to feed two people for a month can be purchased for twenty-five to thirty dollars.

I also like to have supplies of couscous, quinoa, Arborio rice, wild rice, dried and fresh mushrooms, sweet potatoes, celery, dried tomatoes, fresh ginger, lemons, vinegar, olive oil, and canned Italian tomatoes. In the winter I stock a few frozen vegetables, particularly corn and peas.

Stocking a Spice Shelf

The curse of low-fat cooking is that it so often tastes flat. I don't necessarily mean bland—just one-dimensional. Like Hans Christian Andersen's Snow Queen, it has no back. We're all looking for tastes that consist of more than just what you experience the instant you put the first bite in your mouth. Whether you call it depth or substance or complexity, you know what I mean.

Herbs and spices are our major weapon against the backlessness of low-fat vegetable preparations. You'll see recipes in this book that call for fresh cilantro by the cupful and dried oregano by the tablespoon. These are not misprints. We've found a lavish hand with seasoning is essential for producing palatable low-fat meals. Fat is a great carrier of flavor, and if you reduce it significantly without increasing other flavor enhancers, you and your public are going to get bored and cranky.

Ground spices and dried herbs are things you probably have on hand if you've been cooking regularly. Otherwise, purchase a basic supply of these handy flavoring agents.

I'm occasionally asked the difference between an herb and a spice and the answer has always come tripping off my tongue: An herb is a leaf (with its stem if that's edible); a spice is a seed. Now that I'm supposed to be a professional food maven, however, the casual manner in which I'd reached that conclusion began to bother me. So I looked it up in Harold McGee's *On Food and Cooking* and discovered that's precisely the distinction he prefers. It seems to be an adequate definition for culinary purposes, even though, technically, an herb is any annual plant that germinates, sets its seed, and dies in one season.

Fresh herbs are best but they are not always attainable or convenient. Some herbs, however, should always be either fresh or frozen. Dried basil, chervil, and parsley are worthless. Oregano, thyme, and rosemary work very well in their dried forms. Sage and tarragon are all right dried, but they should be used in very small quantities. Don't buy powdered herbs, and discard any you have on hand. They can sometimes pass muster when they're cooked in hot oil, but otherwise they have a nasty bitter taste.

Spices are another matter. They are supposed to be dried and ground. It's preferable, of course, to grind them yourself, but except for black pepper few of us will bother. Black pepper really is an all-purpose spice.

Freshly ground in your own pepper mill, it is good on almost everything but dessert. Red pepper flakes are also useful. I have often used them at the eleventh hour to rescue food from terminal blandness. Don't forget seeds: fennel, cumin, and caraway. Vegetarian-style, low-sodium food can be greatly enhanced by the surprising accents they provide. Useful ground spices, especially if you're cooking Indian or Mexican-style food, include cumin, coriander, turmeric, and chiles.

Try to buy your herbs and spices in a store where they don't look as if they've been hanging around for years. Don't keep them around your house forever either. It's also best not to buy the "gourmet" line in the glass jars if you have any choice. Not only are they absurdly expensive, but they get more exposure to light than is ideal. Herbs and spices retain their flavor best when kept away from light, heat, moisture, and air. Some serious gourmets will tell you everything on your spice shelf that's more than six months old should be tossed out. I think that's ridiculous; if it still smells like what it is, by all means use it. Spices don't rot—they just fade away. If they're old, you need to use more.

All the dried and ground flavoring agents I've mentioned (except those I've specifically denigrated) are used in my kitchen. But before you spend your rich uncle's legacy stocking your spice shelf, let me tell you which ones I consider basic. As long as I have black pepper, red pepper flakes, and dried oregano to combine with some fresh herb from the market, I'll undertake to render palatable almost any food that comes to hand. I might wish for other spices and herbs, but with these three I can handle just about anything. They have been the Big Three on my spice shelf for several decades. My family has consumed many pounds of them. (And, believe me, a pound of dried oregano is an impressive amount.) So if you're just starting out as a cook and aren't yet quite sure of yourself, you can hang out with the Big Three for a while.

I Never Promised You an Herb Garden

If you like to grow things, your eyes may light up at the thought of all those tasty little annuals. However, I recommend growing your own herbs only if you have a real garden. I've tried raising them in pots, but the amounts of basil and parsley and cilantro I use sent my potted plants to the great herb garden in the sky in short order. So grow them if you like plants and you can control yourself—just take a little for the salad. Or grow a nice rosemary bush; it will provide rosemary for all your friends and neighbors. (Of course, dried rosemary is nearly as good. In fact, I can't tell the difference. I only know that a very little rosemary of any kind goes a long way with me.)

One of the reasons I'm always glad when spring arrives is that my frozen herbs are becoming unrecognizable. In summer I haunt the New York greenmarkets and rarely come away without a bunch of thyme, sage, or lovage. Usually a bunch is way too much, even for me, and I end up thrusting the leftovers into a plastic bag and sticking the bag in my freezer. This is not a procedure that's frequently recommended, but it seems to be about as good as any other (although it doesn't work for herbs with big leaves, like basil and parsley), and it's a rough-and-ready way for me to deal with my abhorrence of waste.

There are all kinds of suggested ways to preserve fresh herbs—drying, freezing in liquid, even packing in salt. None of them, to tell the truth, work all that well. Generally, if fresh herbs aren't available, you might as well use commercially dried ones.

I've recently discovered Penzeys, Ltd. (page 303), which is a wonderful source for all kinds of dried herbs (and great spices too) that cost less than they do in the supermarket. The herbs are the tastiest I've found anywhere, and the catalog is full of herb and spice lore—not to mention cooking ideas and recipes—from people who obviously know what they're talking about.

I describe below the herbs that are favorites in my kitchen—the ones I reach for again and again. Don't get hung up on my suggestions of what goes with what, though. I shamelessly use the first herb that comes to hand when I'm in seasoning mode.

So many things work in the kitchen! It's simply amazing.

BARBARA'S *GRETE HERBALL*

Basil: Any sauce containing tomatoes cries out for basil, lots of basil. Basil is an exception to the rule that dried herbs can replace fresh, so it's best to have a serious strategy for prolonging its season. One of the things Tamar misses about northern California is that the one and only season there is basil season. In New York you can get all the basil you want in the summer. In August, in fact, the whole city fairly reeks of it. The rest of the year it is either of very low quality or a stalk with three leaves on it costs as many dollars. A respectable amount would have to be brought home in an armored car.

So what do you do when there's no basil? Basil is not an herb that dries well. You might as well keep a jar of desiccated grass clippings. If you want to preserve fresh basil for winter use, clean it, remove the thick stems, then purée it with a small amount of water or stock in a blender or food processor. Freeze it in ice-cube trays, unmold the frozen cubes into a plastic bag, and store them in your freezer. Then, in the dead of winter, throw a few of the cubes into your sauce.

Parsley: Chances are, even if you're organized enough to process bags and bags of basil in the above fashion, you'll run out before the season comes around again. The best substitute for basil in your red sauce is Italian (flat-leaf) parsley mixed with a teaspoon or two of dried oregano. Parsley, bless its little green heart, is available year-round, and a few tablespoons mixed into almost any dish at the end of cooking will enhance the flavors and mitigate the need for salt. Try not to get stuck with the curly kind with the grassy flavor, and please, no parsley flakes.

Oregano: Tamar and I both use embarrassing amounts of oregano. We buy it in those humongous 4-ounce jars—the ones you look at in the market and say, "Now who would ever want *that* much oregano?" To us Italian food means garlic and oregano—lots of it. None of this subtle northern Italian stuff for the Haspels. I also use a fair amount of oregano in Chinese and Mexican dishes. Through Penzeys, I've discovered Mexican oregano, which is spicier than the standard Greek herb. So that's what I'm putting in my chili these days.

Fresh oregano is a trial to use because it consists of little bitty leaves on inedible sticks. When I buy it, tempted by the idea of the freshly picked version of my favorite herb, most of it is likely to end up in the stockpot. I'm not much for labor-intensive flavoring agents. I do find that my fresh oregano is easier to handle after it's been subjected to my standard preservation treatment. Once it's frozen, the brittle leaves come off the stems fairly easily. But most of the time, oregano that someone else has plucked from its woody stems, dried, and put in jars is just fine with me.

Thyme: Thyme, especially when dried, should be used carefully. The over-thymed dish can develop a distinctly medicinal taste. A little of this herb, however, can help provide that extra layer of flavor in a veggie dish. I especially like it in soups containing legumes. Fresh thyme has the same pesky structure as oregano: tiny leaves on woody stems (again, freezing helps). However, the fact that one of the best places for thyme is the stockpot lessens the difficulty. Pick off a few leaves for your salad and throw the rest into the soup.

Tarragon: I agree with M. F. K. Fisher that the flavor of tarragon is reminiscent of licorice. Like parsley, it seems to lessen the need for salt in a dish. I use fresh tarragon mainly as a salad herb, but it's also nice mixed with basil to season a tomato sauce. Dried tarragon can develop a slightly musty taste and should be used with care, but it can do good things for a soup or sauce. Penzeys sells a good version of the California variety.

Tarragon is the classic herb for flavored vinegar. Insert a large sprig, well washed and dried, into a bottle of wine vinegar of which you've grown tired, and your salads will improve a lot. Keep your tarragon vinegar in a cool, dark place.

Sage: For years I used sage only in poultry stuffing, but now it's playing a much bigger role in my kitchen. It has a real affinity with mushrooms, and I've used it to flavor pasta dishes and rice/lentil combinations in which mushrooms are the main flavor element. I've only used fresh sage for this, but if you can't find any, try a little of the dried kind in your mushroom dishes. And any time you cook poultry, stuffed or not, you can't go wrong with sage.

Cilantro (a.k.a. Coriander): Some writers maintain that the term coriander properly applies only to the seeds of this plant, which have a completely different flavor from the leaves and are a mainstay of Indian cooking. Many people, however, call the leaves coriander as well; and in older cookbooks they're sometimes called Chinese parsley. I always assumed everyone had to love cilantro and I used it by the handful. It has a much livelier flavor than parsley and, unlike that herb, never tastes grassy. I think it goes with everything. For me, the taste and odor are wonderfully fresh and subtly spicy. My family likes it too. Imagine my amazement when I learned that there are people who think cilantro tastes like rubber and smells like bedbugs! (Fortunately, I read this and was not so informed by some hapless guest at my table.) So maybe you should check out cilantro with your eaters before you go all out.

Lovage: Say *what!?* Lovage is a wonderful herb that I find occasionally at my local greenmarket in the summer. I don't think anyone grows it commercially, but someone certainly should. The closest I can come to describing the taste is to say it's like concentrated celery. You know how celery is—the taste is great, but there's so little of it. But *lovage!* There's no better herb to flavor a pasta primavera. It's also great in soup and salad— all manner of things in fact. Because it's so hard to come by, if I had room to grow just one herb, It would be lovage. According to Waverley Root, before lovage fell out of fashion, it was eaten as a vegetable, and the stems were sometimes candied, like angelica.

Kitchen Gadgets: Hall of Fame, House of Shame

The history of labor-saving devices is long and glorious. Think what the automobile and then the airplane did for travel, what the telegraph and then the telephone did for communication. Who among us doesn't remember learning about Eli Whitney, the cotton gin, and the power of innovation? And without the computer, my mother and I can assure you, there would be no *Dreaded Broccoli*. And then where would you be?

Cooking, however, hasn't changed much. Food, knife, and heat are still the basic ingredients, as they were when the heat was an open fire, the knife was a chipped rock, and the food was a mastodon. While our hunting and gathering techniques have improved markedly (now they're planned and mechanized and called "farming"), many of our cooking techniques are only a step away from Stone Age.

It's true that we have found excellent ways of generating and regulating heat (although my stove is emphatically not one of them). Knives are now made of special alloys that keep their edge for decades. Food is much more varied, as we are no longer restricted to what we can hunt or gather in a day's walk. (This is fortunate for those of us who live in Manhattan. I shudder to think of what we'd be eating if we had to find it or kill it.) But the process is the same. Food. Knife. Heat. Dinner.

Improvements in cooking techniques have come in small increments, and some of the smallest have been provided by a varied, and sometimes mysterious, selection of kitchen gadgets. One of my favorite food magazines, *Cook's Illustrated,* has a feature called "What is it?" for which readers send in photos or descriptions of mysterious kitchen gadgets they find in the back of their drawer, or their great-aunt's drawer, or their grandmother's drawer, and which they would like identified. (This seems like the kind of thing we'd write about, only we would call it "What the Hell is THIS Thing?" and it would consist chiefly of idle and indecorous conjecture. *Cook's Illustrated,* however, takes the high road and actually finds out what the thing is.)

Every time I read about one of these obscure gadgets, I am struck by two things: first, the dissimilarity of other people's drawers to my drawers, at the back of which you'd never find anything to send to a magazine, unless it was a magazine you disliked very much, or perhaps a magazine about carbon dating. But I am also struck by the ingenuity of the inventors of these gadgets, who are determined, in their own small way, to contribute to the advancement of cooking. Food. Knife. Heat. Fish scaler, and immortality.

And so we have created the *Dreaded Broccoli* Kitchen Gadget Hall of Fame, to honor the most useful kitchen implements, the ones that are always at the front of the big implement drawer, the ones that are battered from years of use and scores of dishwashings.

And with the Hall of Fame, we bring you the House of Shame, home of the useless, even laughable, attempts at exploiting the cook's endless quest to cut down on kitchen labor.

HALL OF FAME

Garlic press: Until the garlic peeler came along a couple of years ago, the garlic press was my most frequently used kitchen gadget. Now it's second, but my affection for it is undiminished. My garlic press has seen a lot of garlic, and it presses it dependably, with very little oozing out the sides. Periodically I'm tempted by those giant garlic presses that hold five or six cloves, but never enough to buy one. It would be disloyal somehow.

If you don't have a garlic press, get one. If you have one, but it's one of those chintzy ones with plastic handles or an ill-fitting plunger, get another one. A lousy garlic press is actually worse than no garlic press at all, because you spend more time futzing with it than you would just mincing the garlic by hand.

Garlic peeler: First let me tell you what I'm talking about. It's a 4-inch length of plastic tubing. Yup, that's it. Just a length of plastic tubing. You slice the ends off the garlic cloves, insert them in the tube, and roll it around on the counter. Out come your cloves, totally naked. It's the closest thing to magic that I've seen in a kitchen gadget. The first time I used it, the dish I was making ended up being too garlicky even for my tastes, which means it was way too garlicky for most people, but I just HAD to see it work again.

I like this gadget so much that I don't begrudge the inventor, manufacturer, distributor, or retailer one penny of the $5.95 I paid, even though the raw materials must have cost about two cents. Whoever thought of it deserves all that and more.

Potato (rotary) peeler: The best way to cut down on peeling time is to not peel at all, but there are times when even the least fastidious of us (Mom and I compete for this title) has to knuckle under and scrape the skin off a vegetable. The rotary peeler ensures that the job is done with minimum hassle and waste.

Steamer insert: You know what I'm talking about—the little metal basket you put at the bottom of the pot, with the petals that open to adjust to the pot size and fold in for storage. This is a good idea. It fits almost any pot, is easy to use and clean, and doubles as a child's plaything.

Knife sharpener: There are many kinds of knife sharpeners. For those of us with fortitude and dexterity, there is the sharpening steel. For those of us with neither, or perhaps only one, there are many incarnations of sharpener that require varying degrees of elbow grease and precision.

Knife sharpeners hold a special place in my heart since I discovered them fairly recently. I grew up in a house with one "sharp" knife. It was (and still is) a wooden-handled, serrated knife of indistinct origin and dubious quality. It was dull when I was ten. I would speculate that it's even duller now, but I think there is a point after which knives just don't get any duller. For this knife, that point came sometime in the Nixon administration. We no longer refer to it as "serrated." It's wavy.

My knives were headed down the same path until my friend Eli came to visit. Eli, a connoisseur of kitchen gadgets, deplored the state of my knives and bought me not one but two Chef's Choice manual knife sharpeners—one for serrated, one for non. Not for me the wavy knife! My knives can now do anything I ask of them, including slice six-day-old raisin nut bread, which they are called on to do with embarrassing frequency.

Apple corer/slicer: The wagon-wheel apple corer was a fixture of my childhood. We ate a lot of apples, and this device cores them and cuts them into child-size slices in one fell swoop. Perhaps there's a lesson here. It must be easier to get kids to eat fruits and vegetables if you first let them cut them up with a cool gizmo. (I must admit, however, that my mother seldom had any trouble getting me to eat anything.)

I don't even own an apple slicer now. I thought I did, but found out I was mistaken when I excavated my gadget drawer looking for it. Nevertheless, it makes the Hall of Fame riding on its nostalgia value.

Mouli grater: This grater must go by other names, but we always called it the Mouli in our house, to distinguish it from the flat-sided grater (itself a Hall of Fame Honorable Mention). This is the rotary grater with the little compartment for the cheese, which you grate by turning the handle. The Mouli minimizes the chance you'll grate your fingertips along with the Parmesan, and it's easy to bring to the table so each diner can grate his own, thereby sparing you, the cook, the labor of grating for everyone.

Lemon reamer: The lemon reamer is basically just a pointed stick, and it is a very satisfying tool. It's satisfying to hold and satisfying to use. You just impale the lemon half, twist, and lemon juice comes pouring out. How good is that?

Lemon zester: The zester is the tool that removes the outermost rind, or zest, from citrus fruits. It's a handle with several small, sharp metal circles on the end. As you run it over the surface of the fruit, it removes thin strips of the aromatic outer layer of peel while leaving the bitter white inner peel behind.

Fat separator: The best way to skim fat from liquid is to refrigerate it for a while and then just skim the fat off the surface. When time doesn't allow for this method, a fat separator is the next best thing. It lets you pour the liquid from the bottom of the cup, and you stop when you get to the layer of fat that floats at the top.

Splatter screen: Anyone who's ever had a bubbling vat of spaghetti sauce make a huge mess of the kitchen understands the value of a splatter screen. So you left the flame on just a little too high when you went to answer the phone? And you came back 15 minutes later to a kitchen that looked like the scene of a ritual sacrifice? Tomato sauce on the stove, the walls, the floor, the cat? You need a splatter screen, which is just a round screen with a handle that you put on the pot in place of a lid. Unlike a lid, it lets the steam escape so your sauce cooks down, but the splatter is contained.

Jar wrench: There are two kinds of jar opener (if you don't count boyfriends with something to prove), but only one makes the Hall of Fame. It's the kind that is a handle with a series of holes, and a sliding metal stop that adjusts to the size of the jar. The sliding stop gives it an animate quality, like a very thin guy with a very big mouth. This, and not its edge in efficiency over the other kind of jar wrench (which looks like a notched nutcracker), is what lands this wrench in the Hall of Fame.

HOUSE OF SHAME

The Hall of Fame was easy to compile. All I had to do was survey the contents of my big kitchen drawer; the gizmos I used most, or just had an affinity for, made the list. The House of Shame was harder. Every gizmo I've ever actually used that would be a candidate for the House of Shame I've long since thrown away, so research was required. Fortunately, I live right near Zabar's, which stocks every kitchen gadget known to man.

Tuna+: This is the gadget that inspired the House of Shame. It's a device to drain cans of tuna. It has two handles that open with a hinge. One of the handles has a receptacle for the (already opened) can, the other a flat surface to press the lid down. In the history of the world, or at least the history of tuna cans, has there ever been anyone who didn't just hold the lid over the tuna and invert the can over the sink? Maybe if I look around I can find a Tuna+ Plus that I could use to squeeze my Tuna+.

Lettuce knife: This knife is made of special plastic that doesn't turn the lettuce brown. Or maybe it's just ordinary plastic, I'm not really sure. What's wrong with this gadget? It strikes me as silly since I haven't noticed that ordinary knives turn lettuce brown. That doesn't mean they don't; it just means that the problem isn't obvious enough to have caught my attention.

Truffle cutter: A truffle cutter is just a very small slicer that cuts very thin slices. Presumably, you can use it for things other than truffles, things that are also very expensive and are therefore served in very small portions. That doesn't say much for the truffle cutter's overall utility, however, because most things that cost as much as truffles are more likely to end up set in precious metals than tossed with your pasta.

Wine drip collar: This gizmo is certainly aptly named. It's a ring that you put around the neck of your wine bottle to prevent the drips from getting on your clothes or tablecloth. In theory, I don't have a problem with this. I would go so far as to say it's practical. I believe, however, that the dinner table isn't the place for fastidiousness, and the wine drip collar sends the wrong message. When my guests sit down to a meal, I don't want them to be thinking about how important it is to not spill wine on the tablecloth.

Jiff-V-Sealer: This isn't just a gadget, it's a system. It's a plastic bag sealing appliance and a supply of special plastic bag sealers. The point? Keep odor and garbage in. The alternative? Take out the trash.

Lemon juicer: Don't confuse this with the lemon reamer installed in the Hall of Fame. The lemon juicer is a hollow screw of about a half inch in diameter with a little spout on one end. You screw the gizmo into the lemon and pour the juice out the spout. We did a juice-off with this juicer versus the lemon reamer. The reamer takes less time, makes less mess, requires less coordination, and generates more juice.

The Crumbster: What? You've never heard of the Crumbster? Let me tell you about it. It's an igloo-shaped, tennis-ball-size, battery-powered crumb picker-upper. You run it over a surface and *voilà!* crumbs disappear. But better than the gadget itself is the marketing copy on the box.

> The first time you use THE CRUMBSTER, you'll wonder how you ever managed without it! . . . Merely glide THE CRUMBSTER across the table on its sturdy bristle brushes while its powerful motor pulls up crumbs & small pieces of food. . . . It's fun to use too! Everyone will want to help you clean up just so they can use THE CRUMBSTER.

Oh, the shame!

PART THREE

Beyond the Basics: Enthusiasms

THERE ARE MANY, MANY PEOPLE for whom food is merely sustenance. They have to eat enough to fuel their daily activities, and they do, without giving much thought to what it is they're consuming. In college I had a friend named Al who ate exactly the same thing every single day. He said it was because he knew he liked it and that it would get him through the day, so he didn't see the point in experimenting.

Because I get pleasure not just from eating all sorts of food, but from deciding which of those foods is on today's menu, I find Al's mind-set very difficult to understand. To grasp it, I've tried to find an analog in my own life. Food:Al::_____:Tamar.

I can fill in the blank with music. Although I am capable of enjoying music and I frequently have it on in my apartment, it isn't important to me. I tend to play the same CDs over and over (a natural consequence of a CD collection barely out of single digits). I like some music more than other music, but what I like is just as likely to be unmitigated garbage as to be critically acclaimed. No music really engages or excites me, and there are whole genres, jazz, for example, that are completely inaccessible to me. I know myself to be an undiscriminating listener. I simply don't understand music.

People who do understand music don't believe this. I recently tried to explain it to a friend who cares about music. He contends that the only thing that matters is whether you like it or not. "You're overthinking it," he said. Perhaps. But I bet he'll reconsider if he finds my *Archies Greatest Hits* CD.

I'm pretty sure that if I worked at it I could develop some rudimentary appreciation of music. But I would have to listen a lot, pay close attention, and solicit the advice of experts, and I am not interested enough to invest that effort. There are other things I care more about, only one of which is food.

I think food and music appreciation work the same way. I can't be sure, of course, because I have one and not the other, but true enthusiasm for either seems to require some innate component. Although I no longer shake my head and click my tongue in disbelief at people who don't care about food, I continue to feel for them because I think they're missing out on one of life's greatest pleasures. But then they may feel the same way about the pleasures I'm missing out on.

On some level, however, I keep hoping my enthusiasm is contagious. I have a friend who is a very cautious eater (but a remarkable musician). One day both he and a loaf of chocolate bread from a bakery called Ecce Panis were at my house. I offered him a piece, and he declined. "But you have to try it," I said. "It's the perfect balance of bread and chocolate with just the right amount of sweetness." No dice. He wouldn't even taste it.

It wasn't just for his own pleasure and edification that I wanted him to try it, it was also for mine. I didn't just want to eat, I wanted to share, and I wanted to introduce him to something new and delicious.

Eating is only the beginning of the pleasure of food. I've enjoyed a lot of food alone, but any meal is enhanced by the presence of a food-loving friend, and being able to provide the meal, to feed people, is more satisfying yet.

Just eating is the simplest pleasure, and the hardest to describe. I'd love to put my finger on exactly what it is about eating that's so extraordinary, what all great eating experiences have in common, the unifying characteristic. But I can't. The pleasure of eating isn't a concept. It's the mushroom and sage pasta I had for dinner last night, and the striped bass we grilled on Cape Cod this summer.

The pleasure of eating is an amalgam of specifics—elusive specifics. I can remember that I ate a great meal at Chez Panisse last winter, but I can't still taste it. When I think about great food, the great food most likely to spring to mind is the great food I ate yesterday, the food I can almost still taste.

Today, it's nectarines.

I'm writing this on an airplane. In the overhead compartment situated (appropriately) over my head is a shoebox full of Arctic Rose nectarines. I bought them at the farmers' market in San Francisco and I'm bringing them to New York for my parents. These are simply the best nectarines I've ever tasted, and they're up there with the mangoes Mom got from Cushman's (the mail-order fruit company, page 301) as the Best Fruit Ever. They have a wonderful, complex spiced honey flavor and are the perfect balance of flesh and juice. For me, today, they are the pleasure of food.

As a kid, I read a book called *The Search for Delicious* by Natalie Babbitt, about a kingdom that's writing a dictionary. When they get to "delicious," the authors can't agree on one food to use as a definition. So they round up a posse to search the kingdom for delicious and after a long hard search, surprise, they *still* can't agree. After their trek, they return to the castle hot, thirsty, and disillusioned. In front of the castle there's a stream, and as the posse members drink their fill suddenly there is agreement. A cold drink of water after a long, hot, fruitless search is delicious.

The pleasure of eating is immediate and specific. Sharing with others adds to it the pleasure of company and shared enthusiasm. The Muppets said it best in *A Muppet Christmas Carol.* Several pigs are walking out of a restaurant. (These are literal pigs—pink-skinned, blunt-snouted, curly-tailed guys—as distinct from figurative pigs like me and my family, whose behavior in restaurants frequently gets us confused with the real thing.) They're remarking on what a great dinner they just had (okay, they're literal *talking* pigs). They talk about the meal and how full they are and then one asks, "So, what should we do next?" His friend answers, "How about lunch?"

For them, it's not just the food. They're having a grand old time eating together. Such a good time, in fact, that they can't think of anything they'd rather do. Pigs after my own heart.

I was reminded of our close kinship with the animal world one night when my parents, my brother Jake, and I went out for pizza. We all like different kinds of pizza, and we ended up ordering three pizzas for the four of us. When the first two came, the waitress put them down and then pulled a fifth chair up to the table, explaining that there was no room for the third pizza, so we'd have to improvise. When the third pizza came, it went on the chair. This raised the eyebrows of the two guys at the next table, who clearly thought that a reasonable person-to-pizza ratio would be more closely approximated by the addition of another person, not another pizza. To our credit, we took a whole pizza-equivalent home and, when the question of after-dinner activities arose, no one suggested lunch.

Beyond eating and sharing is feeding people, which adds to the pleasures of eating and sharing the knowledge that you have provided for the enjoyment of others. That's why I love to entertain. But not in a Martha Stewart kind of way. In fact, Martha Stewart and I have almost nothing in common. I am terrible at all the things she's good at. Nothing in my house matches. I avoid do-it-yourself decorating projects at all costs. I even avoid get-someone-else-to-do-it decorating projects. My idea of home improvement is vacuuming.

So I hesitate even to use the word "entertain," since it conjures up images of gracious hosts with good manners and expensive clothes. I'm sorry to say that grace, manners, and grooming don't top my list of virtues, but I am undaunted. When I say "entertain" I mean something very specific: I want to feed people.

Entertaining, for me, isn't *just* about food—I certainly want my guests to enjoy the company and conversation at my house—but it is nevertheless feeding them that gives me the greatest satisfaction. Besides, it's a lot easier to enjoy company and conversation in the presence of really good food.

But with feeding others comes responsibility. Eating and sharing are sit-back-and-enjoy pleasures, but you have to work to feed people. You have to plan. You have to cook. If you're anything like me you have to clean your house. (In fact, one reason I entertain regularly is that it forces me to keep my apartment in something resembling order.)

So when it comes off well, you have more than the satisfaction of having had a good meal with friends (a nontrivial satisfaction, to be sure), you have the satisfaction of a job well done. And, of course, the inevitable compliments—no small thing.

I've tried to explain all this to my old friend Hugo, the world's pickiest eater (see page 259). He doesn't understand why making a plain chicken breast for him and serious food for the rest of my guests takes some of the fun out of it. When Hugo is eating in his own little world, spurning the meal I worked hard on for my other guests, my satisfaction is diminished.

When friends and family sit around my table enjoying what I've cooked and each other's company, I have not just the enjoyment of friends and food, but the almost smug satisfaction that comes from knowing I made it all happen.

8.

Fun with Vegetables

AH! ENTHUSIASMS! FUN! That must mean we're about to introduce you to some veggies that are highly nutritious, cheap, simple to prepare, and taste just like sirloin steak. Sorry. This is all common stuff that we like a lot. We're presenting our favorites with preparation hints, an occasional recipe, and a lot of incidental lore. Familiar vegetables but, we hope, some new ideas.

Asparagus: The Thrust of Spring

The force that through the green fuse drives the flower
Drives my green age . . .

—DYLAN THOMAS

Early in life I became aware that asparagus was a spring event. Every summer when I arrived at my great-aunt's farm I hurried to the asparagus patch, hoping against hope that I would find some in its edible state. Alas, all that was ever left were a few seedy, ferny plants.

While I certainly wanted to eat the asparagus (I wanted to eat just about anything that didn't move too quickly), what I was really eager for was a glimpse of the emergent stalks, which had been described to me in lewd terms with many giggles by my friends from the farm across the road. For years I didn't believe them; it wouldn't have been the first time they pulled a fast one on the little city slicker. I had seen asparagus, of course—little tips that came in cans and that I assumed had somehow sprouted from the axils of the great ferny plants. They couldn't really just thrust up out of the ground! Could they? The obscene nature of the query made it impossible to ask an adult. When I was about ten and almost too old to care, it occurred to me to consult the encyclopedia and, sure enough, there was a picture of a whole field of little phallic symbols. So all my life, every spring, the sight of the first fresh asparagus has led me to ask myself that age-old question: Do farm kids really have dirtier minds than other kids or are they just exposed to more inspiration?

But I don't spend much time standing around philosophizing when I see asparagus. I take it home and cook it. Ever seen an asparagus cooker? It's a very tall pot with a very small diameter that many books will say you should use to cook asparagus. I'll bet you don't have one of those. Neither do I. So we improvise.

I break off the woody part of the stalk (they tend to snap naturally at the right point). Lots of people peel asparagus and, if you do, you can leave more of the stalk on without running the risk of overcooking the tips before the stalks are tender. But there are other, less tedious, methods of not wasting asparagus.

You can break the stalks near the tips, slice the edible portion of the stalks in the food processor, and steam the thin slices along with the tips. They will cook very quickly.

If you want nice long spears, but don't want to peel, try this steaming method. Divide your asparagus into three piles and arrange them in your steamer, the tips of each pile resting on the stalks of the adjacent pile (they will form a triangle). This is particularly convenient if, like me, you own a steamer basket with a rod in the middle. Use a pot big enough so that your basket opens all the way, and you'll have room for about thirty spears, approximately a pound. Your asparagus will be done about 5 minutes after it starts to smell cooked. It should have passed its very greenest point but not be edging toward gray. Look and taste as often as you want.

I find this method results in perfectly cooked asparagus about nine times out of ten. If it's that tenth time, the tips will be done and the stalks will still be woody or the peel tough. Don't panic and don't overcook. Dump the asparagus onto your cutting board, cut off the tips with a sharp knife, and serve them in a pretty little bowl. You can save the stalks for soup.

Asparagus can handle flavorful or spicy treatment. It's good steamed, and then briefly sautéed with sesame oil, ginger, and a little soy sauce.

Asparagus cooked by any method can be served cold or hot with a mustard-based dressing or a plain vinaigrette. Combine it with some strips of roasted red pepper. Asparagus can also stand up to the acidity of citrus—try adding some orange or lemon zest (and even a little bit of juice) and a few slivered almonds.

Asparagus is also one of the few green vegetables that takes well to roasting. If you're roasting root vegetables—potatoes, turnips, parsnips, rutabagas—throw in some asparagus toward the end of the cooking time (about 15 minutes in a 400°F oven) to give your roast some variety and color. The hardiness that makes asparagus stand up to roasting also makes it a particularly good addition to risotto, because it cooks long enough to impart some of its flavor to the other ingredients.

While the classic asparagus accompaniments, like hollandaise and mornay sauce, are off-limits to the fat-conscious, any yogurt-based dressing works well for cold asparagus (those dressings tend to break apart when put on hot foods). Try the mint-yogurt dressing in the chopped salad recipe on page 220.

Experiment with your asparagus—you'll soon find your favorite preparation. I have to admit that mine is simply steamed with a little lemon juice and some freshly ground pepper.

A Peck of Peppers

Columbus seems to be responsible for more than his share of the confusion in the world. Determined to believe himself in India, he called the islands he explored the West Indies, the people he met Indians, and the chiles he was served "peppers." As it happens, those chiles were totally unrelated to the black peppercorns Columbus was hoping would help make him a rich man. But the name stuck, and today is applied not only to hot chiles, but to all the other capsicums of the New World.

All capsicums are American in origin. Wherever you find them in the world's cuisines—and they are ubiquitous—they got there from here. For some palates, hot chiles are overwhelming, but the sweet bell pepper is virtually a universal taste. The raw ones have just enough spiciness along with their satisfying snap to make them interesting. Sautéed they retain their color and flavor and make admirable additions to stir-frys and sauces. Roasted they have a sweet unctuousness that can take the place of oil in a variety of dishes.

Green bell peppers are available year-round, usually at reasonable prices, and they are a staple in my kitchen. But it is the ripened peppers, which are usually red but also come in purple, orange, and yellow, that are the real prizes. With their sweet, rich, mellow flavor, they can contribute immeasurably to the quality of your cooking. The bad news is that, except for local harvests in the fall, most peppers are picked green. There are exceptions, most of which come all the way from Holland, but they tend to be very expensive. The good news is that if you roast a lot of ripe peppers while they're in season, you can freeze them and have them all through the winter.

STUFF IT!

There's something appealing about the idea of stuffed green peppers. I look at the nice chunky peppers and at my leftover grain and legume combination and it occurs to me that they would contain it rather nicely. When I start thinking along those lines, I just sit very still (as someone said about the urge to do aerobic exercise) and wait for the feeling to pass. I have never stuffed anything smaller than a large chicken. Never have. Never will.

I'll admit that in my childhood I adored stuffed peppers. They were the most exotic dish my grandmother ever cooked, and I loved the idea of a food with an entirely different food inside. I loved their aroma while they cooked, and I loved the subtle flavor the peppers imparted to the stuffing. My children, however, were deprived of the stuffed pepper experience.

This is dreaded veggie prep at its worst. You have to cut the tops off the peppers, reach inside to remove the seeds and membranes without cutting the flesh, and then you're not done yet! If you want advice from someone who has never stuffed a pepper, I'll tell you I think you should always choose green peppers for stuffing. Not only are their walls somewhat firmer than those of the ripe ones, but the subtleties of the latter are wasted by this mode of preparation. Your peppers should be lightly steamed after the innards are removed, then filled with whatever you like inside them (it should be precooked). Replace the tops and bake them at 325°F or so for about 20 to 30 minutes, depending on the size of the peppers. You could also nuke them in the microwave.

But if you're the kind of person who wants to stuff peppers, you'll find these instructions grossly inadequate. Besides, why should you trust someone yammering away about a procedure she's never performed? I can't be all things to all men. That's what you've got real cookbooks for.

PEPPERS: A ROASTING ANOMALY

Roasted peppers are a useful garnish to almost anything and can also be puréed with roasted garlic to make a pasta sauce. It's traditional to use the sweet red ones, but any kind of pepper that's big enough to hold up under charring and peeling can be roasted. Roasting hot peppers like jalapeños, however, is not especially rewarding. Done indoors, it can fill the house with fumes that resemble tear gas. Besides, peeling hot peppers can be hell on your fingers, so if you want to preserve them, either dry them in a hot oven (about 150°F) until they are thoroughly shriveled or just put them, raw and uncut, into the freezer. Bits can be sliced off them very easily in their frozen state.

I recommend confining the roasting procedure to sweet peppers. Get yourself some—red, yellow, purple, white, or green. You'll make your life easier if you use largish ones with flat sides. I always roast at least four or five at a time. Late summer and early fall, when the local ones are plentiful and cheap, is the best time.

Actually, even when you take into account how loose the term has become, it's odd to call this method roasting. It's more like charring followed by steaming. But peppers cooked this way are always called roasted, so it's no use swimming against the stream. Just remember, you can't extrapolate. This procedure is not useful for roasting potatoes or turkey.

I use either the broiler or a charcoal grill to roast peppers, but an electric grill or gas burner—anything that will char the skins without instantly reducing the pepper to a pile of ashes—will do. A good time to roast peppers on a charcoal grill is after whatever you're having for dinner has been removed. We all know that's the time when the coals are in their prime. There are drawbacks. You have to remember to turn your peppers occasionally. And, of course, after dinner, when everyone is drinking coffee and liqueurs and having a high old time out on the patio, you'll be in the kitchen pulling the skin off hot peppers. But you're a cook. You're accustomed to life among the cinders.

HOW TO ROAST A PEPPER

Leave the peppers whole with the stems on but trim away any blackened or soft spots. Place them an inch or two from the source of heat. Cook the peppers, turning every 3 or 4 minutes, until all surfaces are charred.

Immediately place the peppers in a paper bag and close it tightly so the peppers steam. (Alternatively, a bowl covered with a plate can be used. This has the advantage of preserving all the juices.)

When the peppers are cool enough to handle, pull off the skins and remove the stems, seeds, and interior membranes. Do this over a bowl in order to catch any liquid that may have accumulated inside the peppers. You can just add it right away to any stock or sauce you may be saving or reserve it to put into whatever container is going to hold the peppers. Don't worry about any skin that doesn't come off easily. This need not be a painstaking procedure. Pepper skin is not offensive. Just concentrate on getting most of the charred bits. You may have seen a recipe that advised peeling the peppers under running water. This is a sinful waste of flavor and nutrients and displays a neurotic fear of charred pepper skin. Don't let me catch you doing it.

Cut the roasted peppers into strips or chunks and store them in jars with a little of their own juice. I've found that they keep at least a week in the refrigerator. If you add some vinegar to the jar they'll keep longer, but they'll taste like vinegar, which may or may not be desirable on any given day. (Of course, the vinegar will taste like peppers, and can be used to dress a green salad.) Roasted peppers can be frozen, with surprisingly good results. If you freeze them in a plastic container, in layers interleaved with plastic wrap or waxed paper, you'll be able to remove them as you need them. (It's actually worth the extra trouble to do this. Being confronted with a quart-size red pepper brick at mealtime overtaxes my gifts for culinary improvisation.) They can be thawed out without much loss of texture. I've found that thawed-out roasted peppers are good enough not just for soups and sauces, but for salads.

ROASTED PEPPER SOUP
Makes 3 generous or 4 rather mean servings

2 garlic cloves

1 medium onion

1 teaspoon olive oil

1 large carrot

2 celery stalks

4 cups chicken or vegetable stock

½ teaspoon dried thyme leaves

6 red bell peppers, roasted, seeded, peeled, and quartered

1 cup buttermilk

1 teaspoon freshly ground pepper or to taste

Salt to taste

1 to 2 teaspoons lemon juice or vinegar (optional)

1 small bunch basil, large stems removed

2 scallions

1. Mince the garlic and onion. (The chopping blade of the food processor is fine for this.)

2. Heat the olive oil in a large nonstick skillet and add the garlic and onion. Cook over medium heat until soft, about 5 minutes.

3. Chop the carrot and celery fairly fine. (Use the food processor for this also and, for heaven's sake, don't clean the bowl first—or after— you're going to use it again.) Add them to the skillet and continue to sauté another 2 or 3 minutes, stirring frequently. Add the stock and thyme. Raise the heat to medium and simmer for about 25 minutes. Add the peppers and continue simmering for 5 minutes more. Let cool slightly.

4. Transfer the mixture to your food processor and purée until smooth. (A blender will work even better for this step, but your blender isn't dirty yet and you don't want it to be.) Pour the soup into a saucepan, stir in the buttermilk, and warm over medium-low heat. Do not allow to boil.

5. Add the pepper, then taste and correct the seasoning. If the soup seems a bit sweet and bland add more pepper, a little salt, or some lemon juice or vinegar.

6. Chop the basil and scallions together in your trusty food processor and use them to garnish the soup.

120 calories, 1 gram fat, 0 grams saturated fat per serving of 4

ROASTED PEPPER RED SAUCE
Makes 4 cups, enough for about ¾ pound pasta

2 or 3 red bell peppers, roasted, peeled, seeded, and quartered

2 garlic cloves

1 small onion

One 28-ounce can crushed tomatoes

1 to 2 teaspoons dried oregano

½ teaspoon dried thyme

½ teaspoon dried rosemary

½ cup dry red wine (optional)

Juice of ½ lemon

Freshly ground black pepper to taste

1. Chop the peppers, garlic, and onion in the food processor.

2. Place the mixture, along with the tomatoes and herbs, in a saucepan and simmer, uncovered, over low heat for at least 30 minutes (an hour is better), stirring and adding red wine (if drinking) occasionally.

3. Just before serving, add the lemon juice and pepper.

NOTES: Make a double batch of this sauce if you like it. It will keep several days in the refrigerator.

This sauce will taste even better if you sauté the garlic, onion, and dried herbs in a little olive oil before adding the tomatoes and peppers, but it won't be quite so quick.

80 calories, 0 grams fat, 0 grams saturated fat per cup

Exploring Your Roots

Roots are primal food. Before our ancestors became agriculturalists, even before they became hunters, they probably dug their main subsistence out of the soil. And those roots most likely bore a strong resemblance to modern turnips and parsnips. Digging sticks—for prying roots from the ground—have been discovered among the remains of paleolithic communities. We recognize them because modern hunter-gatherers use almost identical tools.

Although innumerable roots have been consumed in the course of human history, root-eating has, at least in recent centuries, not been considered quite the thing. In Europe they were the food of domestic animals and the poor. Aristocrats ate game and scorned fiber, which may explain why we see so few aristocrats around nowadays.

Roots made us what we are today. So if you've been limiting your acquaintance with these plants to potatoes, carrots, and perhaps an occasional radish, strap on your gathering pouch, pick up your digging stick, and let's go forth.

PARSNIPS

> Yet a perfect parsnip is delicious, sweet, nutty, and aromatic. I would like to say a good word for it, but, as Sir Walter Scott reminded us, "Fine words butter no parsnips."
>
> —WAVERLEY ROOT

A parsnip looks like a bleached carrot, but it has a lot more flavor. To me, the taste is reminiscent of horseradish, albeit much milder. Tender young parsnips are the best; in fact, stay away from them if they are more than 6 inches long. Large parsnips are woody and somewhat bitter.

I have been slicing raw parsnips into winter salads for years, and they have been received without comment. I believe my family regards them as a kind of radish. Parsnips are also excellent in vegetable soup. Slice them thin and add them during the last 20 minutes or so of cooking. They bake well, both in the clay pot or in a Root Roast (page 185).

Until recently, I had not realized the degree to which our ancestors were nourished by parsnips. The parsnip has been cultivated since Roman times. At the end of summer the solids of the root consist largely of starch, but after the root is exposed to temperatures near freezing for a few weeks, much of the starch changes to sugar, improving its eating quality. The parsnip can be left in the ground through much of the winter, undamaged by hard freezing of the soil. A handy little food-storage package.

According to Waverley Root, the heyday of the parsnip was the Middle Ages, when fast days, especially Lent, were rigorously observed. Obliged to renounce meat, fasters turned to fish or vegetables. Naturally, the filling, starchy parsnip found favor, especially since it was one of the few vegetables available in the Lenten season. The German botanist Hieronymus Trager wrote in 1552 that parsnips and the European broad bean were the basic foods of Lent.

When Europeans finally worked up the courage to eat potatoes, their neutral taste, which permitted them to be combined with almost any other food, quickly eclipsed the pungent parsnip. It's now possible to browse through a large stack of cookbooks, many of them vegetarian, and find scarcely a parsnip recipe. But don't let that stop you. Just about anything you can do with a carrot, you can do with a parsnip. Put some in your stir-fry; they have a real affinity for ginger. Put some parsnip sticks on your next plate of crudités. Mystify your friends.

RUTABAGAS

Many people, especially outside of Scandinavia, think the proper vocation of the rutabaga is to serve as fodder for animals, but others actually prefer it for their own eating to the smaller garden turnips.

—WAVERLEY ROOT

With all due respect to Root I must point out that the rutabaga is not a turnip. It's often called a swede turnip, a yellow turnip, a waxed turnip, and other even less pleasant names. But the rutabaga cannot be hybridized with any variety of turnip. It has thirty-eight chromosomes, the true turnip seven. It is a vegetable in its own right, a vastly unappreciated one. As Root goes on to say, "a root more admired a century or two ago than it is now."

When I was a child, I actually liked rutabagas. (And I was outside of Scandinavia, although perhaps not in a cultural sense.) My grandmother used to cut them up and boil them for what I'm sure was an inordinate amount of time, but they managed to retain a pleasant texture and a distinctive flavor. A forgiving beast, the rutabaga! I ate them mashed, with butter, of course; now I enjoy them with horseradish or mustard.

Oddly, all the time my own children were growing up, I never even thought of cooking a rutabaga. I'm sure this was in part because I had walked away from the culinary tradition in which I was raised—bad Norwegian—and shut the door firmly behind me. However, if the rutabagas available in the supermarket hadn't been big, ugly brownish globes covered with a thick coating of wax, they might well have called to me. It was only when I began to shop at the farmers' markets in New York and saw rutabagas that looked and smelled like the ones I remembered from childhood that they reentered my life. I almost always cook them along with other vegetables—in the clay pot or as part of a Root Roast (page 185).

TURNIPS

> I give you these roots, friends of winter and of rime; Romulus ate of them at the table of the Gods.
>
> —MARTIAL

Martial is said to have accompanied the words above with a gift of turnips. Your friends might rather you didn't follow his example. Even among turnip lovers, to make them pass for a gift takes considerable chutzpah (something that Martial apparently had plenty of).

Like parsnips, turnips have been eaten in Europe for many centuries, and have fallen into ill repute since the rise of the potato. They are said to come in a number of colors and shapes, but the only ones I've ever seen in the market are the globular white ones with the purple tops.

Francophiles sometimes wax rhapsodic over the virtues of the *navet,* or French turnip. It is said to be white, carrot shaped, and altogether more refined than the ordinary round turnip. (Sounds like a parsnip to me, but what does a rutabaga eater know, even if she is outside of Scandinavia?)

Young turnips, the ones you get in the spring, can be used much like parsnips—sliced in salads, soups, and stir-frys. Most people—if they tolerate turnips at all—think these are the ones to go for. I rather like more mature turnips, the ones that come around in the early part of the winter and have achieved about 3 inches in diameter. They roast well and have an earthy taste that I think is what turnip eating is all about.

Either kind of turnip—and rutabagas, too—can be turned into a satisfying side dish. Just cut them into baby-carrot-size pieces and boil them (about 12 minutes for turnips, 20 minutes for rutabagas). Drain them, and sauté in a little olive oil with garlic, pepper, salt, and the herb of your choice. If you can find lovage, try it—the celery flavor is a good complement. If you can't find lovage, flat-leaf parsley or cilantro makes an admirable substitute. Leeks and shallots also combine nicely, not just with turnips, but all kinds of roots.

ROOT ROAST
Makes 2 large servings

4 small red potatoes
½ pound parsnips
1 celery root
1 rutabaga
3 medium turnips
2 large carrots
1 to 2 tablespoons olive oil (or a bit less if you're really into lowfat)
6 thyme branches, or ½ teaspoon dried
½ teaspoon dill or fennel seeds
Salt and freshly ground pepper to taste
4 small yellow onions
1 garlic head
2 bay leaves

1. Preheat the oven to 425°F.
2. Remove any woody portions and tough peels from the vegetables. Don't try to scrape the celery root thriftily. Trim it viciously and save the trimmings for the stockpot.
3. Cut the vegetables into respectable-looking pieces (a large carrot, for example, should probably be quartered). So that everything will be done at the same time, try to make the pieces more or less uniform.
4. Place the vegetables in a large bowl with ½ to 1 tablespoon of the olive oil, half the thyme, half the dill or fennel, a bit of salt if you want it, and plenty of ground pepper. Toss well to coat your roots with the oil and seasonings.
5. Coarsely chop the onions. Remove as much of the papery coating from the head of garlic as comes off easily and rub it with a little oil. Do not separate the cloves.
6. Put a few tablespoons of water or stock and a teaspoon or so of olive oil in the bottom of a nonstick roasting pan. If you have one large

enough to hold all the vegetables in a single layer, that's great, but it's not essential. Scatter the onions over the bottom of the pan along with the bay leaves and the rest of the seasonings. Spread all the cut vegetables on this bed of onions and tuck the garlic into the pan.

7. Cover the pan (a sheet of aluminum foil is probably best for this) and bake the vegetables for 30 minutes, then remove the pan and stir them around gently. Cover, return them to the oven, and bake about 20 minutes more. Remove the foil to brown the vegetables slightly. This step will take about 10 minutes. If they're not soft enough or brown enough at this point, continue to bake them until they seem right to you. A loaf of bread, a green salad (perhaps with a few chickpeas in it), and a glass of good red wine and you've got dinner.

600 calories, 10 grams fat, 2 grams saturated fat per serving

ROOT SOUP
Makes abut 1½ quarts

1 medium onion, coarsely chopped

1 teaspoon olive oil

2 medium potatoes, peeled and chopped

2 parsnips, peeled and chopped

½ fennel bulb, chopped

1 large celery root, peeled and chopped (or just brutalized)

1 teaspoon salt, or to taste (see Notes)

1 teaspoon dill seed, fennel seed, or a combination, ground or
     crushed, or just use a lot of fresh dill and fennel tops

2 cups stock or water

2 cups buttermilk (preferably nonfat)

Freshly ground black pepper to taste

Sprigs of fresh dill and/or some leafy fennel tops

1. In a large nonstick saucepan, sauté the onion in the oil about 5 minutes, until translucent but not browned. (Add a little stock if necessary to prevent sticking.)
2. Add the potatoes, parsnips, fennel bulb, celery root, salt, herbs, and spices. Sauté 10 minutes or so, adding small amounts of liquid if necessary.

3. Add the stock or water and cook, covered, on low heat 20 to 30 minutes.
4. Let cool slightly and purée in a blender or food processor with the buttermilk until the mixture is smooth and thick.
5. Reheat gently, seasoning with pepper, fresh dill, and fennel. Do not allow to boil.

NOTES: Even if you don't ordinarily cook with salt, a soup like this cries out for it. Simple, low-fat vegetable purées like this one can taste surprisingly rich and satisfying, but without salt they just don't achieve their potential. If you're seriously restricting your sodium consumption, better make something else. If you don't care, you may want to use a bit more salt than I've recommended.

This is a fine recipe for mixing and matching your roots. A small rutabaga or medium turnip can be substituted for the parsnips. I think this soup is also good with a large rutabaga instead of the potatoes, but then I'm a big fan of that particular tuber.

640 calories, 3 grams fat, 0 grams saturated fat per quart

Garlic, Mon Amour

"Why is this so good?"

I've already told you about the question I addressed to my mother as I was making my eager and uninhibited way through my first plate of real Italian spaghetti—at least it was as real as an Italian restaurateur dared to make it in Minnesota in 1948.

She smiled. My food passions were already a family legend. "Well, I guess they use spices Grandma and Aunt Dag don't have. Italian things."

But I wasn't listening. I was poking through the remains of the sauce, tasting individual particles, trying to discover the source of my taste buds' joy. Eureka! "It's this stuff," I said, extending a small whitish oval on my fork.

"Ah!" said my mother, "Garlic."

So began a lifelong love affair.

Oddly, it never occurred to me that this wonderful new taste could be brought into my grandmother's or great-aunt's kitchen. Garlic existed on the other side of a magic curtain, in a culinary kingdom of which I could only catch rare glimpses. I knew I would get there someday, and it would be full of wonderful tastes, foods I'd never dreamed of. I did and it was, but none has proved better than garlic.

I am not alone. Garlic, as far as I know, is the only vegetable with its own fan club—it's called Lovers of the Stinking Rose. But thirty-five years ago when I first began to cook, garlic had yet to find favor in this country. Recipes that included garlic typically specified half a clove in a recipe meant to serve six. Or the garlic was to be sautéed and discarded prior to adding other foods. (O! Iago, the pity of it!) I'm glad to say I always knew better than that. Typically, I would quadruple the amount of garlic in a recipe. However, there was a lot I didn't know about garlic in those days. A head of garlic could last as long as a month in my kitchen. Much as I loved it, I didn't realize it could be a vegetable in its own right.

James Beard's forty-clove-garlic chicken was my introduction to garlic in really satisfying quantities. I moved on to garlic roasted in the embers of the charcoal fire, then found I could duplicate the effect in the oven. Now a week rarely goes by that we don't use up a whole head or two. I would find it a lot harder to give up garlic than I did to give up saturated fat.

What about the smell? Well, I can't tolerate most commercial soaps or read magazines that come with perfume inserts. My children, annoyed at my ability to detect illicit substances, used to call me the Bionic Nose. However, I am oblivious to the odor of garlic unless it's cooking—in which case I find it ambrosial. I'm sure this is because my body is totally saturated with the stuff. Fortunately, everyone who knows me well enough to tell me I smell bad eats as much garlic as I do. No one moves away from me in exercise class, but that may be because New Yorkers develop insensitive noses, iron self-control, or both. I have read that if you really eat a lot of garlic all the time your metabolism changes and you no longer exude a garlicky odor. I'd like to believe this, but as far as I know there's no real supporting evidence and I don't want to encourage you to inhabit a fool's paradise. I suggest you do as I do and choose your friends among the garlic eaters. They're the best people anyway.

WHAT TO DO WITH GARLIC

Except in the dessert chapter you'll rarely find a recipe in this book that doesn't call for quite a lot of garlic. But my favorite use of this wonderful vegetable is just to roast it and squeeze out the cloves onto bread or potatoes. I also have been known to squeeze out the pulp with my teeth the way you'd scrape an artichoke leaf. Relatively freshly picked garlic is best for this purpose; after it begins to sprout, it's better to slice it up and sauté it.

To roast a head of garlic, remove the loose, papery, outer coating. Don't peel or separate the cloves. Cut off just enough of the top of the head so that the tip of each clove is exposed. This makes it easy to remove the pulp after roasting. Rub it with a little olive oil if you wish, place it in a shallow baking dish or on a cookie sheet, and bake at 325°F for approximately 45 minutes or until the head is yielding to the touch (squeezable). Precise timing is not critical. You'll discover with a bit of practice how soft you like your roasted garlic. Just be careful not to let it get dried out or scorched.

You can cook garlic very quickly in a microwave (this is one of the few things this appliance is good for), but it will taste more steamed than roasted. Just trim the head as above, put it in a 2-cup container with ¼ cup chicken or vegetable broth and a teaspoon or so of olive oil. On high power allow 4 minutes cooking and 5 minutes standing time. (That's normal. My wimpy microwave requires about 7 minutes.) Before you do this, be sure you cut off enough of the top of the bulb to expose all the cloves. Petrified traces of a garlic explosion adhere to the roof of my microwave to remind me that this step is important.

If you like the taste of garlic enough to eat it raw in your salad, you'll want a garlic press. That way you don't even need to peel the cloves. The garlic press has rather a bad name among certain elitist gourmets. They claim it makes the garlic taste rank and bitter. I contend that what they're complaining of is oxidation and it comes from their failure to get the garlic into some liquid (preferably a little olive oil) immediately after pressing. The same problem exists when garlic is sliced or minced, but it is less evident because not as much of the cut clove is exposed to air. If you saw the movie *Goodfellas,* you may remember the gourmet gangster making pasta sauce and slowly slicing garlic with a razor blade. That, he maintained, was the only way to make it thin enough. However, he was depositing the slices on his cutting board where you could almost see them oxidizing. "Get that garlic into oil, you turkey," I wanted to shout at him. I guess most people were impressed by the rather graphic scenes of violence in that movie. Me, I remember the abused garlic.

If you want to get serious about garlic, try the recipe for All-Purpose Garlic Sauce on page 190. This sauce will keep for several days in the refrigerator, but it is best when freshly made. It can be used to moisten and flavor all kinds of grain/legume/vegetable combinations. Along with a few drops of olive oil and some balsamic vinegar it makes a good salad dressing. It is an excellent topping for pasta. When made with the best summer basil, it comes as close to real pesto as I ever expect to get again. (A little grated Parmesan cheese, of course, is a great enhancer.) With cilantro, it becomes vaguely Asian, especially if you add a little ginger or curry spices to whatever you're cooking.

One recent night at our house, we ate refried potatoes and carrots. When the vegetables were done, I added a can of tuna, a couple of chopped anchovies, and a cup of the all-purpose garlic sauce made with cilantro and a little ginger. Sounds too weird? What can I say? We liked it a lot.

ALL-PURPOSE GARLIC SAUCE
Makes about 2 cups

1 garlic head, roasted (page 188)

1 cup nonfat buttermilk

1 to 4 cloves raw garlic (optional; only for serious garlic eaters)

2 scallions

½ jalapeño or other hot pepper, or a sprinkling of red pepper flakes

1 teaspoon dried oregano

½ teaspoon dried thyme

1 large bunch basil or cilantro, or 1 small bunch Italian parsley,
thick stems removed

1. Separate and peel the roasted garlic cloves or squeeze the pulp out of the peels into a blender or food processor. Add the buttermilk, raw garlic if using, scallions, jalapeño, and dried herbs. Process briefly.

2. Add the fresh herbs and process until the leaves are chopped fairly fine.

110 calories, 0 grams fat, 0 grams saturated fat per cup

The Wonderful World of Beets

Two! Two! Two Veggies in One!

Beet roots are just about the only vegetables I can think of that aren't substantially improved by the addition of fat. They are moist, sweet, flavorful, and nonabsorbent—all qualities that recommend themselves to fat-free preparation. I like to roast beets, slice or dice them, toss with some vinegar and mustard and a few chopped scallions, and serve warm or at room temperature. You can add beets prepared this way to a green salad or combine them with another vegetable, but be sure to do it just before serving, as beets turn the whole world purple. (Including your urine. Don't be alarmed.)

Try to learn to appreciate beet greens as well. They taste good raw or cooked, and they far surpass beet roots nutritionally. Because, unlike most of us, they don't turn bitter as they age, they are one of the best greens to cook now that you're not using cream or bacon drippings. Young beet greens are a fine addition to salads.

Whether or not you want to eat beet greens, it's best to purchase beets with the leaves on. Their condition is a reliable guide to how long ago the beets were picked. To use the greens, remove the thickest part of the red stems unless you're making soup stock. I've had decent results chopping these stem ends and throwing them into a stir-fry, but first test them for toughness while they're raw. If you can't bite through them easily, they belong in the stockpot—or the garbage.)

Beets should always be cooked whole and unpeeled. Leave an inch or so of greens attached. Most borscht recipes tell you to peel and grate the raw beets, but that's tedious and unnecessary.

We have a beet conflict in our family. I believe beets should be roasted until they are fairly soft, which brings out the sweet earthy flavor. Chuck prefers them rather hard, like the pickled beets of his childhood that preserved their integrity through months in the jar. The consistency of cooked beets is more a function of method than of duration. Boiled beets always have a smoother texture and (to my mind) a blander taste than roasted ones. I have resolved our dilemma by making borscht. Tamar likes beets both ways, but often goes the pickled route because it's easy and fast.

Beets are actually more versatile than their distinctive color and unfortunate reputation would have you believe. Middle Easterners combine beets with yogurt, garlic, and lemon juice—served cold, it's a salad; puréed, it's a dip. If you have a high beet-to-yogurt ratio, it's a good accompaniment for a spicy couscous dish. Greeks combine beets with the thick potato paste called skordalia. Beets can also simply be roasted with a wide variety of other vegetables—turnips and potatoes work well, just be prepared for them to turn pink from the beet juice. My personal favorite is beets roasted with sweet onions, served with just a little balsamic vinegar.

BORSCHT
Makes about 2 quarts

1 pound beets (about 4 medium)
1 large onion
1 teaspoon olive oil
1 medium carrot
1 medium parsnip
1 teaspoon caraway seeds
1 teaspoon dill seeds, or 1 tablespoon chopped fresh dill
6 cups stock or water (beet cooking liquid is good)
2 tablespoons red wine vinegar
Freshly ground black pepper to taste
Nonfat yogurt cheese (page 271) for garnish (optional)

1. Preheat the oven to 375°F.
2. Scrub the beets well and place them in a shallow roasting pan. Add ½ inch of water, cover with aluminum foil, and bake until the beets soften slightly, about 20 minutes. Allow to cool, reserving the liquid in the bottom of the pan. Peel the beets unless they are very young and tender. I find that the best way is to hold the beet in both hands and work the peel off with my thumbs. Quarter them if they're large. (All this beet preparation can be done hours or days in advance.)
3. Slice the onion fairly thin. It and all subsequent vegetables can be processed in your trusty food processor using the slicing blade. Heat the oil gently in a large soup pot. Add the onion and sauté very slowly, stirring frequently to prevent sticking, until soft and fragrant.
4. Slice the carrot, parsnip, and partially cooked beets about ¼ inch thick. Add them to the onion along with the caraway and dill. Sauté, stirring frequently, over medium heat, until the vegetables begin to smell cooked. (Sautéing the vegetables isn't strictly necessary. I think it releases more vegetable flavor into the soup than simply adding the vegetables and stock at the same time and bringing them to a boil, but it's a marginal advantage and not worth doing if you're pressed for time.)
5. Add the stock a cup or two at a time, allowing each addition to come to a simmer before adding the next cup. Don't forget to add the liquid from the roasting pan. Cover the pot, lower the heat, and simmer for about 45 minutes.
6. Stir in the vinegar and pepper and serve with a dollop of yogurt cheese if you like it.

240 calories, 2 grams fat, 0 grams saturated fat per quart

FAUX PICKLED BEETS
Makes 6 side-dish servings

8 to 10 small or 4 to 6 large beets

2 tablespoons balsamic vinegar

1 tablespoon wine vinegar

2 teaspoons prepared horseradish

Pinch of sugar (optional)

1. Clean and trim the beets in preparation for boiling them. If you plan to use the cooking water for soup or stock, clean them thoroughly. If not, there's no need to be fastidious. Beets only come clean with serious scrubbing.

2. Boil the beets until tender in enough water to generously cover them. Small beets will cook in 35 to 40 minutes; larger beets 45 to 50 minutes. If you're not sure they're tender, err on the side of more time as it's just about impossible to overcook a beet. They're done when you can easily spear them with a fork. Drain the cooked beets and put them in a bowl of cold water until they're cool enough to handle.

3. Peel the beets and cut into slices or thick julienne strips. Combine with the vinegars, horseradish, and sugar if using. Adjust the seasonings to taste. Refrigerate the beets for at least several hours. Overnight is better. Serve chilled.

20 calories, 0 grams fat, 0 grams saturated fat per serving

BEET SALAD WITH APRICOTS
Makes 4 to 6 side-dish servings

5 large or 9 small beets (enough to make 4 cups sliced)
½ cup dried apricots, sliced
2 tablespoons balsamic vinegar
2 teaspoons olive oil
Pinch of sugar
¼ cup coarsely chopped pecans or walnuts

1. Wash and trim the beets. Put them in a medium pot with enough water to cover them generously. Boil until the beets are tender, about 35 to 50 minutes, depending on the size of the beets.

2. Immerse the beets in cold water until they're cool enough to handle. Peel them and cut them into bite-size pieces. Add the apricots, vinegar, oil, and sugar and mix well. If you're planning to use the salad within an hour or two, let the mixture stand at room temperature. Otherwise, refrigerate it and remove it from the refrigerator about an hour before serving (the flavors work better at room temperature).

3. About 15 minutes before serving, toast the nuts by spreading them out on a cookie sheet and putting them in a 350°F oven for about 10 minutes, until they smell toasted. Add the nuts to the salad (if you add the nuts earlier, they'll get soggy). Serve at room temperature.

100 calories, 6 grams fat, 0 grams saturated fat per serving of 6

I Say Potato . . .

All the time I was growing up, I thought there were only two varieties of potato, the Large Brown Kind and the Small Red Kind. An heirloom potato was, for me, the surprise at the bottom of the bin, the forgotten spud looking like a holdover from the previous generation. In fact, there are hundreds of varieties of potato, and each has a slightly different taste and texture. (At least they're supposed to; I suspect, however, that there is a serious limit to the number of different tastes and textures a potato can have.) Potatoes run the gamut from the familiar Russet Burbank to the less familiar, or perhaps completely unknown, Superior or Kennebec. A type that has recently come to the fore is Yukon Gold, a good-tasting, all-purpose, medium-textured potato.

One of the best places to find out about potatoes is your local farmers' market. Go visit the Potato Guy (at my farmers' market he's between the Mushroom Guy and the Lettuce Lady). He'll tell you with pride about the varieties he grows and their differences and uses. If you don't have a local farmers' market, or your market doesn't have a Potato Guy, try a produce market that specializes in organic or esoteric fruits and vegetables.

The most important factor that differentiates potatoes (aside from the obvious size and color) is texture. Potatoes range from mealy (the kind that breaks up easily and has a grainy texture when cooked) to waxy (the firmer kind that sticks together and has a—you guessed it—waxy texture). Texture correlates roughly to starch content, the starchier potatoes being mealy and the less starchy waxy.

I know, I know. "Mealy" and "waxy" aren't the most appetizing terms to apply to food. Waxy makes it sound like you're eating one of those decorative candles you see at craft shows, and mealy is like those end-of-season peaches you throw away after the first disappointing bite. But those seem to be the technical terms, and who am I to buck the system?

Mealy potatoes are useful for baking and mashing. Waxy potatoes are better for gratins or potato salads. This is intuitive; the kind that fall apart are good for dishes in which they're expected to fall apart and the kind that hold together are good for the dishes in which they're expected to hold together. Use your judgment and don't be intimidated. If you use the wrong kind, it's unlikely anyone will say, "Gee, this potato salad is pretty good, but it could definitely have been improved by the use of a waxier potato." If you've read this page, you know more about potatoes than 98 percent of the population.

So, you ask, how can I tell a waxy potato from a mealy potato? According to Harold McGee, author of *On Food and Cooking,* there is a way. Make a saltwater solution of one part salt and eleven parts water. Drop your potatoes in. The mealy, denser ones will sink and the waxy ones will float. I'm naturally skeptical, so I decided to test this out. I bought four different kinds of potatoes: Russets, White Rose (a smooth-skinned, light yellow potato), small red potatoes, and baby red potatoes. I filled a pot with 11 cups of water and 1 cup of table salt, stirred it until the salt was dissolved, and dropped the potatoes in. Imagine my disappointment when they all floated.

My experience with my local supermarket potatoes told me that they tended toward the mealy, and my high school physics (and summers on Cape Cod) told me that the saltier the water, the more buoyant an object placed in it is. So I gradually added water to make the solution less salty to see if it would then distinguish among the potatoes. Voilà! After I had added about a cup more water, the Russet and the red potato sank, the baby red floated, and the White Rose turned vertical and hovered, with one end trying to float and the other trying to sink (I'm not quite sure what that meant). You might want to try this experiment at home with your local potatoes. It might even be appropriate for children, as it is quite safe, makes only a limited mess, and has a marginally interesting outcome.

Nutritionally, the potato is an excellent food. A 6-ounce potato has about 110 calories, 23 grams of carbohydrates, 3 grams of protein, no cholesterol, and almost no fat. If you have had it beaten into your food consciousness that potatoes are fattening, beat it out again. It simply isn't true. Potatoes can be an integral part of a low-fat diet and are an excellent choice for the weight conscious.

Potatoes are also a good source for many vitamins and minerals including, surprisingly, vitamin C (one potato has about half the vitamin C of an orange). The peel, by weight, contains more of the nutrients than the flesh of the potato, and is an especially good source of fiber. If possible, leave the peel on. If you or your family are just too fastidious for potato peel, however, don't take potatoes off your list—the flesh is good food too.

The only nutritional problem with potatoes is that they scream out for high-fat condiments. You can almost hear them crying, "Butter! Sour Cream! Cheese!" as you pull them out of the oven. Be strong! You are the Condiment Czar and need not take orders from your potatoes (or your toast or your vegetables or your pasta). One of the recurring problems of a low-fat diet is that almost every low-fat food can be improved by the addition of fat, but that's where free will comes in. The whole point is to make the most of these low-fat foods without succumbing to butter or cream.

POTATO CARE

Potatoes should be stored in a cool, dry, dark place (ideally 45°F to 50°F). If they're stored in the refrigerator, some of their starch begins to convert to sugar, and you end up with a sweetened potato (although this process will reverse if the potatoes are left out at room temperature again). No matter where you keep them, don't store your potatoes in plastic bags. They are best stored loosely in bins or paper bags.

Potatoes are best eaten within a couple of weeks of purchase, although they will keep longer. Once the skins begin to get that greenish tinge (caused by exposure to light), you should probably just throw them out and start fresh. The green color betrays the presence of toxic alkaloids, and, while the cooking process will kill the alkaloids, they may leave you with a bitter-tasting potato. Better just to toss it (or feed it to the pigs, if you happen to keep pigs). Similarly, potato sprouts are toxic and should be thoroughly dug out before the sprouted potato is used. None of these "toxic" potato by-products, however, is poisonous enough to do any serious harm (I know, I've eaten many a green-skinned potato), so don't expect to commit the perfect crime by feeding your least-favorite family member a salad of potato sprouts.

YAM OR SWEET POTATO?

Once and for all, what's the different between a yam and a sweet potato? A sweet potato is the tuber of a member of the morning glory family, and is what we all think of when we hear either "sweet potato" or "yam." A yam is actually the tuber of a genus of tropical climbing plant. A genuine yam can weigh up to one hundred pounds (and you thought roasting a turkey was cumbersome). Everything we see in our supermarkets that's marked "yam" is, in fact, a sweet potato. (Actually, I can't guarantee that. You may shop at a market that specializes in obscure tropical tubers, and the yams may indeed by yams.)

Sweet potatoes are highly nutritious—an excellent source of beta-carotene. They are higher in sugar than regular potatoes and consequently higher in calories, about 160 for a six ouncer. Don't be quick to renounce them on the basis of their caloric content, however. Because they are sweeter and have a smoother texture, they have a more satisfying feel than regular potatoes, and fare better without added fat. So, although the sweet potato itself may be higher in calories, you may very well come out ahead because you're less inclined to add that extra pat of butter.

You've probably discovered that when you eat a really healthful diet there are some delicious foods you must simply resign yourself to living without. Occasionally, however, you'll run across a food you never liked that you now have an excellent excuse *not* to eat. For me, candied sweet potatoes fall into that category. Although they're not usually appallingly high in fat, they're high enough in empty sugar calories that you can in good conscience refrain from eating them for health reasons.

POTATO TOPPINGS

Potatoes, both the regular and sweet varieties, are a dinnertime staple, and they can take many forms. Given that we eschew the high-fat kinds like french fried and au gratin, Mom and I are by default potato traditionalists. We like 'em just plain baked. The question then becomes "What do we put on them?" rather than "How are we going to cook them?" Here are some suggestions.

The basis for many excellent potato toppings is yogurt cheese, which is just yogurt with the whey drained off, so only the solids are left (see The Way to De-whey, page 271). As a rule, anything you dip vegetables in can also be put on a baked potato, so dips and potato toppings are generally indistinguishable. By adding the herbs, vegetables, and condiments of your choice to yogurt cheese, you can create substantial mouth-pleasing potato toppings.

Some possible additions to yogurt cheese are:

- Chives
- Cilantro
- Scallions
- Parsley
- Salsa
- Roasted garlic

(If you use dried herbs, leave some time for the mixed-in herbs to absorb some of the moisture of the yogurt cheese and soften up. Otherwise, your topping will taste like yogurt cheese with iron filings in it.)

Other potato-topping possibilities are:

- Chutney
- Salsa
- Low-fat gravy
- Low-fat cheeses (there are actually a few good ones on the market—at last! See page 270.)

Because not everyone's eyes have been opened to the life-extending benefits of a low-fat diet, we suggest that, on special occasions, you also set out butter and sour cream for those of your guests who couldn't conceive of a holiday meal without them. Or, if you really want to impress such types, try the recipe below.

POTATO AND MUSHROOM PIE WITH POLENTA CRUST
Makes 4 main-dish or 6 side-dish servings

For the filling
½ ounce dried porcini mushrooms

1 cup hot water

2 pounds new potatoes

1 tablespoon plus ½ teaspoon olive oil

1 medium onion, diced

4 garlic cloves, pressed

1 pound fresh shiitake mushrooms, stems discarded,
    caps sliced

1 teaspoon dried thyme

¼ teaspoon cayenne pepper

1½ tablespoons all-purpose flour

Salt to taste

1 cup tiny green frozen peas

For the crust
3 cups water

¼ teaspoon salt, or to taste

¾ cup cornmeal

1. Soak the porcini in the hot water for at least 1 hour. Remove the mushrooms from the water and purée them, first removing any hard or fibrous parts. Strain the broth through a fine sieve.
2. Preheat the oven to 425°F.
3. Cut the potatoes into bite-size pieces. Lightly oil a 9 x 9-inch roasting dish. Add the potatoes and roast until tender, about 35 minutes. Stir them once or twice during roasting to prevent sticking and to brown all sides evenly. (The potatoes can be roasted several hours in ad-

vance, or even the preceding day. Consider making extras. Roasted potatoes are great enablers of pantry momentum.)

4. Meanwhile, heat the ½ teaspoon olive oil in a large nonstick skillet. Add the onion and garlic and sauté over medium heat until wilted. Add the fresh mushrooms, thyme, and cayenne; cook until the mushrooms have softened and shrunk to about half their original size, about 15 minutes.

5. In a separate skillet, heat the remaining 1 tablespoon olive oil over medium heat. Make a roux by adding the flour and stirring until it begins to turn brown. Add the roux, mushroom broth, puréed porcini, and salt to the mushroom mixture and cook until the liquid reduces by about one-third, about 5 minutes. Add the frozen peas just before you take the mixture off the heat.

6. Remove the potatoes from the oven and lower the oven temperature to 350°F. Add the vegetables to the potatoes in their pan.

7. For the crust, bring the water and salt to a rolling boil in a saucepan. Add the cornmeal slowly, stirring constantly. Lower the heat to medium and cook, stirring constantly, until the mixture thickens and begins to pull away from the sides of the pan, 10 to 20 minutes.

8. Spread the polenta over the vegetables and potatoes and bake until the top is lightly browned, about 15 minutes. Remove from the oven and let sit for at least 15 minutes before serving.

250 calories, 4 grams fat, 1 gram saturated fat per side-dish serving

COLD POTATOES

As a child, one of the few foods I couldn't get behind was potato salad. Despite my eagerness to sample all the world's edibles, I remained a potato conservative. Potatoes should be hot, I was convinced, and they should be accompanied by butter. Cream and cheese were also desirable. Cold potatoes drowned in mayo struck me as belonging in the same league as the culinary travesties concocted by my great-grandmother in her final years. In fact, I first sampled potato salad at her table and for some time labored under the delusion that she had invented it—perhaps on the same day she first combined cabbage with rhubarb.

The years passed, and I learned that some potato salads are better than others. Less mayo, potatoes that aren't overcooked, some onion and celery to enhance the flavor—all these alterations helped create much more acceptable versions than my great-grandmother's. I especially appreciated German potato salad—hot and no mayo. There was a deli in Poughkeepsie where they really knew how to make it. Chuck, however, prefers the cold mayo-ridden kind. I learned to produce a sort of compromise: firm potatoes, room temperature, plenty of onion and celery, a touch of oil and vinegar, and then light on the mayo. So by the time we got into serious low-fat eating, I had eaten, and prepared, a lot of potato salad of the kind that lends itself to nutritional correctness. No one who eats my potato salad believes it's low in fat. One guy who did threatened to take it out and have it analyzed. Try the recipe. It really works.

THE DEFINITIVE POTATO SALAD
Makes 4 servings

> 2 pounds firm waxy potatoes (most new potatoes are suitable;
>   Red Bliss work well)
> 1 to 2 teaspoons extra-virgin olive oil
> Salt and freshly ground black pepper to taste
> 1 small onion or 3 or 4 scallions, chopped
> ¼ cup chopped celery
> ½ cup plain nonfat yogurt (see Notes)
> 1 tablespoon mustard (I prefer a whole-grain type
>   such as Pommery, but a Dijon-style mustard like
>   Grey Poupon is fine)
> 1 tablespoon wine vinegar
> 1 small bunch basil, cilantro, or Italian parsley,
>   finely chopped

1. Boil or steam the potatoes in their jackets. Let cool slightly. Cut them into bite-size pieces, removing whatever skin loosens in the process. (I usually end up with about half the skin on the potatoes, half in the garbage.) While the potatoes are still warm, toss them with the oil and pepper. Let stand at room temperature for up to an hour or two.
2. Add the onion and celery. Mix the yogurt, mustard, and vinegar in a small bowl. Add half of it to the salad, mixing well. Add the fresh herbs if using. Continue adding dressing until the mixture looks like potato salad to you.

NOTES: If your yogurt seems watery, drain it (page 271) to remove some of the whey.

To my mind, this salad tastes best if served at room temperature within a couple of hours after the potatoes are cooked, but there's no harm in making it ahead and refrigerating it.

If you're looking for something a little jazzier than traditional potato salad, try serving your cold potatoes with tomatillo sauce. Tomatillos look like green tomatoes, but are actually related to gooseberries. They're much firmer than tomatoes, and stand up well to even fairly lengthy cooking. They're very acidic, but the flavor is different from either vinegar or lemon. I love the taste, but if you find your finished sauce is mouth-puckering, add a pinch or two of sugar. The recipe makes more than you'll use on two pounds of potatoes. Leftovers are good in soup or sauce—a fine tool for pantry momentum.

Prepare your potatoes as for the recipe above, but omit the celery and raw onion from the salad. Add some blanched frozen peas if you want.

TOMATILLO SAUCE
Makes about 1½ cups

4 garlic cloves, peeled
2 jalapeño or other hot peppers, seeds and
    veins removed
1 tablespoon olive oil
½ to 1 teaspoon ground cumin (optional)
10 tomatillos, papery husks removed
1 small red bell pepper
½ medium onion
1 small bunch cilantro, large stems removed
Salt to taste
Pinch of sugar (optional)
1 to 2 tablespoons white wine or nonfat yogurt (optional)

1. Chop the garlic and jalapeño peppers rather coarsely (use the food processor).
2. Heat the oil in a nonstick skillet over medium heat and add the cumin if using, the garlic, and the peppers, cooking until the vegetables are softened but not browned.
3. Meanwhile, insert the slicing blade into your machine and process the tomatillos, bell pepper, and onion. Add this mixture to the skillet,

continuing to cook over medium heat until it is soft and fragrant, about 10 to 15 minutes. Let cool slightly.

4. Return the mixture to the food processor fitted with the chopping blade. Add the cilantro and the salt. Process until fairly smooth. Add sugar if needed, and a little wine or yogurt if you feel the mixture is too thick.
5. Add the sauce to the potatoes a little at a time until the salad looks and tastes right to you.

N O T E :　A variant of this sauce works well on pasta. Add a cup of white wine (red is okay, but doesn't look as nice) to the sauce as it's cooking. When the sauce is done, purée only half the mixture. Return the puree to the skillet with the rest of the sauce and reheat before saucing your pasta.

190 calories, 11 grams fat, 1 gram saturated fat per cup

Knowing Your Onions

> Let onion atoms lurk within the bowl
> And, scarce suspected, animate the whole
>
> —SYDNEY SMITH, RECIPE FOR SALAD, *LADY HOLLAND'S MEMOIR* (1855)

History's testament to the onion includes five thousand years of cultivation, an appearance in the Code of Hammurabi (which decrees that the poor should get a regular allowance of bread and onions), and the occasional onion-worshiping religion. Onions were the breakfast of ancient Romans, the funerary offerings of the Egyptians, and the scurvy-fighting weapon of sailors everywhere. Marco Polo discovered onion eaters in Persia, Cortez found them in Mexico, and Père Marquette was reportedly saved from starvation by the onions native to North America. According to Waverley Root, the city of Chicago takes its name from the Indian word for the smell of onions. (I was skeptical of this claim, so I looked it up. *Encyclopedia Britannica* says, "The name is derived from an Indian word of doubtful origin, meaning, according to some, 'skunk' or 'wild onion,' but more likely 'powerful.'" That's close enough for me; I'm with Mr. Root.)

It's no wonder that onions crop up so often and in so many places in history. Onions are magic. No cook I know, even the least adventurous, doesn't count the onion as a kitchen staple. Even those who shy away from garlic (imagine!), onion's potent cousin in the house of *Allium,* will use onions with a free hand. I put them in almost everything savory I cook because, as Sydney Smith understood, they provide a robust but unobtrusive backbone.

They help fill in the holes that stronger flavors, like hot pepper or ginger, invariably leave. They're a crucial ingredient in stocks and reductions.

But there's another side to onions. If you use enough of them to go beyond unobtrusive, you end up with a sweetness you can't get from anything else in the vegetable world. Instead of being a background flavor, the sweetness of onions can be a dish's reason for being. Onion soup and onion tart, for example, are all about onions.

It is unfortunate that onions' virtues are obscured by the distinctiveness, shall we say, of their smell and flavor when raw. Instead of being properly admired, the onion is viewed with suspicion. It will make your eyes water. It will make your breath smell. It will offend the people around you.

So the onion is often rejected. It happens every day. Somewhere, at some deli, someone decides not to put onions on his sandwich because he's got an important meeting that afternoon and doesn't want to offend his clients with onion breath. Or maybe it's a big date that evening. Or maybe just a general feeling that one shouldn't subject one's friends and neighbors to such a pungent odor. Every day, onions are spurned on the basis of a perception of general offensiveness. Come on, fess up, you've done it.

But I have a theory. I think onion breath is a myth. Ask yourself: Have you *ever* been offended by the smell of onions on someone's breath? I never have, and neither has Mom, but we've always put that down to the fact that we eat so many onions that no one else's onion breath could penetrate the fog of our own. But then I got to thinking, Maybe that's not the reason. Maybe the reason I've never smelled onion breath is that onion breath doesn't exist. You can see how the myth could get started. Onions certainly smell strong. When they're raw, they have an assertive flavor. Sometimes you can taste them long after your sandwich is gone. It would be logical to assume that the smell also lingers, and that those around you can discern it.

I think this misconception is up there with the great myths of history, like pyramid power, the Bermuda Triangle, and one size fits all. In the absence of hard data, of course, this is merely an assertion. And I can assure you that there is, indeed, an absence of hard data. So I did what all good theorists do when they can't find data—I made it up. Er, I mean, I conducted some original research.

I understand the importance of research methodology, so I conducted my survey in the most scientific way possible. I e-mailed twenty of my closest friends. I asked them several questions regarding onions and garlic, the most important of which was:

Q: Have you ever actually noticed onion breath on anyone else? (Think hard, now. This question refers specifically to being able to smell actual onions on someone's breath, and does not cover generic bad breath with possible vegetal overtones.)

The results confirmed my suspicions. Sure, there were a couple of people who claimed that they had occasionally smelled onion on someone's breath. In the market research world, there's a term for respondents who don't want to go along with the general thrust of your survey—they're called "outliers," meaning that their responses are so far away from the range of other responses that they have to be discarded or accounted for in some other way. Once I discarded these outliers, I was left with unanimous agreement that onion breath is indeed a myth.

I also asked my respondents whether they had ever avoided onions because they feared onion breath. Only about half of them had, but I have to admit there may be some sample bias here. Many of my friends are the type who refuse to take such mundane considerations as bad breath into account when they're deciding important things like what's for lunch. However, among those who did report that they had occasionally passed on onions, several said they would eat them more freely if they were convinced that onion breath is indeed a myth.

When I extrapolate these results to the general population, it's clear that millions of people will be eating more onions now that I've published the definitive study exposing the myth of onion breath. It's a new day for the house of *Allium*.

ONIONS WITH CHICKEN
Makes 3 main-dish servings

2 teaspoons olive oil

5 garlic cloves, chopped

1 teaspoon dried thyme

5 medium onions, thinly sliced

2 cups chicken stock

1 to 2 cups dry white wine

Dash of Worcestershire sauce (optional)

1 pound fresh spinach, washed and stemmed

¾ pound skinless, boneless chicken breasts, cut into thin strips

2 ounces low-fat goat cheese or ricotta (optional)

1. Heat the olive oil in a large nonstick skillet. Add the garlic, thyme, and onions and sauté over medium heat until the onions are very limp and brown, about 40 minutes. If they stick, stir in a little stock or wine.
2. Add the chicken stock and 1 cup of the wine. Cook until the liquid has reduced by about half. Taste. If the wine hasn't counterbalanced the sweetness of the onions, add more wine until it does. You can also use Worcestershire sauce to help.
3. Add the spinach and cook until it wilts and turns dark green, 2 to 4 minutes. If excess liquid accumulates, pour some off.
4. Push the onion mixture to the sides of the pan and add the chicken in the middle. Cook until the meat is no longer translucent in the center. If you've cut the chicken in thin strips, this will only take a minute or two. If the strips are thicker, it takes a little longer.
5. Add the goat cheese or ricotta if using and stir until thoroughly combined. Serve over rice, pasta, or barley.

340 calories, 5 grams fat, 1 gram saturated fat per serving

Plugging Leeks

LEEK LORE

Apicius, a notorious gourmand who wrote and reveled in the days of Caesar Augustus, knew his leeks. A leek pie, the recipe for which was said to have been retrieved from his works, used to be a favorite at New York's Four Seasons restaurant. Leeks were around, however, long before they became an ingredient in the *haute cuisine* of the Roman Empire. Although their time and place of origin are lost in the mists of time, they may well go back to the early Bronze Age. The earliest dated reference is 2100 B.C., when Ur-Nammu of Ur grew them in his garden. We know they were plentiful in the British Isles at least by the early Middle Ages. When the Welsh fought the Saxons in 640, they wore leeks in their caps so that they could distinguish each other from the enemy. They gained a great victory, and the leek has been an emblem of Welsh national pride ever since.

In Shakespeare's *Henry V,* the comic but gallant Welsh captain, Fluellen, is greeted by Pistol with the insulting words, "Hence! I am qualmish at the smell of leek." Whereupon Fluellen redeems the honor of his country by forcing Pistol to eat a leek. Pistol's dislike of the smell of leek is enough all by itself to make his character suspect. The leek's odor is one of its noble qualities. It is reminiscent of onion but much more subtle and earthy. And while the onion comes on like gangbusters when you cut it up and begin to cook it, then becomes sweet, tame, and rather dull as it continues to be exposed to heat, the leek will at no time bring tears to your eyes but will retain its tantalizing odor throughout the cooking process.

It is the practical French—perhaps the world's most serious cooks and eaters—who have made the leek the undisputed monarch of the *Allium* family, which also includes onions, garlic, and chives. They have, as far as I know, no highfalutin leek legends. They know how to keep vegetables in their place—the kitchen. The three recipes in this section are French-inspired. They are our adaptations of simple, classic dishes as interpreted by great cookbook writers like Julia Child, Elizabeth David, and Richard Olney. These are not recipes for special occasions, although any discriminating guest will certainly appreciate them. The *potage bonne femme* is eaten nearly every day in many French households, its variations limited only by the imagination of the *bonne femme* and by the vegetables available in her market or garden.

FIXING LEEKS AT HOME

Leeks, although as common as dirt in France, were so rare in this country only a generation ago that Waverley Root could write that Americans who wanted leeks had better grow their own. Now they are available in any good produce market, but often cost even more than asparagus. They are best in the fall and spring and can usually be had a bit more cheaply then, especially if you have access to a farmers' market. Nutritionally, they will never win any prizes, although they do contain a reasonable amount of potassium, some calcium, and a little protein. And, like all their relatives, they are virtually free of fat. But no one tells her children, "Eat your leeks. They're good for you." Flavor is the be-all and the end-all here.

Leeks are striking vegetables, a little like scallions on steroids. The white portion is often two inches in diameter, terminating in a flat plate with fine protruding roots. The dark green leaves are broad and flat. Select leeks with very white white parts and very green greens. Also, it is best not to purchase leeks if the roots have been trimmed very close or most of the greens chopped off. This usually represents an attempt to disguise those that have passed their prime. Although one of their many virtues is that even rather old ones have plenty of flavor left, leeks are too expensive for you to settle for them at less than their best. They keep pretty well and will hang out in the vegetable crisper of your refrigerator (in a plastic bag with a few air holes punched in it) for at least a week.

Wash your leeks well. Grit works its way down between the layers, often further down than you would ever suspect. Slice off the tops about an inch above the white portion, stand the leek on its root end, and make a single vertical cut down to within about an inch of the base. Rinse each leek thoroughly in cold water, gently separating the layers with your fingers and inspecting for dirt. Don't try to watch television while you do this. Close scrutiny is everything when it comes to cleaning leeks.

Except for the scallion-size leeks you can occasionally find in the spring, this is a vegetable that ought to be well and thoroughly cooked. You should not need a steak knife to cut up your leeks vinaigrette. For those occasions when you want to serve them whole, you'll find it is easier to achieve leeks that are intact but well softened in a pot of boiling water than in a steamer. You can trim off the dark green leafy tops and the hairy bottoms and tie what remains in a bundle (to keep them from falling apart) before you put them in the boiling water if you want. That is the classic technique. However, we find it simplifies our lives to leave the root ends on until the leeks are boiled. Then drain them, let them cool down a bit, and it's easy to trim them. This is also the time to remove the outer layers if you find they aren't easily penetrable with a knife. The root ends and the tougher outer layers will keep your leeks from falling apart while they're cooking, and there's no need to bundle them.

Save the water in which you've cooked your leeks for the soup pot. You should also save any trimmings you remove before cooking, provided they aren't yellow or wilted. Put a few pieces of leek leaf in the water when you're cooking grains and dried legumes. Almost anything that cooks in liquid for a fairly long time will be enhanced by the addition of a little leek.

POTAGE BONNE FEMME
Makes 6 servings

> 1 teaspoon salt, or to taste
> 1 pound potatoes, peeled and cut into bite-size pieces
> 1 pound leeks, tough green parts removed, cleaned and thinly sliced
> 7 cups boiling water, chicken stock, or a combination
> ¼ cup chopped Italian parsley (optional)
> 1 tablespoon butter (optional)

1. Add the salt and vegetables to the boiling water or stock, lower the heat, cover the pot, and cook at a low boil until the potatoes are quite soft, 25 to 30 minutes.
2. Either add the parsley and butter if using and serve at once, or let the mixture cool slightly and purée all or part of it in a blender or food

processor. Be careful not to overblend or the potatoes will turn sticky. Reheat if necessary, add the parsley and butter, and serve.

80 calories, 0 grams fat, 0 grams saturated fat per serving

VARIATIONS: You can add carrots, green beans, cauliflower, broccoli, or anything similar that takes your fancy to this soup. Additions can be cooked separately or in the soup, puréed with other ingredients or not. An especially nice variation, recommended by Julia Child and by us, is the addition of a packed cup of watercress leaves just before puréeing the soup. A little evaporated skim milk (or an ounce or two of heavy cream if your diet can accommodate it) is very nice in this watercress version.

LEEKS VINAIGRETTE
Makes 4 to 6 servings

3 pounds small leeks (no more than 1 inch in diameter and
*   all more or less the same size), cleaned (page 206),*
*   root ends left on, trimmed so that about an inch of*
*   green remains, and cooked in boiling water for*
*   approximately 10 minutes or until fairly soft*

Vinaigrette
1 tablespoon white wine vinegar
1 tablespoon dry white wine
1 tablespoon extra-virgin olive oil
1 tablespoon Dijon mustard
½ cup chopped Italian parsley
Salt and freshly ground black pepper to taste

1. Drain the leeks carefully. Cut off and discard the root ends and remove any tough outer leaves. Arrange the leeks in a serving dish. Mix the vinaigrette. (Using a blender or food processor can save you from having to chop the parsley, but a small bowl will do just fine.) If you'd like more sauce, or it seems too thick with parsley, add a bit more of any of the liquid ingredients.
2. Spoon or pour the vinaigrette over the leeks, turning them gently in the dish until they are well coated. Allow to stand for a few minutes before serving. This dish tastes best at room temperature.

90 calories, 2 grams fat, 0 grams saturated fat per serving of 6

LEEKS IN RED WINE
Makes 4 to 6 servings

*1 tablespoon olive oil (a bit more if your diet accommodates it, a bit
    less if you're avoiding fat)*

*3 pounds small leeks (no more than 1 inch in diameter and all more or
    less the same size), cleaned (page 206), root ends left on, and
    trimmed so that about an inch of green leaf remains*

1 cup good-quality dry red wine

½ cup water or stock

1. Heat the oil in a skillet large enough to hold the leeks in a single layer.
   (If your skillet has a nonstick surface, you'll be able to use less oil.)
   Add the leeks in a single layer and sauté over medium heat about five
   minutes, or until they are very lightly browned on all sides. If they
   show any tendency to stick add a tablespoon of wine or stock.
2. When the leeks are browned and slightly softened, add all the wine
   and stock and bring to a boil. Cover the skillet, lower the heat slightly,
   and simmer for about 10 minutes, turning the leeks once during the
   process.
3. Remove the leeks to a serving dish and cut off and discard the root
   ends. Boil the sauce a few more minutes to reduce it, pour the sauce
   over the leeks, and serve. This dish is good hot, cold, or tepid.

100 calories, 2 grams fat, 0 grams saturated fat per serving of 6

Mushroom to Maneuver

When you stand in the produce section of the supermarket and see the
neat plastic-wrapped containers of mushrooms nestled between the carrots and the cabbage, you probably think of them as just another vegetable. Perhaps you should get some for the stir-fry you're planning—or
maybe you'll just make do with zucchini. But mushrooms are not vegetables. Nor are they fruits, though they are the fruiting bodies of filamentous
fungi. Mushrooms are saprophytic, a fancy word meaning that they don't
photosynthesize sugars, preferring to nourish themselves with the decay-
ing remains of other organisms. The very cell walls of fungi are chemically
distinct from those of the higher plants, being composed not of cellulose
but of chitin, which is the same stuff that forms an insect's exoskeleton.
That's why mushrooms contain more protein and less carbohydrate than
the general run of vegetable.

There are a lot of mushrooms in this book. We regard mushrooms as one of the basic food groups. Many people who are vegetarians—total or almost—seem to agree with us. Mushrooms have a vaguely meaty taste and texture that make them unlike anything else you'll be eating if you give up fleshy foods. There are folks who swear by soy products to stand in for meat, but we think things like seitan and foods made from textured vegetable protein entirely lack meaty succulence. A grilled portobello, on the other hand, can satisfy even a serious carnivore. (Perhaps not every day, but at least once.)

Until recently, mushrooms, for most of us, meant the common white kind. Extremely common, as the gourmets love to sneer. Pay them no mind. If you cook those little white guys right (the mushrooms, not the gourmets), you can intensify their flavor considerably. That's not to say, however, that there wouldn't be big gastronomic rewards in the enlargement of your mushroom repertoire. Try some dried mushrooms and you'll find that your soups and sauces develop a new layer of flavor, a depth that's hard to get when using vegetable stocks.

You might also want to explore some of the exotica of the mushroom world that have probably invaded your supermarket by this time (see 'Shroom Boom on page 217). They can taste very good indeed. A large grilled portobello mushroom cap can give you the feeling of having eaten a substantial dish at the cost of almost no fat or calories. You can also feed one or two to your seriously carnivorous relatives, and they'll feel almost as satisfied as if you had served up a slab of sirloin. (At least, they'll be more satisfied than they ever expected to be at your house.) Oyster mushrooms, morels, porcini, chanterelles, shiitakes—each of these has its own flavor and texture. However, there are several things you should take into account when considering the purchase of one of the elite fungi. First of all, they are expensive. Second, depending on where you live, they may not arrive at your market in the peak of condition. And, finally, you may not notice all that much difference between their flavor and that of the plain old white mushroom, *Agaricus supermarketus.*

A significant difference between mushrooms and many vegetables is that delicate flavors in mushrooms are enhanced by prolonged cooking. To make the most of your supermarket mushrooms, slice them thin or dice them and sauté them in a nonstick skillet with a little olive oil (a teaspoon or two for each pound) and some finely chopped onion and garlic over medium-high heat. Add the mushrooms gradually so as not to crowd the skillet (you don't want them to steam), letting each addition cook down somewhat before adding more. Stir frequently and add small amounts of wine or stock periodically to prevent sticking. Cook until nearly all liquid is evaporated, 15 to 20 minutes.

These cooked mushrooms can be stored in the refrigerator for several days or even frozen successfully. The addition of a few (or a lot) of them will enhance almost anything—with the possible exception of your breakfast cereal.

It's best to cook all mushrooms within a day or two of purchase. Until then they should be stored in paper bags in the refrigerator. Leave a 'shroom languishing in plastic and it'll drown in its own juices, often in a matter of a few hours.

Clean mushrooms gently. Just brush them off with a damp paper towel or, if they seem really filthy, run them briefly under running water. When asked what people should do who were really grossed out by the culture medium (sterilized manure), Jay Bertoglia, who farms mushrooms in Pennsylvania (see East Coast Exotics on page 301), had two words: "Eat shiitakes." Even if you aren't all that fastidious, it's good advice. Not only do shiitakes grow on nice clean blocks made of hardwood sawdust, they are, for our money, the absolute monarchs of the mushroom world.

Lots of medical claims have been made for shiitakes, and there's some provocative data that indicates that they may actually lower cholesterol. They do contain more fat than other mushrooms, but it's unsaturated. They are also expensive, but they are so flavorful and sturdy that just a few go a long way.

For cooking any and all exotics, you can't go wrong with the slow sautéing that brings out the flavor of the common whites. As their moisture content is not as high, you will need only about half as many. Only the caps of shiitakes should be included, but the stems of most other mushrooms, unless they are dry and woody, can be incorporated. Your results will be more interesting if you break up the caps of your exotics with your hands to leave uneven surfaces. This also applies to common white mushrooms, but the difference is so slight that we don't think it's worth the trouble. Just wipe them off if they're dirty and let the slicing blade of your food processor do the rest of the work.

Most exotic mushrooms have to be cooked longer than standard-issue supermarket mushrooms. Chanterelles, particularly, don't begin to earn their reputation (or their purchase price) until they have been cooked at least 30 to 40 minutes. Longer is often better. An undercooked chanterelle tastes like dirt and might put you off exotics for good. Don't risk it; cook them a good long time.

A mushroom need not be psychedelic to expand your consciousness. Nothing smells like a mushroom. Nothing tastes like one. Nothing feels quite like one in your mouth. Surrender yourself to the mushroom experience.

DRIED MUSHROOMS

Almost every recipe that includes dried mushrooms will tell you to soak them in boiling (or very hot) water for 20 minutes or so, then cut them up and treat them more or less like fresh mushrooms. Sometimes this works, but even when it does you may be somewhat disappointed in the result.

You'd think from reading your cookbooks that what you were doing was reconstituting your mushrooms, but that's not so. The structure of mushrooms is irrevocably altered by drying. Soaking leaches most of their flavor out into the water and often renders their flesh mushy, stringy, or chewy. This is not such a bad thing, however. The mushrooms may be of minimal use after soaking, but the broth you've produced in the process is precious.

No two dried mushrooms are created equal. It helps a little to know what species you're dealing with. Dried shiitakes have an exceptionally firm structure and actually do seem to reconstitute. This is the variety you're most likely to be familiar with, especially if you've done much Asian cooking. Dried porcini (a.k.a. cèpes) make a wonderfully intense broth but are liable to have an earthy taste that can ruin a dish if you don't exercise moderation. Then there are the inexpensive, anonymous dried mushrooms you find huddled in little plastic containers on the supermarket shelf. You bring them home and hope for the best, but they may be good for very little once they've been in water for half an hour, and even their broth may be on the wimpy side.

To prepare any dried mushrooms, begin by soaking them in hot water. Two cups water to 1 ounce mushrooms is usually about right. Let your mushrooms stand for half an hour or so. Then you've reached the point when your discretion must come to the fore. The first step is to see that they are completely clean. Swish them through the broth with your fingers, feeling for grit, and check the bottom of the container. If very little debris has collected, you can be fairly confident that your delectable mushroom dish won't be ruined by sand.

The next step is to test for palatability and texture. Taste both the broth and the mushrooms. If you're trying, for example, to produce a sauce with a fairly delicate flavor, and your dried mushrooms and broth have a very earthy taste, use only a portion of them, reserving the rest for a more robust concoction. They will keep in their broth, in the refrigerator, for 2 or 3 days, somewhat longer if you add a few drops of vinegar.

Occasionally your packet of dried mushrooms will contain stems and other fibrous bits that will never soften and should be weeded out as you run your fingers through the soaked mushrooms. Be fairly ruthless about this. Don't count on them to soften as they cook. They never do.

Finally, remove the mushrooms, set them aside, and strain your broth through a fine sieve, a piece of cheesecloth, or a coffee filter. All this is not as hard as it may sound. It's not a test of your dexterity or your patience—only your judgment. And when you're done you've got an ingredient that can work magic in your soups and sauces.

BASIC SAUTÉED MUSHROOMS
Makes 2 servings as a principal ingredient, 4 as a bit player

½ to 1 tablespoon olive or canola oil or butter

1 small onion, finely chopped

2 garlic cloves, finely chopped or minced

1 pound common white mushrooms, thinly sliced or diced

½ cup dry white wine

1. Heat the oil or butter in a large nonstick skillet over medium-low heat. Add the onion and garlic and cook until the onion is soft and translucent, about 5 minutes. Raise the heat slightly and add the mushrooms, stirring so that they cook evenly and don't steam in their juices. When they stick, add a little white wine. Continue cooking over medium heat for about 20 minutes, or until the mushrooms are fragrant and very soft and nearly all liquid is evaporated. Stir frequently and add wine when necessary to prevent sticking. (If you want to, add any remaining wine when the mushrooms are nearly done and continue cooking until it is mostly evaporated. Otherwise, just drink it.)

N O T E :   As this is a basic, all-purpose recipe, we've restricted the seasonings to good ol' onions and garlic. However, depending on how you want to use your mushrooms, you may want to add things like thyme, oregano, tarragon—not to mention salt and freshly ground pepper. A good rule of thumb is to use ½ teaspoon of any dried herb and add it to the oil at the same time you add the onions and garlic. Use at least twice that quantity of any fresh herb and add it at the end of cooking. It's also best to add salt and pepper to taste when the mushrooms are nearly done.

80 calories, 3 grams fat, 0 grams saturated fat per serving of 4

BAKED MUSHROOM OMELET
Makes 3 main-dish or 6 side-dish or appetizer servings

1⅓ cups skim milk

1 large egg

3 large egg whites

¼ teaspoon salt if not using cheese

¼ teaspoon freshly ground black pepper

¾ cup all-purpose flour

1½ pounds common white mushrooms, prepared as directed for Basic
  Sautéed Mushrooms (see page 213) with 1 teaspoon fresh
  thyme, tarragon, rosemary, or a combination (or ½ teaspoon of
  any of the same herbs, dried)

2 to 3 tablespoons freshly grated Parmesan or Gruyère cheese
  (optional)

1. Preheat the oven to 350°F.
2. Spray a 10-inch quiche pan or pie plate or any shallow baking dish
   that holds at least 2 quarts with vegetable spray, or grease it with butter in the old-fashioned style.
3. Combine the milk, egg, egg whites, salt, and pepper in a blender or
   food processor. With the machine running, add the flour. Process just
   until thoroughly blended, about 30 seconds.
4. Pour about half the egg mixture into the prepared pan and top with
   the sautéed mushrooms, reserving a few for garnish if desired. (If you
   have any wine left, you can use it to deglaze the mushroom skillet,
   boiling it down rapidly until less than a tablespoon of liquid remains.
   Add it to the mushrooms.) Sprinkle with the cheese if using and pour
   the remaining egg mixture over the top.
5. Bake until the omelet is browned and slightly puffed, about 45 to 50
   minutes. Allow to cool about 10 minutes before serving. Garnish with
   the reserved mushrooms and a few fresh thyme sprigs, if desired.

130 calories, 2 grams fat, 0 grams saturated fat
per appetizer serving

WILD RICE PILAF WITH MUSHROOMS
Makes 4 to 6 servings

3 cups hot water
1 ounce dried porcini mushrooms
4 to 6 garlic cloves
4 to 6 scallions
1 tablespoon olive oil
2 cups wild rice (see Note)
½ teaspoon dried thyme, or 1 teaspoon fresh
½ pound fresh shiitake mushrooms, thinly sliced or diced
1 large red bell pepper, thinly sliced
½ cup dry white wine
½ cup chopped parsley or cilantro
Salt to taste

1. Pour the hot water over the dried mushrooms and allow to soak for at least 1 hour. Remove the dried mushrooms, reserving the liquid, and immerse them briefly in clean water, swishing to be sure they are clean. (If you see almost no dirt in the bottom of the soaking liquid, you can omit this step. Just stir the mushrooms in the liquid before you remove them to dislodge any lingering dirt.)
2. Chop half the porcini mushrooms, 2 garlic cloves, and 1 scallion fairly fine. (The chopping blade of your food processor is ideal for this chore.) Heat about half the oil in a saucepan large enough to hold the rice, add the mushroom mixture, and sauté, stirring often, over medium heat until softened. Add the wild rice and cook briefly, stirring to coat the grains.
3. Add enough water to the mushroom broth to make about 3¼ cups. Strain into the rice pot. If using dried thyme, add it now. Bring to a boil, lower the heat, cover the pot, and simmer until the grains are fairly tender, but try not to let them split. Usually this takes about 30 minutes.
4. Meanwhile, finely chop the remaining garlic and scallions. Heat the remaining oil in a large nonstick skillet, add the garlic and scallions, and sauté until they are just wilted. Add the fresh mushrooms and bell pepper and cook over medium-low heat until they are soft, about 20 minutes, adding small amounts of wine to prevent sticking. If the soaked dried mushrooms taste good (not too earthy), chop them and add them to the fresh mushrooms about halfway through the cooking

process. Otherwise, save them for a spicy sauce or soup where their faults won't be evident.

5. When the mushrooms and rice are done, add the rice to the mushrooms in the skillet, stirring to coat the grains. (This will take only a minute or two unless the rice is still a little wet. If it is, add it to the skillet a little at a time and cook, stirring, until all the liquid has evaporated.)

6. Off heat, add the parsley or cilantro and fresh thyme if using. Add salt if necessary. Serve warm or at room temperature.

NOTE: Wild rice isn't a requirement for this recipe—just adjust the cooking time and liquid to suit whatever rice you're using.

250 calories, 3 grams fat, 0 grams saturated fat per serving of 6

CLAY POT CASSEROLE WITH SHIITAKES
Makes 3 to 4 main-dish servings

1 cup dry white beans, such as Great Northerns or small limas, or 2
   cups precooked or canned

2 tablespoons dried oregano

1 bay leaf

½ teaspoon olive oil

2 large onions, diced

5 garlic cloves, minced or pressed

¾ pound fresh shiitake mushrooms, stems discarded, caps sliced

1 large eggplant, cut into ½-inch cubes

One 28-ounce can crushed tomatoes

1. If using dry beans, soak them in water to cover for 6 hours or overnight. Drain them, cover with fresh water, and add the oregano and bay leaf. Simmer, covered, until the beans are soft, 1 to 2 hours.

2. Meanwhile, heat the olive oil in a large nonstick skillet, add the onions and garlic, and sauté over medium heat until the onions are wilted. Add the mushrooms and eggplant and sauté until they soften slightly. Add the tomatoes and simmer until the eggplant is tender, about 20 minutes.

3. While the mushroom/eggplant mixture is simmering, submerge your clay pot in cold water for about 15 minutes.

4. Drain the beans and add with the mushroom mixture to the clay pot.

Put the clay pot in a cold oven, set the oven temperature at 425°F, and bake for 40 minutes. (Or preheat the oven to 350°F and bake in a covered baking dish for about the same length of time.)

....

340 calories, 3 grams fat, 0 grams saturated fat per serving of 4

....

'SHROOM BOOM

....

AARGH! THERE ARE WEIRD FUNGI in the supermarket! Don't be intimidated by strange-looking mushrooms. More or less the same rules for selection and cooking apply to them all. It's usually best to choose mushrooms that look plump and fresh, with rounded caps folded around the gills. A mushroom that has flattened out, exposing the gills, is generally past optimum maturity.

Common White: Your basic generic mushroom. Always available, always the same, always an asset at dinnertime. The only mushroom you should even consider eating raw.

Cremini: Originating as Italian field mushrooms, cremini range in color from light tan to a rich brown. A more intense version of the basic mushroom, with a somewhat richer flavor and a firmer texture.

Portobello: Cremini allowed to fulfill their potential. They have grown up—sometimes to a diameter of 6 inches—and developed a more intense flavor. If you want to grill them (an excellent idea), there's nothing wrong with selecting flat mushrooms, especially if you plan to cook them right away. Portobellos are, by nature, very mature mushrooms; and specimens that have opened fully taste fine and are easier to grill evenly.

Shiitake: The classic mushroom in Asian cooking but very good in almost any mushroom dish. Tan, umbrella shaped, rather flat capped, so that the gills are exposed even in youth, they have such a distinctive flavor and firm texture that a few go a long way.

The stems are tough and fibrous and are good only for flavoring stock.

Oyster: Shaped like the bivalve from which they get their name, oyster mushrooms are small and delicate, with an almost sweet flavor. They are delicious combined with seafood and pasta.

Porcini (a.k.a. Cèpe): Dark brown and earthy. You may have only encountered them dried, but if you can find fresh ones, snap them up. They can be the foundation of a sauce that tastes wickedly rich.

Chanterelle: Beautiful, pale red or yellow, trumpet-shaped mushrooms. They look delicate but have a robust flavor that mellows with extended cooking. They have thus far resisted attempts at cultivation, so they cost a lot. If you ever indulge in butter, cream, and eggs, the day you find chanterelles is the time to do so. They are perfect combined with rich scrambled eggs or as an omelet filling.

A Tomato Lament

I moved to San Francisco right out of college and lived the first eleven years of my adult life there. I loved it. It's a beautiful city, and I was lucky enough to find an apartment that showed it to its best advantage. The weather's perfect most of the year. I made friends. My father would have you believe that I mellowed. I drove a convertible.

So it was with some trepidation that I moved back to New York a few years ago. I worried about leaving eleven years' worth of a life behind, and I worried that those eleven years had made me irredeemably West Coast. Frequent travel throughout my California residency had fostered an illusion of dual citizenship, but the move back would put it to the test. Was I still a New Yorker?

I was. As much as I enjoyed my San Francisco tenure, in retrospect it seems like it wasn't quite right. When I left New York, I was warned that Californians were different, and that New Yorkers often had trouble adjusting. I dismissed this as hooey, but it wasn't. It's not for nothing it's gotten to be a cliché that California is slow and friendly. I distinctly remember not thinking warm happy thoughts the first time the supermarket checkout clerk seemed more interested in how my day was than in how quickly my groceries were bagged.

I wasn't a perfect fit. I argued too long and too loudly. I slept too late. I walked too fast. I shunned soy products. I still do those things, but I'm surrounded by a city's worth of people who do them too. I am indeed a New Yorker.

I do miss San Francisco, though. I miss my friends and I miss the weather. If pressed, I'll admit that I miss my car. I miss my Bay view. And I miss the tomatoes.

It's not just the tomatoes, it's all the produce, but the difference between California and New York produce is most apparent in the tomatoes. This is because tomatoes vary in quality more than any other vegetable. The good ones are so very good, but the bad ones are inedible. And in most places, for most of the year, all you can find are the bad ones.

But in San Francisco, nearly all summer, you can get superb tomatoes at the Embarcadero greenmarket. The tomato stand I frequented was in the southeast corner of the market, and they regularly had a startling array of tomatoes in all sizes, shapes, and colors. Little pear-shaped yellow ones, orange cherry-size ones, normal-looking red ones, and striped, stippled, misshapen heirloom varieties. I tried them all. Truth be told, I didn't just try them, I wallowed in them. One day, strolling around the market, I ate almost two pounds of the little orange ones, like grapes, straight out of the bag.

It must say something unflattering about my character that one of my enduring San Francisco memories involves shameless piggery, but there it is. I can almost taste those tomatoes. Almost. In order to really taste them, I'm afraid I have to go back. But that's okay—I'll be just about due for a visit when tomato season rolls around.

WE HAPPY FEW

If you're fortunate enough to get your hands on some really good tomatoes, and you're planning to cook them, stop! Unless you have a true tomato glut—more than you, your family, and friends could possibly consume in a reasonable time period—it's a waste to cook really good tomatoes. This is my opinion, of course. Others may tell you different, and they can put their opinions in their books. For my money, the only way to eat good tomatoes is raw.

The appeal of a good tomato is a combination of taste, texture, and smell, all of which are transformed by cooking. The perfect tomato has a balance of sweetness and acidity, flesh and juice. It smells like the ground it grew in. Once cooked, however, it's flat and lifeless.

Let me be clear that my objection to cooked tomatoes does not extend to tomato sauce. On the contrary, I am one of tomato sauce's biggest fans. Once a tomato is turned into sauce, it's something quite different from a fresh tomato. Only when it's cooked just enough to lose its freshness but retain its tomatohood do I object to it.

This is not to say you have to eat them out of the bag at the greenmarket. You can take them home and cut them up and combine them with other things in a very civilized way. Just don't cook them.

Tomatoes combine well with almost any other vegetable and any kind of herb. The recipes below use basil, mint, and cilantro, but rosemary, tarragon, and parsley work just as well. Because they're soft, juicy, and red, tomatoes are an excellent complement to vegetables that are firm and green. Tomatoes combine well with other raw ingredients (lettuce, peppers, cucumbers, radishes) or with cooked ingredients. Steamed asparagus, green beans, or leeks, chilled or at room temperature, all work well with tomatoes. And, of course, good fresh tomatoes are the basis for good fresh salsa. Combine with some finely chopped hot pepper like jalapeño (be careful of the superhots like habanero—a little goes a very long way), some bell pepper, scallions or onions, and cilantro. For a little variety, try lime juice or mint.

CHOPPED TOMATO AND TUNA SALAD
WITH MINT-YOGURT DRESSING
Makes 2 large servings

For the dressing
½ cup mint leaves, loosely packed
2 tablespoons plain nonfat yogurt
1 tablespoon balsamic vinegar
2 teaspoons olive oil
Pinch of sugar

For the salad
2 tomatoes
1 yellow bell pepper
One 4-inch piece cucumber
Half a 14-ounce can hearts of palm
3 scallions
1 celery stalk

2 ounces feta cheese (optional)

One 6½-ounce can tuna

1. To make the dressing, mix all ingredients in a blender or food processor until the mint has been chopped quite small and the dressing has
   emulsified. This dressing benefits form sitting in the refrigerator
   overnight—the mint flavor infuses the other ingredients—so make it
   the day before if you can.
2. Chop all the salad vegetables and cheese if using in small pieces. If
   you don't like the watery innards of the tomatoes, you can seed them
   before you chop them. I usually just chop them and try to leave most
   of the seeds and liquid behind on the cutting board when I transfer
   the tomatoes to the bowl.
3. Add the tuna. Dress and toss.

NOTE: A recipe for something like chopped salad is obviously just a
suggestion. You can add pretty much anything you like or just happen to
have lying around. For example, you can turn this salad into a substantial meal by adding chopped cooked potatoes. You can liven it up with
anchovies or substitute cooked chicken or small shrimp for tuna. You can
also change the dressing by using a different herb—basil works well—or
use a different dressing altogether. It's salad. Anything goes.

250 calories, 6 grams fat, 1 gram saturated fat per serving

MARINATED TOMATO/SEAFOOD SALAD
Makes 2 to 4 servings

For the dressing

½- to 1-inch length fresh ginger, peeled and grated (see Notes)

½ cup chopped cilantro (see Notes)

2 teaspoons olive oil

3 tablespoons rice wine vinegar

For the salad

*1½ pounds assorted cooked seafood (scallops, shrimp, mussels,
    clams, and calamari all work well; see Notes)*

3 large ripe tomatoes, chopped

½ medium red onion, finely chopped

1 yellow bell pepper, chopped

1. Combine the dressing ingredients and mix well. Put the salad ingredients in a bowl, add the dressing, and stir to combine. Let the salad marinate in the refrigerator for 1 to 2 hours.

NOTE: To make the dressing, it's easiest just to throw everything—the chunk of ginger, a small bunch of cilantro with its tough stems removed, and the liquids—into the food processor. Use the chopping blade.

If you're starting with raw seafood, it's easy to steam it, but you should do each ingredient separately since they have different cooking times. Start a pot with enough water to steam several shifts of seafood, and use a removable steamer insert or basket. Large scallops steam in about 5 minutes, shrimp in 3 or 4, calamari in 6 to 8. Clams and mussels vary from just 1 or 2 minutes to almost 10. Scallops, shrimp, and calamari are done when they lose that translucent look. Clams and mussels are done when they open (discard any that don't). You can also use cooked fish in this recipe—it's a great way to use up leftovers.

275 calories, 4 grams fat, 1 gram saturated fat per serving of 4

TOMATOES VINAIGRETTE
Makes 4 side-dish servings

2 pounds or more ripe tomatoes, cut in thin wedges

2 tablespoons balsamic vinegar

2 teaspoons extra-virgin olive oil

3 tablespoons chopped fresh basil

2 scallions, or 1 shallot, finely chopped

Salt and freshly ground pepper to taste

1. Combine all ingredients and let marinate for at least 1 hour. Serve chilled or, as I prefer, at room temperature. If your tomatoes released a lot of liquid while they marinated, drain some of it off before you serve them. Save the liquid for the soup pot or to help dress a future green salad.

70 calories, 3 grams fat, 0 grams saturated fat per serving

All-American Corn

> Some people take the whole stem and gnaw [the kernels] out with their
> teeth . . . It really troubles me to see how their wide mouths . . . raven-
> ously grind up the beautiful white, pearly maize ears.
>
> —FREDERICK BREMER (VISITING AMERICA IN 1850)

> People have tried and they have tried, but sex is not better than
> sweet corn.
>
> —GARRISON KEILLOR

That's the kind of thing people say about corn. None of this highfalutin ro-
mantic stuff. Not that you won't find a lot of references to corn in European literature, but the authors are talking about wheat or sometimes
barley or oats—whatever cereal grain was most familiar in their localities.
What Americans call corn, Europeans call maize or Indian corn. The alien
corn amid which Ruth stood weeping was probably Mesopotamian
wheat. Corn in Old English meant a small, worn-down particle—it could
be sand, salt, or a cereal grain. Corned beef, for example, has nothing to
do with corn. It is simply beef preserved with salt. Corn rye is a term for
bread made from whole grain, a fact that, when I learned it a few years
ago, answered a question that had puzzled me since childhood: "Why
can't I taste the corn in this bread?"

Corn was the grain of the Incas, Mayans, and Aztecs. Without it, they
would not have been able to establish permanent settlements and develop complex cultures. But the story of the domestication of the corn
plant, like most of the rest of their story, is lost because of their lack of
written history. So for us, the history of corn begins when Europeans discovered it.

CORN ON THE COB: GROSSING OUT GENTEEL EUROPE

Frederick Bremer was just one of a long series of European visitors who
were shocked at watching Americans "take the whole stem and gnaw"
their corn. What all these well-bred folk failed to understand was that the
minute sweet corn is picked the clock starts running—the sugar in the kernels begins turning to starch. In the presence of high temperatures the
process takes place very rapidly indeed. The quicker the kernels get from
the stalk in the field to the mouth of the eater the better they will taste. By

not removing the corn from the cob, thus eliminating a stage between picking and eating, you can speed the process along considerably.

When you are fortunate enough to acquire good sweet corn, all your efforts should be devoted to cooking and eating it at the earliest possible moment and to keeping it cool until that moment arrives. If you drive to a farm stand or farmers' market, take along a cooler filled with ice in which to bring home your corn.

Cool days are best for buying sweet corn. Never purchase ears that have been sitting in the hot sun. Buying it early in the morning and eating it for lunch gives you the best chance of an uplifting corn experience. When you get home, put your corn in the refrigerator instantly and don't take it out again until your water is boiling or your grill or oven is hot.

Sweet corn is best cooked by steaming. Bring an inch or so of water to a boil in a large pot, add the shucked corn, cover the pot, lower the heat, and simmer for no more than 3 or 4 minutes. Very young, tender corn can even be eaten raw, although I admit I am partial to the slight chewiness that develops when it is heated.

My great-aunt Dag always cooked the corn from her garden (picked after the water was boiling) with the husks on, and I'm convinced that this is the best method of conserving the sugar. However, it requires larger pots than most of us have, and removing the silk from the hot corn is something of a hassle, not to mention a way to gross out people a lot less sensitive than Frederick Bremer. Seeing me in a corn trance, covered with cornsilk and melted butter, my uncle Frank used to refer to me affectionately as the Greasy Hairy Beast.

It is, of course, possible to desilk corn without detaching the husks, but I suspect that some of the sugar-conserving virtues of the cooking method are lost this way. It's a useful technique if you want to bake or grill your corn, however. Roll back the husks, remove the silk, wet the ears with cold water to prevent charring, and reclose the husks over the ears. (Some people tie them with strings, but that seems unduly tedious.) You can bake corn prepared in this fashion in a 350°F oven for about 15 minutes or place the ears in the coals at the edge of your charcoal fire for about the same length of time, turning them every 5 minutes or so.

The habits of my childhood notwithstanding, good sweet corn does not need butter. It is best totally unadorned. For those who must have some seasoning, a little salt and perhaps some freshly ground pepper should be sufficient.

Everything I've said so far applies only to traditional sweet corn, the local stuff that's available just a couple of months a year—August and September in most localities. But agriculture marches on. Recently developed supersweet corn can have a sugar content as high as 30 percent, and the sugar-to-starch conversion takes place much more slowly than in the old sweet corn we all know and love. These new varieties can be as much as five times as sweet as regular sweet corn and stay that way for two weeks longer. Until my favorite Cape Cod produce vendor (Georgia at Quail Hollow Farms in Sandwich) introduced me to this type of corn a few years ago, I was convinced that I would never eat corn on the cob except in the late summer and early fall. What was Georgia, who respects seasons and doesn't sell any bad stuff, doing with corn at the end of June? Shipped up from Tennessee, she told me, and delicious. Sure. But I took a chance, took some home, and, lo, it was very good.

Supersweet corn (that's an official designation in the trade; you can ask for it by name) is almost too sweet. It lacks some of the satisfying corniness of the old-fashioned varieties. However, it's available virtually year-round if you know where to look, and unless it's really ancient, it will always taste good. I recommend cooking it by laying the naked ears directly on the barbecue grill. The sugars caramelize and the slight charring brings out the latent corn flavor. Recently this corn has added a new dimension to New York street fairs—a food that's worth eating and isn't dangerous. Vendors actually grill the corn before your eyes and, if you can catch them before they baste it with the greasy sauce, you'll have a fine snack.

Whichever type of good sweet corn you can lay your hands on, gnaw away. The American approach to food may not always be the best in the world, but we certainly know how to eat sweet corn.

Cabbage: A Tepid Enthusiasm

"Well," said Mom, when I suggested that cabbage should be included in this chapter, "I certainly can't get excited about it. You're on your own."

I'll admit right off the bat that I am not as enthusiastic about cabbage as I am about other vegetables like asparagus, beets, and mushrooms. But there is one particular kind of cabbage I am inordinately fond of—the braised red kind you (or at least I) always associate with German food. I can trace the association easily. We never had cabbage at home, so the only time I ever ate it was at the best (and possibly only) German restaurant in Poughkeepsie, the Little Brauhaus. We didn't go there often, but when we did it was a bonanza for those in our family who possess the sausage gene. Those Germans sure know their sausages.

If I didn't order the bratwurst or the knockwurst or the weisswurst, I got the sauerbraten, and it came with braised red cabbage. It's possible that one of the reasons I liked it so much was that it was an integral part of the sauerbraten experience, but I don't like to examine my motives too closely. I prefer to believe that I like the vegetable on its own merits.

Until I went to college, that was about the limit of my cabbage experience. And even in college, I didn't go out of my way to find it. Occasionally, however, I had it thrust upon me. I spent two of my four college years living in a cooperative called Von Cramm. There were about thirty of us, and we were responsible for everything from keeping the house clean to fixing the plumbing to electing new members. The majority of our house time, however, was spent planning and preparing meals.

We at the Cramm were divided into seven teams of four or five people. Each team had one day of the week (which rotated, so no one got stuck with Friday every week) to cook dinner (we were on our own for breakfast and lunch). The team was responsible for preparing, cooking, setting tables, serving, and cleaning up. We weren't so culinarily naive as to count on the teams to plan the meal—we had a steward who did that.

Most teams had their share of kitchen talent, so there were very few disastrous meals. There was, however, one legendarily bad cook in our house. His name was Joe, and he was one of the nicest people I've ever known. He just couldn't cook his way out of a wet paper bag.

On one Wednesday night that would go down in Von Cramm history, Joe's team was in charge and stuffed cabbage was dinner. As usual, the team scanned the menu to find the most foolproof task for Joe. With stuffed cabbage, it was easy. Joe was assigned to fill and roll the cabbage leaves. It was a job tailor-made for Joe. It wasn't like cooking at all. It was more like wrapping presents.

Joe proved to be good at wrapping presents, and the stuffed leaves went into the oven looking great. It was only after they came out that we realized Joe had failed Vegetable Identification 101 and we had thirty entrées of stuffed iceberg lettuce.

Perhaps that meal left an emotional scar because when I decided to write about cabbage I realized that I had never actually cooked one. To be fair, though, I don't think Joe had anything to do with it. I just never got around to it.

Now, many cabbages later, I feel like quite an authority. Which just goes to prove that, when it comes to vegetables, expertise comes easily. Good thing, too.

BRAISED RED CABBAGE
Makes 6 servings

1 teaspoon olive oil
1 large onion, chopped
1 small apple, peeled and chopped
2 cups dry red wine
1 cup chicken or vegetable stock
5 whole cloves
5 whole allspice berries
1 cinnamon stick
1 medium head red cabbage, trimmed, quartered,
    cored, and thinly sliced

1. Heat the olive oil in a large nonstick saucepan. Add the onion and apple and sauté over medium heat until limp, about 10 minutes.
2. Add the wine, stock, and spices and bring to a boil. Lower the heat, stir in the cabbage, cover, and simmer, stirring occasionally, until the cabbage is tender, about 45 minutes. Serve hot or cold.

80 calories, 1 gram fat, 0 grams saturated fat per serving

Strictly for Carnivores

I'VE SPENT MOST OF MY LIFE on the coasts, primarily in New York and San Francisco. Most of what I've seen of America's heartland I've seen from 35,000 feet. This has warped my perspective.

I thought the standard American diet (meat, starch, veg) was a thing of the past, that pretty much everyone had gotten with the less fat, more fiber, heavy-on-the-produce program.

I thought it was easy to find good vegetables and fruits. It know it's true in New York because I live five blocks from Fairway, the famed Manhattan produce store. I know it's true in San Francisco because the farmers' market on the Embarcadero is open every Saturday, year-round. It's true on Cape Cod, where we go in the summer, and it's true in Miami, where my parents go in the winter (I'm not old enough yet—I'm always carded at the airport and sent home). It's true everywhere I go.

Then I went to Cleveland.

I went at the invitation—no, more like the behest—of my good friend Eli. Eli has lived in Cleveland all his life, and has spent no small part of the many years I've known him telling me what a great place it is. And he's right. Cleveland is a fine city. There's a lot of money there, much of it left over from the heyday of John D. Rockefeller and Standard Oil, and the money has been well spent. The city has art and music, sports and theater. And meat. Lots and lots of meat.

I was only in Cleveland for a weekend, which is not long enough for serious eating, but I tried to make up for the lack of time by spending as much of it as possible in restaurants and markets. I grant that this isn't too much different from the way I usually spend my weekends, but this time I had an excuse.

My weekend disabused me of the idea that meat was no longer at the forefront of the American diet. In the restaurants and markets of Cleveland, meat of all kinds is very much in the spotlight. Most of my Saturday morning was spent at the West Side Market, which is where Clevelanders who care about food go to shop. It's housed in a cavernous building designed for the purpose, and on the day I was there, it was mobbed. The main building is essentially a big open hall, and each vendor has a semi-permanent booth. Throughout, there are terrific terra-cotta relief tiles of fruits, vegetables, and animals built into the walls and columns. The building, the clientele, the atmosphere are the epitome of marketness. But almost all the booths had meat.

There was beef and pork and lamb in every conceivable cut. There were calves' feet and pigs' knuckles and brains and hearts and livers. There were chickens and turkeys and capons and squabs. There were chops and steaks and whole halves of things that were way too readily identifiable as four-footed creatures. There were many, many sausages.

Interspersed among the meat and poultry booths were a few cheese booths, several bread booths, and a pasta booth. Tucked away in an obscure corner was a lone fish booth with a few milky-eyed pike and an unpleasant smell.

No vegetables?

Yes! There are vegetables! They're in the produce annex outside. And while there is an excellent selection of fruits and vegetables in the annex, produce is clearly a second-class citizen at the West Side Market. Inside the main building, vendors have tiled walls and well-constructed booths and glass display cases. In the annex, they have plastic walls with zip-out windows, and the vegetables are piled on wooden platforms and produce crates. There is no question that meat is cock of the walk.

The low status of vegetables at the West Side Market may have as much to do with what's locally produced as with what's most prized. Cows grow in Ohio in March. Asparagus does not. But if Ohioans were eating a diet heavy on vegetables and light on meat, it would undoubtedly have been reflected in the products at the market and the menus at the restaurants. The Invisible Hand would see to it. Meat is predominant because it's what people eat.

SATURATED FAT: DANGER! DANGER!

While much of the news on the nutrition front has been confusing and even contradictory, among the few incontrovertible facts is that saturated fat, the kind that predominates in meat, is very bad for you. It significantly raises your risk for many diseases, heart disease and cancer among them. While food and nutrition experts may argue how much olive oil is okay and whether the Mediterranean diet is the healthiest, they are almost unanimous in their condemnation of saturated fat.

So, given the perils of saturated fat, you might expect the meat chapter in a book about healthful cooking to be brutish and short. "Chapter 9: Meat. Don't eat it." The truth of the matter, however, is that there is no reason you have to eliminate meat from your diet altogether. Instead, you need to find the lowest-fat kinds, and learn to use small quantities to optimal advantage.

Red meat is usually named as the prime suspect in the overconsumption of saturated fat. And, while it's certainly true that most red meat contains distressingly high amounts of it, poultry is not blameless. Dark meat chicken is worse for you than some cuts of beef, and some kinds of red meat are as harmless as white meat turkey. Unless you're committed to avoiding meat and poultry altogether—and I'm not—it's useful to understand your options.

(If you're inclined to avoid meat and poultry on moral, rather than on nutritional, grounds, see Mom's Pig Girl's Manifesto at the end of this chapter.)

CARNIVOROUS SURVIVAL STRATEGIES

I think there's a reason the phrase "red meat" has become so prevalent. It's just graphic enough to remind you what it is you're actually eating. Beef is something you eat. Lamb is something you eat. Red meat is something you avoid. What else explains that ad campaign for pork, "the other white meat"? The National Pork Board doesn't want pork to be tarred with the red-meat brush.

Giving up red meat comes more easily to some than to others. There are people in this world (the same ones who love lentils and brown rice—you know who you are, MOM) who decide to eat better, forgo beef for a few weeks, and then say things like, "I just stopped wanting to eat red meat after a while." Well bully for them. I suggest the rest of us bundle all those people off to an island somewhere to live on jícama and tree bark and see how they like *that*. Me, even though I'm not in the T-Rex Carnivore Club, I still like a hamburger every now and then.

If you are one of those people who have no desire to eat red meat, by all means don't. Skip the rest of this section, which is for people who would like to incorporate some beef or lamb or pork (I don't care what they say—it's red to me) into the occasional dinner.

From the standpoint of minimizing saturated fat intake, negotiating poultry is straightforward: Eat the white meat, eschew the skin and dark meat. Negotiating red meat is harder. There are three basic strategies:

STRATEGY 1: USE MEAT AS AN INGREDIENT, NOT A CENTERPIECE.

Centerpiece meat is the slab in the middle of your plate. It's a steak or a hamburger or a slice of a roast. Ingredient meat is the little pieces incorporated into another dish, like chili or stir-fry or spaghetti sauce.

Centerpiece meat is the kind you really should just resign yourself to not having, except on very special occasions. There are, however, all sorts of interesting things you can do with ingredient meat. Small quantities of beef, pork, or game can add heft to a stir-fry, soup, or pasta sauce. Rice can be turned into a substantial side dish with the addition of a little meat and a few vegetables. Meat combines particularly well with root vegetables like potatoes, carrots, and parsnips. Leftover beef or game can even work in a cold pasta salad. The key is to think about it as an ingredient in a dish that gets most of its substance from other ingredients. You'll be surprised at how little beef you need to make a truly beefy beef stew. Give it a shot—just don't give any to my mother until she finishes her tree bark.

STRATEGY 2: USE THE LEANEST CUTS OF BEEF AND PORK.

Some parts of cows and pigs are fattier than others. The cuts of beef lowest in fat (5 to 7 grams of fat in a 4-ounce serving) are eye round and top round (sometimes disguised as London broil). There are also some producers who specialize in breeding and raising leaner animals. If any such meat is available in your area, it will be clearly marked at your market or butcher shop.

For pork, go with the tenderloin or center loin, but keep in mind that even the leanest cuts of pork have about 50 percent more fat than the leanest beef. (One surprise: Lean cured ham is relatively low in fat, with only 5 grams in a 4-ounce serving. The sodium content, however, is another story.)

STRATEGY 3: EAT GAME.

Most "game" available in markets isn't wild at all—the venison and buffalo come from commercially raised animals. Both buffalo and venison have about half the fat of beef, so you needn't be so careful about selecting cuts. In fact, you're unlikely to have much of a choice; even in my superduper urban meat market, I can only get one cut of each.

Not every carnivore likes to venture beyond traditional barnyard choices. If Old MacDonald didn't have it, they aren't eating it! Both buffalo and venison have a gamy flavor that doesn't appeal to everyone. (It does to me.) However, when you're cooking with just a little and hoping it will impart flavor to an entire dish, a strong taste can work to your advantage. Encourage your Old MacDonald carnivore to experiment, just this once.

Buffalo: At Home, on the Range

Buffalo's fat content, like beef's, varies, but it can be as low as turkey breast, which is to say very low in fat. And it has a definite edge over white-meat turkey in that it actually tastes like something. Turkey, of course, has the advantage of being inexpensive and available in every supermarket. Although buffalo has become more common in the last few years as its benefits become better known to increasingly health-conscious consumers, it's still not that easy to find, and it's still expensive.

Venison is even less widely available, but if you can get it, try it. Use it the same way you'd use buffalo.

Below you'll find some suggestions for using buffalo (or venison or lean beef) as ingredient meat. I've discovered that game has a couple of advantages over beef in these recipes. Although venison and buffalo are lower in fat than even the leanest beef, they can be more tender. They work particularly well when they're simmered a long time in liquid (as in either the chili or the stew). Beef can get quite tough, and although it will soften somewhat with extended cooking time (several hours), it is never as tender as buffalo or venison.

The other advantage to game is that you don't have to carefully defat it. Although it exudes some liquid as it browns, just as other meats do, so little of that is fat that you don't have to drain it or blot it up with paper towels as you do with beef. And, although this defatting procedure is effective with beef, it takes some of the flavor with it.

If you can find buffalo, venison, or any other kind of game at your local market, you'll find that it's similar enough to the beef you're familiar with that you'll get the hang of cooking it right away.

BUFFALO CHILI
Makes 8 main-dish servings

1 pound dried kidney beans
2 teaspoons olive oil

2 large onions, chopped

5 garlic cloves, chopped

1 jalapeño or other hot pepper, minced, with seeds

4 tablespoons chili powder

2 teaspoons ground cumin

2 teaspoons dried thyme

1 teaspoon red pepper flakes or cayenne, or to taste

Three 28-ounce cans crushed tomatoes

1 pound ground buffalo, venison, or lean beef

Salt to taste

1. Put the kidney beans in a pot, cover with at least 3 inches of water, and let soak overnight.
2. Drain the beans, cover them with at least 3 inches of fresh water, and bring to a boil. Reduce the heat, cover the pot, and simmer the beans until tender, 45 to 60 minutes. Drain the beans.
3. Heat the olive oil in a large pot over medium heat. Add the onions, garlic, hot pepper, chili powder, cumin, thyme, and red pepper and sauté until the onions are wilted, about 15 minutes. Add the crushed tomatoes and beans.
4. In a nonstick skillet, sauté the meat, breaking it up into small pieces as it cooks, over medium heat, until most of the red is gone. Make sure not to overcook it, or it will get tough. If you're using buffalo or venison, simply add the meat and all the pan juices to the chili. If you're using ground beef, drain the meat well in a colander lined with paper towels and add it to the chili.
5. Taste the chili and adjust the seasonings, including the salt, as necessary. Keep in mind that chili powders vary widely—some are much spicier than others—so any quantity you find in a recipe is just a guideline. Cover and simmer the chili for about 45 minutes. Serve over rice.

410 calories, 3 grams fat, 2 grams saturated fat per serving

BEEF (OR BUFFALO OR VENISON) STEW
Makes 4 or 5 main-dish servings

4 teaspoons olive oil

3 medium onions, chopped

5 garlic cloves, minced

1 pound fresh shiitake mushrooms, with stems removed, caps sliced

3 tablespoons chopped fresh thyme, or 2 teaspoons dried

1 pound buffalo, venison, or low-fat beef (eye round and
  top round are lowest in fat)

All-purpose flour for coating

2½ cups dry red wine

4 cups beef stock

One 14-ounce can crushed tomatoes

1 pound small red potatoes, cut into bite-size pieces

3 large carrots, sliced thick

Salt and pepper to taste

1 cup pearl barley

1. Heat 2 teaspoons of the olive oil in a large pot over medium heat. Add the onions and garlic and sauté until the onions are translucent. Add the mushrooms and thyme and continue sautéing until the mushrooms are soft, about 15 minutes.

2. After trimming all visible fat from the meat, cut it into 1-inch cubes. Coat the cubes with flour.

3. Push the mushroom mixture to the sides of the pot, clearing as big a space as possible in the center of the pot. In the center, add 1 teaspoon of the remaining olive oil and heat it. Add as many cubes of meat as will fit comfortably in one layer. Sear the cubes on all sides, and remove them from the pan. Sear the remaining meat in one or two more batches using the remaining oil, then return all the meat to the pan. If your pot isn't big enough for searing the meat while the vegetables are still in it, or your vegetables are in danger of scorching, remove the veggies before you sear the meat. (Scorching shouldn't be a problem—the liquid in the veggies usually prevents it—but keep your eyes open.)

4. Add the wine, stock, tomatoes, potatoes, and carrots. Bring the stew to a boil. Reduce the heat, and simmer for at least 2 hours. If the stew is too liquid, cook it longer. If the stew gets too thick as it cooks, add more wine or stock. Season with salt and pepper. (If you're using beef,

the meat will be more tender if you cook the stew for about 3 hours. To do that, just put a lid on the pot once the stew reaches the consistency you like, and cook it over very low heat for the remaining time.)

5. As the stew cooks, bring about 6 cups of water to a boil in a large pan. Add the barley and simmer until it's tender, about 35 minutes. Serve the stew with the drained barley.

530 calories, 7 grams fat, 2 grams saturated fat per serving of 5

It Tastes Like Chicken

This winter was a bad flu season in New York, but I wasn't worried. I never get sick. And I still believe that, if circumstances hadn't conspired against me, I wouldn't have. But I got hit with a one-two punch. First, I got food poisoning. That depleted my disease-fighting resources. Then I got on an airplane, which exposed me, no doubt, to a wide variety of opportunistic pathogens. Then I got the flu. I was miserable—feverish and nauseated and weak—but also surprised. I was sick.

Aaron, Jake, and I have always been healthy. Mom puts it down to hybrid vigor. Our genetic mixture of Eastern European and Scandinavian is good at warding off disease. But that's not the only benefit to a hybrid family—it's very useful in Division of Chicken. Dad's ancestors apparently liked white meat, and Mom's liked dark. I inherited my mother's tendency, Jake got Dad's, and Aaron hasn't yet noticed a significant difference between white and dark (if you see him, please don't tell him, as it will upset our delicate balance). And so one large chicken feeds our family quite nicely, with no squabbling.

We don't serve a whole chicken for dinner all that often, though, because of dreaded saturated fat. Both Mom and I cook our chickens the same way—baked in a clay pot—and we always bake them with large quantities of filling vegetables, so we leave the table satisfied without having eaten a pound of chicken. The chicken's appearance at table could be even rarer, however, if it weren't for its utility for pantry momentum. Not only can you make leftover chicken classics like sandwiches and hash, you can use the veggies in soups and stews, and the carcass and the cooking liquid for stock. As far as pantry momentum is concerned, leftover chicken is a boon.

CLAY POT CHICKEN
Makes 4 to 6 main-dish servings

1 large chicken (4 to 5 pounds)

3 medium sweet potatoes, cut into 2-inch chunks

1 pound small red potatoes, cut in half if they're bigger than golf balls

3 large carrots, cut into 1-inch pieces

1 onion, peeled and quartered

½ pound whole white mushrooms

1 garlic head

½ cup beer, dry white wine, or chicken stock

1. Submerge a 4-quart clay pot (see Note) in water and let it soak for at least 15 minutes.
2. Rinse the chicken and remove the giblets.
3. Drain the pot and put some of the vegetables in a layer in the bottom of the pot. Put the chicken, breast side up, on the vegetables, and pack the remaining vegetables around the chicken.
4. Pour the beer, wine, or stock over all, cover it, and place the pot in a cold oven. Set the oven temperature at 450°F. Roast for about 1¼ hours, until the juices run clear when you pierce the thigh joint with a knife. To brown the chicken, remove the cover for the last 15 minutes.

N O T E : If you don't have a clay pot, you can use a Dutch oven or another large ovenproof pot. The cooking times are about the same, but you should use a slightly lower temperature (425°F works well) and preheat the oven. Leave the lid of the pot slightly ajar so moisture can escape and your chicken won't steam.

410 calories, 5 grams fat, 2 grams saturated fat per serving of 6

DUMB CHICKEN JOKES

MY FIRST JOB OUT OF COLLEGE was with IBM, and I spent most of my six years there selling small computer systems to manufacturers and wholesale distributors. The owners of those companies didn't know anything about computers, and didn't want to know anything about computers, so I found out quickly that our common language would have to be the language of *their* business. I learned about inventory control and order entry and accounts payable. I found out about carrying costs and obsolescence. I learned to drive a forklift. After about a year in the field, I could pass myself off as a knowledgeable insider.

Most of the businesses I sold to were pretty prosaic: hardware distributors (the hammer-and-nail kind, not the computer kind), wire-mesh wholesalers, garment manufacturers. I found, to my surprise, that I was genuinely interested in these businesses. I enjoyed getting familiar with them and figuring out what might make them more profitable and competitive. But there was always a special place in my heart for the food businesses. I called on produce wholesalers, sausage makers, and specialty food importers. There were candy manufacturers and juice juicers and meat distributors. There were bakeries, one of which had a super-duper pie-making machine where you essentially poured all the ingredients in one end and waited for the pie to come out the other. Just like the Jetsons. There was even a caviar distributor. Hell would have to freeze over before they bought a computer, but if I stopped by at the right time in the afternoon, I could usually get a sample.

And then there was the Modesto Poultry company. I never called on them because, geographically, they weren't in my territory, but I saw their trucks go by all the time (reading trucks is one of the habits you develop when you sell to wholesalers). I always thought somebody at that company must enjoy his job, because the motto on their trucks was "Poultry in Motion." To this day, I can't carry a chicken home from the store without smiling to myself. Poultry in motion.

Talking Turkey

My relationship with turkey is the classic one of familiarity breeding contempt (on my part, that is; no one has asked a turkey's opinion). Nearly every festive family occasion for the last thirty-eight years has featured roast turkey; the cook for every one of those occasions has been me. I figure one hundred turkeys, give or take a few, have died just so that the

Haspels would have a place to sit and fight about politics. No substitutions were permitted. It had to be a turkey. How can you call your brother a purveyor of pernicious cant unless you can wave a drumstick at him while you're doing it?

So for many years I didn't really take turkeys seriously as food. They were holiday props. I considered the dark meat worthy of a certain minimal respect, but my interest in turkey breast went only so far as to wonder why anyone would want to eat it. Hence the following conversation with my daughter:

TAMAR: Mom, I roasted my turkey upside down and the white meat was really good, not dry at all. You should try it. Just . . .
MOM: Never mind. I never touch the stuff and Dad *likes* it dry.

That was then. Circumstances have since forced me to produce meals extremely low in saturated fat. I have confronted the virtues of turkey breast. There are two: 1) It contains only about 1 gram of fat per ounce. 2) My husband likes it.

I have found that there are ways to make turkey breast more flavorful. Unfortunately, nearly all of them, including roasting your turkey upside down so that the fat in the lower regions runs into the breast, involve adding fat. But unless you have someone in your family, as I have, who must restrict fat intake severely and who *likes* it dry anyway, roasting upside down is a reasonable option. Turkey's fairly low in fat throughout. Your bird will emerge looking like a victim of the Inquisition with iron grill marks on its pale pathetic breast, but if you turn it over for the last half hour of roasting its appearance will improve somewhat. James Beard recommends roasting it upside down for the first hour, then for 45 minutes on each side, with the rest of the time right side up. I'm not even tempted to try that. It's too hard to handle a large turkey in a hot oven.

I subscribe to the relatively low-temperature (325°F) theory of turkey roasting. It seems to me that this method produces a more tender bird than high-temperature roasting. The bird also looks more attractive and smells better while it's in the oven. On festive occasions such cosmetic virtues are not to be despised. There is a downside here. The turkey is likely to dry out—something it can ill afford to do. This effect can be mitigated, however, by some fairly simple measures. Chief among them is taking care not to overroast. Bad jokes aside, I do try to take care of my turkeys—even their Styrofoam breasts. I see people eating them, so I know they're food. All food, even the two or three things in the world I'd rather not eat, puts me on my cook's mettle. My turkeys have been widely praised—sometimes even by people who weren't bound to me by ties of love or kinship.

The following sequence of steps has evolved in my kitchen over the years with the help of a few suggestions from the likes of James Beard and Julia Child.

STEP 1: A TURKEY IN YOUR FUTURE? THINK STUFFING.

Make a lot of bread crumbs. You'll need about 10 to 12 cups. About half of these should be fine crumbs made in the blender or food processor and half should be ¼ inch cubes. For several weeks prior to Turkey Day save odds and ends of bread. Don't discard the crusts. Any decent bread is fine—the more different kinds the better. Just remember that some whole-grain breads contain quite a lot of sweetener. You don't want your stuffing to taste of honey, so use such breads judiciously. If you're efficient, you'll make crumbs from the bread *before* you stick it into the freezer. If you're not, at least cut it into pieces small enough for the food processor. Stuffing half a loaf of stale frozen bread into your turkey in a solid chunk will probably not produce a satisfactory result.

There are stuffings other than bread stuffings, but not in my family. And I've been able to reduce the fat in my bread stuffing to a remarkably low level without generating complaints. If your family has its own traditional nonbread stuffing, however, I suggest you not switch to mine. You may think your daughter is a wild-eyed radical, but just try changing your turkey stuffing and she'll turn into Anita Bryant before your eyes. But you too can probably cut back on the fat. Most stuffing recipes contain more fat than is optimal for taste, let alone health. They were developed in northern Europe and America at a time when few herbs and spices were available or widely used. Butter, bacon fat, and cream were the chief weapons in a very small arsenal of flavor enhancers. Take a look at the stuffing recipe on page 244 with its suggestions for flavoring agents and textural variations.

If you're very concerned about pathogens spreading from the turkey to the stuffing, and thence to the intestines of your family, you can cook all your stuffing in a casserole. It will take about half an hour at 325°F. I think, however, not only that stuffing tastes a lot better if it's been in the bird, but that a stuffed turkey has a festive air that can't be matched by an empty one. By all means take sensible precautions. Cook your stuffing just before you put it into the turkey and then get the bird into a hot oven immediately. Also, remove all the stuffing from the carcass after the meal.

STEP 2: GET A TURKEY.

Try to get one that's fresh, i.e., not frozen. Free-range turkeys usually taste best (not always—see Turk LaLanne on page 245) but the price difference is dramatic. Just the other day I acquired a supermarket turkey, the only kind available off-season in my neighborhood. The 12-pound bird cost me $9.50! Last Thanksgiving a fancy-shmancy bird that was only slightly bigger set me back $42.

I have my own reasons for preferring free-range poultry. If I'm going to eat one of my fellow creatures, I like to think it had a decent life before I got my knife and fork into it. And I can spare $42 for luxury housing for my dinner. The $42 turkey was better, but the difference was marginal. The flavor was somewhat more intense and the texture was meatier. The most significant difference was a thicker layer of subcutaneous fat on the supermarket turkey. Much more fat was rendered during roasting than was exuded by the pricey turkey, and when I removed pieces of skin from the roasted bird a visible layer of fat still adhered to it. Birds that move around are leaner than those that don't. (Remember that the next time you don't feel like getting up for aerobics class.) I have to assume that the meat and the stuffing of el cheapo turkey absorbed more fat during roasting than that of my elite bird. However, I did notice that most of the fat was under the skin of the dark meat of the supermarket turkey. The breast meat may well be nearly as low in fat as that of its free-range cousin. I say: If the $42 causes you pain, go for the $9.50. The only turkey I've ever had that was orders of magnitude better than any other was one hand raised by a friend. Generally speaking, like you may have said about your sister's boyfriend, "Put him in a thousand-dollar suit. Buy him a seat on the Concorde. He's still a turkey!"

If you must use a frozen turkey, allow at least two days for it to thaw in the refrigerator. You can speed up this process by filling your sink with cold water and immersing the turkey (in its plastic wrapper) for several hours, but that's strictly an emergency measure.

I suggest a bird between 11 and 16 pounds. Any smaller and you'd be better off with a chicken or two. Larger ones tend to be a bit tough, not to mention hard to handle. It's no joke wrestling a hot 20-pound bird onto a platter in a kitchen where you've probably used up all available workspace with other elements of your gala meal. You'll also simplify your life considerably if you get a few ancillary pieces of equipment: a roasting pan with an adjustable rack, four or five small skewers (the kind that come with string for trussing), a bulb baster, a meat thermometer, and a gravy-skimming cup.

STEP 3: PRODUCE BROTH.
You'll use it for stuffing, basting, and gravy. If you have homemade chicken or vegetable stock around the house, fine. If not, you may want to have a can or two of chicken stock on hand. In any case, save odds

and ends of vegetables during the week prior to Turkey Day. The day before, or at least two hours before your bird will go into the oven, reach into its body cavity and remove the neck and giblets, which will doubtless be enclosed in a little bag, sometimes two little bags. Discard the liver unless you have a domestic animal salivating at your feet, or you have very low cholesterol and consider turkey liver a treat.

Place the neck, heart, and gizzard in a large saucepan along with 2 quarts of cold water or stock and trimmings from your stuffing vegetables and from your refrigerator. Don't forget the stems from the bunch of parsley you used in the stuffing. Add an onion, a carrot, and a couple of celery stalks, all coarsely chopped. Add 4 or 5 whole cloves (if you have them) and some peppercorns (which you should have). Bring to a boil and allow to simmer at least 2 hours. Now the broth is ready to deglaze your stuffing and, a bit later, to baste your turkey. Keep the pot on the stove, over a very low flame, adding more liquid occasionally if necessary.

After 3 hours or so you may want to strain out the solids. The giblets can be chopped up for the gravy if you wish. Discard the neck and vegetables. Return broth to the low heat. Do not cover. You want it to reduce, intensifying the flavor. On the other hand, you don't want it to reduce to nothing, so keep your eye on it. If it's in your way at any point, just stick it off to the side somewhere. You don't have to keep it simmering constantly. As long as you bring it back to a boil before you eat it, any nasty bacteria will die.

STEP 4: STUFF AND TRUSS.
When your stuffing (see recipe on page 244) is cool enough to handle, and you're about 5 hours—more or less, depending on the size of the bird—from the time you want to eat, take your turkey out of the refrigerator and unwrap it. Preheat your oven to 325°F. I like to put my turkey in the sink, resting on its plastic wrap, while I stuff it. This keeps it from contaminating other surfaces, a real concern with raw poultry, and the plastic catches stray bits of stuffing. Run some cold water through the cavity, reaching in to loosen any stray bits of fat or foreign objects. Dry with paper toweling. Tilt the bird in the sink, cavity up and open, and stuff. Your hands are the only appropriate tools for this operation. Pack the stuffing loosely. Truss.

Don't let trussing intimidate you. All it really means is that you should find a way to keep the limbs of the turkey from flopping around and the stuffing from falling out. People who butcher turkeys have wised up in recent years and have made this fairly easy. Most often you will find the legs of your turkey held close to the body with a flap of skin. Simply remove the ends of the legs from the flap while you stuff and replace them in the flap when you've finished. Unless you're an extraordinarily neat person, you'll find this is adequate both to hold in the legs and contain the stuffing.

The extraordinarily tidy can sew up the cavity. This can be done with a sturdy needle and heavy-duty thread. It's also possible to purchase skewers and string for this purpose where kitchen supplies are sold. They come in sets on a little card with a picture of a roasted turkey on it. You can't miss them. It's a good idea for even the extraordinarily sloppy to obtain one of these sets. They're very useful for the other end of the turkey.

Once the leg end of the turkey is well secured, turn it over so that the small neck cavity is tilted up. If you can manage it, you want the breast facing away from you. However, it may be safer to lay the turkey on its side in the sink and stuff from that angle. When you've loosely filled the breast cavity, pull the flap of skin that covers it fairly tightly over the back of the turkey and secure it with one or two skewers. If you've neglected to acquire skewers, simply tie a piece of string around the turkey, securing both the skin flap and the wings close to the body.

Carefully transfer the turkey to a rack in a roasting pan. You're in luck if your rack is a V-shaped adjustable one. You can bring the sides up close to the sides of the turkey. It will hold everything in place and cover a multitude of trussing sins.

Rub the breast with a small amount of canola or olive oil. This prevents scorching at an early stage.

Get the beast into the oven and discard the plastic wrapper and paper towels and anything else you can't wash that touched the raw turkey. Clean your work area thoroughly with soap and water. Wash your hands well.

Collapse for an hour.

STEP 5: ROAST AND BASTE.

After about an hour, check your turkey. Probably nothing much is happening, but if there's any sign of browning at this stage, it's a good idea to cover the bird loosely with a sheet of foil, shiny side up. If you keep it tented during most of the roasting period it will require less basting. Just don't make the tent airtight so that the bird ends up in a steam bath rather than a sauna. (Actually, anything as large as a turkey will be exposed to quite a lot of steam in a space as small as your oven. Don't worry about it. We do our best with the tools we've got.) If you tent after the first hour you can safely ignore the beast for another half hour or so.

About 1½ hours into the roasting process, you'll want to start to baste. Remember the pan of broth. It's time to return it to the top of the stove. Strain out the solids if you haven't already done so. Using a bulb baster, baste the turkey with the broth. Once every 20 minutes or so is about right. When a lot of broth, fat, and turkey juices have accumulated in the roasting pan, get your basting liquid from there.

About 3 hours into the roasting process—less for a smallish bird— remove the foil. You want your turkey to get nicely browned. At this point add about a cup of water or stock to the pan to extend the juices.

Your 11- to 16-pound stuffed turkey will probably be done in about 3½ to 4 hours. How can you tell? It looks done. It smells done. It has exuded brown juices into the roasting pan. The legs are loose in their sockets. If you cut the skin where the thigh joins the body, the juice will run fairly clear. A meat thermometer inserted in the thickest part of the breast will register between 162°F and 170°F.

Remove the bird from the oven, cover it loosely with the same foil you used in the oven, and let it rest at least half an hour before carving.

STEP 6: GRAVY.

Gravy is not a low-fat food. It just isn't. Forget about imitation gravies— stocks thickened with flour and cornstarch. They can make you lose your will to live. What I'm going to propose is low-fat by gravy standards, but it tastes like real gravy. Begin by pouring the fat and juices left in the roasting pan through a strainer into your gravy-skimming cup. (If you don't have one, use a fairly small, narrow jar.) To deglaze your roasting pan, use ½ cup of either turkey broth or a dry wine. Quickly bring the liquid to a boil in the roasting pan, scraping to loosen the drippings. Boil for 2 to 3 minutes, stirring and scraping constantly. Gradually add 2 tablespoons flour (browned flour, see page 133, is good for this but not necessary) and cook, stirring constantly, for 3 to 5 minutes. Gradually add 2 cups stock to the roasting pan and bring to a boil. Pour the hot liquid into a saucepan and continue to simmer over low heat. Add the defatted juices you skimmed from the roasting pan. (If you use a jar rather than a gravy-skimming cup, reach into the bottom with your bulb baster and suction up as much of the juice as possible. If you have no bulb baster, consider saving the juices for a second round of gravy. Refrigerate the jar and you'll be able to spoon off the hardened fat tomorrow. In that case, add a cup or so of stock to the saucepan. Use canned chicken stock if that's all you've got.) Taste for seasoning. A little salt and some freshly ground pepper, perhaps even a shot of Worcestershire sauce, may well be needed. If you like objects in your gravy, cut up the giblets from the broth or add some sautéed mushrooms. Cook over low heat for at least 5 minutes, stirring frequently, to meld the flavors.

By now your turkey should be ready to carve. Find someone else to do it. No cook should have to carve. Enlist Man the Hunter. Bon appétit!

TURKEY STUFFING
Enough for a 12-pound turkey (10 to 12 servings)

2 to 4 cups sliced firm vegetables
     Mandatory: 1 cup onion, ½ cup celery
     Optional: Carrots, garlic, mushrooms (shiitake preferred), bell peppers, fennel, celery root, chestnuts
1 tablespoon canola or olive oil
1 cup turkey broth (see Step 3 in Talking Turkey, page 240)
1 small bunch Italian parsley, stemmed, leaves chopped
Suggested herbs: 1 tablespoon fresh sage, or 1 teaspoon dried (traditional and highly desirable), thyme, and/or oregano
½ to 1 teaspoon freshly ground black pepper
½ to 1 teaspoon fennel seeds (optional)
10 cups bread crumbs (see Step 1 in Talking Turkey, page 239)

1. About an hour before you plan to stuff your bird, start preparing the stuffing. Slice all the vegetables. The slicing blade of your food processor works well for this.
2. Heat the oil in a large nonstick skillet over medium heat. Add the vegetables and sauté, stirring frequently, until wilted, about 10 minutes. When the vegetables show a tendency to burn or stick (and they will), add an ounce or so of stock. A bulb baster is ideal for this, especially if your stock is cooking while you're making your stuffing.
3. Add the herbs and spices. Reduce the heat slightly and add the bread crumbs, about a cup at a time, alternately with small amounts of stock. Toss to combine crumbs and vegetables, keeping the mixture slightly moist as you work. If not all the crumbs will fit in the skillet, finish mixing in a large bowl off the heat.
4. Stuff the turkey as soon as the stuffing is cool enough to handle. Stuffing that doesn't fit into the turkey can be baked in an uncovered casserole dish. Moisten with an ounce or two of stock and bake at 350°F for about 30 minutes.

380 calories, 4 grams fat, 1 gram saturated fat per serving of 12

TURK LALANNE

A COUPLE OF YEARS AGO, we shifted the venue of family dinner from my parents' house to mine. There were a couple of reasons for this. First, I have more places to sit. My parents' apartment doubles as their aerobics studio because their personal trainer, Lori, comes twice a week to put them through a vigorous workout. To facilitate that, Mom and Dad try to keep their furniture to a minimum. They have only one and a half real chairs. The full chair is a recliner they've had for thirty-five years, during which it has suffered at least five reupholsterings and countless child- and pet-related indignities. The half chair is a fold-up job that consists of black padded fabric held to a collapsible metal frame with thick black elastic. At least the elastic used to be black. Soon after they bought the chair, the elastic started to break. Some of it had to be replaced, but my father couldn't find black elastic to make the repairs, so he settled for white. This makes the chair look silly, but it works fine. On the plus side, the white elastic has already turned gray, and is well on its way to black, whereupon it will match the rest of the chair.

I don't have a personal trainer, so I am free to furnish my living room with esoteric amenities like a couch.

The other reason we use my house is that my kitchen is just a little bit bigger than Mom's. No one who's ever been to my house thinks that my mother's kitchen could possibly be smaller, but then they go to her house and become true believers. My slightly larger kitchen houses a slightly larger oven which can, in turn, house a slightly larger turkey, so we cook at my house.

The first year we did this, Mom and I divided dinner responsibilities so that we each had absolute control over part of the meal and we'd never have to be in the kitchen at the same time. I took dessert and clean-up. She took everything else. (Come on, she *is* the mom.) Once the pies were cooling on what we euphemistically refer to as the sideboard (it's really the radiator cover), Mom took over with the turkey. She made the dressing, stuffed the bird, and put it in my slightly larger oven. We sat down with the newspaper and waited for that tantalizing beginning-to-cook turkey smell.

Sure enough, after about an hour we started to smell it, but it wasn't quite right. And the noise wasn't right either—there was none of the crackling you hear as fat starts to render out of the bird. When we opened the door, we realized why that was. There was no fat in the bird to begin with.

I mean this literally. There were no drippings in the pan. There was no glistening on the skin of the bird. This "free-range" turkey had obviously taken advantage of its freedom to reduce its body fat to almost nothing. We assumed it had done this with a rigorous combination of diet and exercise and, perhaps taking a cue from my free-range parents, had gotten itself a personal trainer. And so we named the bird after legendary bodybuilder Jack LaLanne.

One of the reasons turkey is so popular with the health conscious, of course, is its low fat content, but what little fat there is makes it possible to distinguish turkey from Styrofoam. No fat, no distinction.

Mom saved the turkey. She basted it constantly and injected olive oil under its skin. She made gravy from what little drippings there were combined with the cooked giblets and some leftover chicken stock. Not only was the bird edible, my father even thought it was good. He didn't notice that it squeaked between his teeth.

The ABC of Moral Reasoning: A Pig-Girl's Manifesto

Uncle Frank looked down at the platter from which he had just taken the last rasher of bacon. "So," he asked, "is that the last of Cornelius?"

"Just about," said Aunt Dag, giving him a look implying that the fate of Cornelius might be in store for *him* at a fairly early date.

Uncle Frank gave me a worried glance. He and I both knew what my aunt's look meant: "Not in front of the child!"

"Barbara knows where bacon comes from. She wasn't born yesterday. Right?" He turned to me anxiously for confirmation. He was a man of infinite kindness and the idea that he might have distressed me was a prospect even worse than his wife's wrath.

"Sure," I replied, poker-faced, determined to endure adult scrutiny and give nothing away. Not for the world would I have confessed to what I instantly recognized as rank stupidity. Every summer when I arrived at the farm from the city, there was a new pig. Where had I thought they all went? I had read about children who had ruined everyone's Christmas dinner when they suddenly learned they were chowing down on Tom, the pride of the poultry yard—the good old bird that had eaten corn from their hands. I had felt nothing but contempt for such wimps. Besides, I didn't want to get Uncle Frank into trouble.

Cornelius had been the pig of the previous summer. Caring for him had been my favorite chore. I had hauled out the kitchen slops and giggled at his joy in consuming them—it was easy for me to feel kinship with an enthusiastic eater. I had spent hours scratching his back with sturdy sticks that I'd scrounged for the purpose. But this year I was performing the same services for Damian! Why had I never come to the obvious conclusion? How could I have been so dumb?

I guess my excuse was that I learned about the pig succession when I was too young to be analytical. By the time I was ten, it was just part of my general knowledge. I had met Xerxes when I was four. The next year I became acquainted with Yousef. Then there was Zachariah, and I was too interested in the alphabetical progression of names to question the fate of the animals. It fascinated me that Uncle Frank had been farming so long that he'd gone through the whole alphabet and come back to the beginning.

The years had passed; Abednego and Benjamin had come and gone. My responsibilities had expanded, and the summer of Cornelius found me big enough to carry largish buckets of slops out to the pig enclosure. So Cornelius became my special friend. I was even allowed to let him follow me to the little pine grove behind the chicken yard when I read there after supper. He rooted among the pine cones or lay at my feet like a dog while I scratched his back.

But this was the year of Damian and time for me to ponder the realities of the carnivorous lifestyle. It was clear to me right away that If you were going to eat pigs—or any other creature, it made no sense to make exceptions for your friends. A pig was a pig. I was sure all pigs must have friends. No one I knew had more than a few pigs and they all had names and got respect.

The possibility of not eating pigs never occurred to me. I had heard that bread was the staff of life, but I thought that was just someone's odd whimsy. The staff of life was meat. When Chuck and I reminisce about our respective youths in St. Paul and get to the kind of snack on which we spent our allowances during the hungry years between ten and thirteen, he remembers fifty-cents' worth of day-old doughnuts (that was a lot of doughnuts back in olden times), but I remember plunking down my half-dollar for a bag of six White Castle hamburgers. At ten, if I had even heard of the existence of vegetarians, I certainly considered them as exotic as whirling dervishes or men who lay on beds of nails.

So I concluded that the only thing to be done for animals whose lives were going to be tragically foreshortened was to make them as happy as possible while they were among us. Damian's quality of life, of course, was my personal responsibility. I was the one who fed him and supplied him with companionship. You will understand that I led a very happy and sheltered life when I tell you that the need to brighten Damian's brief earthly sojourn was the most onerous moral burden I had borne in all my ten years.

Damian was not an easy pig to love. Cornelius had been quiet, well-mannered, and meditative—the perfect companion for quiet evenings in the pine grove. Damian was restless—much given to aggressive rooting and sudden loud snorts. He was also fond of poking me with his snout when he wanted my attention, occasionally knocking me down. By the end of the summer he was quite large and I was a little afraid of him. He would never have injured me deliberately, but he seemed totally oblivious to his own weight and strength. As pigs went, Damian was no rocket scientist. Still, I persevered.

"Damian would really like some of that," I would say, and Uncle Frank would often hand over an extra ear or two of corn, only grumbling that his was the only pig in the world with a lawyer. (Aunt Dag, on the other hand, usually replied, "So would we, dear," and consigned whatever kitchen tidbit I had my eye on to the refrigerator.) Fortunately, I had not read *Charlotte's Web,* and the makers of *Babe* had probably not yet been born. If I could have imagined an alternative destiny for Damian, I would undoubtedly have taken on even more demanding pig-related tasks: pro-pig propaganda and special pig training.

As it was, I neglected my friends at the farm next door just to hang out with that obnoxious pig. After all, I reasoned, Lois and Arlette probably weren't destined to die over the winter. I parted from Damian that fall with decidedly mixed feelings. I was truly sorry he was going to become pork, but I couldn't claim I would miss him. I had done my best for him, but I was beginning to suspect that my best was more than he was equipped to appreciate.

By the next summer, I was ready to treat Ethan more casually. He was a nice pig, I took good care of him, and we got along fine, but I didn't feel I owed him inordinate compensation for his pending premature demise. After all, he didn't know it was coming. Just a nice normal piggy life struck me as being good enough.

I would like to claim to be a more succinct moral reasoner now than I was when I was ten. Oh, my knowledge of vegetarianism has expanded and my metabolism has slowed down to the point where eschewing meat seems like a viable option. I guess that makes my present position even more wishy-washy than the one I reached while I sat on the fence keeping Damian company.

Get a load of my ringing moral statement (sure to be embraced by all crusaders for animal rights): I don't want any creature I eat to have led a miserable life. I avoid all red meat most of the time and veal entirely. Whenever possible, I buy free-range chickens and turkeys. And I don't want several sentient lives to have been extinguished to make my dinner. About ten years ago I ordered quail in a restaurant and was appalled to see the corpses of four birds on my plate. Oh, I ate them. Not to have eaten them would have added gratuitous waste to excessive carnage. But since then I have mostly consumed small pieces of large animals, although I make an exception for fish and shellfish, for which I can't summon up very much fellow feeling. Mostly I eat vegetables. Nothing dies, and they're better for me anyway.

10.

Something Fishy

Very Finny! A Glimpse of Basic Fish Cookery

JUST ABOUT ANY KIND OF FISH IS GOOD FOR YOU. The lean ones are very lean and the fats in the fatty ones are omega3 fatty acids, which seem to be useful in preventing coronary artery disease. So mastery of a variety of methods for cooking these creatures can make meals in a flesh-eating household more nutritious.

We've all heard the standard advice about fish: It should be impeccably fresh and never overcooked. The first requirement is pretty much a matter of finding a fishmonger you can trust. There are lots of bargains in the world, but few of them are in seafood. Usually the best fish store in town is also the priciest. So you blow your week's food budget on a piece of fish and all the way home you worry lest you ruin it. It's enough to make you settle for rice and beans again. Often, however, a successful seafood meal is just a matter of a proper match between method of preparation and the particular fish you've acquired.

Maybe you've been afraid of cooking fish because you're not sure how to tell that it's done. But it's easy to test fish for doneness. The flesh separates naturally as it cooks, and all you have to do is gently pry it apart at the thickest point and peer in. When it's opaque, it's done. That's how all successful fish chefs cook, including the ones in four-star restaurants. There are no magic fish-cooking times.

Here you have a distillation of my own experience and that of James Peterson, the author of an extraordinarily useful book entitled simply *Fish and Shellfish.* Naturally, I've confined myself to the cooking methods that require little or no added fat. The guide below is by no means exhaustive. If you want exhaustive, get Peterson's book. I don't always agree with him, and I find some of his recipes needlessly fussy. (But then, whose recipes *don't* I find needlessly fussy?) The book, unfortunately, lists at forty dollars (no bargains in seafood *books* either); but it explains fish cookery in such detail that you won't be afraid to tackle modes of preparation you've never tried. It includes a finfish dictionary that will help you identify and cook any fish you might meet in your market, and additionally provides you with a lot of fishy lore with which to regale your friends and family if they don't like dinner.

Grilling. If your grill is the old-fashioned charcoal kind, buy the briquettes that light right up without lighter fluid. Let them burn for at least 20 minutes before you cook to rid them of all chemical odor. We think the fancy stuff to throw on the fire—expensive wood chips, vine clippings— is a waste of money. None of us can discern any taste advantage in the finished dish, although the fire does smell good.

Avoid the trauma of turning delicate fish on the grill by using a grilling basket. Marinate your fish briefly in a little olive oil (add a little white wine and some herbs if you like), or just spray it with a thin layer of cooking spray, and put it in the basket. Position whole fish or thick fillets (¾ to 1 inch) about 4 inches from the coals, thinner steaks or fIllets about 6 inches. James Peterson says whole fish take about 10 minutes per inch at the thickest point, steaks and fillets about 6 minutes. We've found ours take nearly twice that long, and we cook our fish until it's barely opaque. He must achieve a much hotter fire. If you've got a covered grill, don't use the cover when you cook fish. Foods with short cooking times get a sooty taste when covered.

BEST BETS: Any whole fish, fish steaks, or thick, firm-fleshed fillets, preferably with the skin on one side (score the skin with a knife before you cook as sometimes it shrinks). Wild striped bass fillets are superb grilled.

Broiling. A poor substitute for grilling, especially if, like me, you have a cheap wimpy stove and the broiler doesn't get very hot. I would really only consider this method for a thick fish steak—something that would brown in my broiler before it dried out. As you would for grilling, marinate your fish or spray it with a little oil. Then place it on a piece of aluminum foil (so you won't get an awful fishy mess) and put it—if it's a steak an inch or so thick—on the broiler pan about 3 or 4 inches from the heat. Turn after about 5 minutes, cook the second side 3 minutes more, and then crouch down on the floor to check for doneness every 30 seconds or so until you're satisfied. Next time maybe you should light the grill.

BEST BETS: Steaks of halibut, swordfish, tuna, salmon, or other firm fish.

Sautéing/Pan-Frying. This method is dead-easy and, in a nonstick pan, requires only a teaspoon or two of olive oil (there's no need to use your best extra-extra-virgin for this), most of which can be patted off the fish with a paper towel when it's done. Dry the fillets thoroughly, sprinkle both sides with salt and pepper, and slide them into the hot pan as soon as the oil is hot enough so you see ripples on its surface. James Peterson suggests moving the sauté pan back and forth while adding the fish so that it's moving over the surface of the hot pan for the first 5 or 10 seconds of cooking. I'm more likely to maneuver it gently with a plastic spatula. A fillet half an inch thick will cook in about 6 minutes; turn it after 3 minutes and watch it closely thereafter. If your fillets are very thin and delicate, cook them for 2 minutes on one side and, instead of turning them over, turn off the heat, cover the pan, and let them steam to finish cooking. Fish prepared in this way is a good foil to a meal that is otherwise spicy and assertive. Salsa, in my opinion, is its best sauce.

BEST BETS: Any relatively thin, skinless fillets.

Poaching. Fish is poached by simmering it gently in just enough liquid to cover. If you like this method of preparation, a fish poacher—a long pan with a rack inside—is a great amenity.

A simple vegetable broth is the best liquid for fish poaching. Just chop up a couple of onions and carrots, along with some celery and/or part of a fennel bulb. Put them in about 4 cups of water. Add some herbs like thyme and parsley and simmer for about 20 minutes. Then add a cup or so of white wine and simmer for 10 minutes more. This makes enough for about 1½ pounds of fish. Once the fish is in the broth, you can add a little boiling water if you need to. Fish broth—or just plain old water—can also be used as poaching liquid.

Slide the fish into the simmering liquid, being sure to have a plan for getting it out again. I use two pairs of kitchen tongs to lift the rack out of the fish poacher. If you're poaching without a rack, form a long strip of aluminum foil, folded so that it's thick enough to support the fish. Place the fish on the foil in the pan and use the ends of foil as handles to lift the fish when it's done. If you have no removal plan when your fish begins to cook, you have about 8 to 10 minutes per inch of its thickness to think of one.

BEST BETS: Salmon, cod, or grouper fillets—thick enough to be fairly sturdy—or any whole fish that will fit in your poacher.

Steaming. Quick and easy. Only moist air touches the fish. James Peterson recommends a large couscoussière as the best utensil for steaming fish, but a less expensive option is a set of those Chinese bamboo steamers that you can stack on top of each other. These are handy because you can steam vegetables in the bottom layer of the steamer and put the fish above them. It's best to use as little liquid as possible for steaming fish, because then it's possible to boil it down to concentrate the flavor, add some herbs and spices, and either use it to sauce the fish or freeze it for some later date when you need fish stock. Just be sure there's not so little liquid that it boils away. I've found that a fillet about half an inch thick steams in about 5 or 6 minutes. Peterson suggests 8 minutes for each inch of thickness for a whole fish, but I think 10 minutes may be more realistic. After the first 5 minutes, check your fish often.

BEST BETS: Sturdy fillets—snapper, blackfish, and striped bass are good choices—about ½ inch thick, or any whole fish that will fit into your steamer, such as sea bass, grouper, snapper, or tilapia.

Baking/Roasting. This is one of the easiest—and least time-critical—methods of fish preparation. Fish cooks fairly slowly in the oven, so you have a bigger window of opportunity between raw and dry. Preheat your oven to 400°F, rub your fish with olive oil, add some pepper and a few herbs if you want, and place it in a lightly oiled pan. Allow about 15 minutes per inch of thickness for fillets, a little more for whole fish.

As a variation, try cooking a whole fish in one of those baking bags with some aromatic vegetables and a little wine or broth. Preheat your oven to 375°F and bake 15 to 20 minutes for each inch of thickness. You can also make individual servings sealed in parchment or foil, but you should sauté your vegetables first, as the cooking time will be fairly short—about 8 minutes at 400°F for ½-inch-thick fillets.

BEST BETS: Anything but the most delicate, thin fillets.

LOOKING YOUR FISH IN THE EYE

Nothing is easier than cooking a cleaned whole fish. You just put it down anywhere it'll fit—on the grill, in the oven, in the poacher—and turn the heat on. It's not nearly as likely as fillets to overcook, as the presence of the whole skin, the head, and all the bones helps to preserve its moisture. Choosing it at the fish store is also easy. You can see right away if its eyes are bright and its skin is shiny and taut. Even if you don't want to cook your fish whole, it is still best to buy it that way and have the fishmonger fillet it for you. It should look as much like a live fish as possible, hence the potential discomfort.

James Peterson says he finds a whole fish without its head a little depressing. I must admit that I am a little depressed by a whole fish *with* its head. (No, let's call things by their right names. What I am is a little *squeamish*.) When dealing with a whole fish, I have been known to cover the head with a lettuce leaf or a paper towel. Occasionally, I do delve into the cooked head of a fairly large fish to extract the cheeks, but most often I decapitate it the moment it is cooked and toss the head into the garbage pail, greatly relieved by its disappearance.

On a few occasions in the remote past, I obtained fish heads for making stock. The stock was good, but I didn't enjoy preparing it. In addition to its having what seemed to be at least a thousand eyes that stare up at you from the pot (I actually closed my eyes while I strained it), fish stock smells up your house. Even though its cooking time is fairly short, the odor can linger for hours. Fishmongers, who have plenty of fish heads and bones just lying around, and whose premises already smell of fish, seem to have plugged in to the demand for instant fish stock. These days, in New York City, I buy mine at Citarella's (Broadway and 75th) or Jake's (Broadway and 89th). If your fishmonger hasn't moved with the times, I suggest substituting chicken or vegetable stock (perhaps mixed with some bottled clam juice) in recipes that call for fish stock.

One Fish, Two Fish, Monkfish, Bluefish

Monkfish and bluefish are two of the most distinctive denizens of the deep. When you tackle these guys, you can forget almost all of what we've told you about fish cookery so far. They are both much more forgiving of cooking errors than most fish, which may be why Tamar and I like them so much.

MONSTER OF THE DEEP

If you've ever heard anything about monkfish, you've probably heard one, or maybe both, of two things: They're ugly and they taste like lobster. The first is true. The second is not, although I can see how such a rumor got started.

First, the ugliness. I didn't think I'd ever seen a monkfish, but then I read that it's also called an anglerfish and realized I'd seen them in aquariums. Now I know why they only sell the fillets at the fish market; this is one scary-looking fish. It's very spiny and its head is bigger than its body—the kind of anatomy we usually associate with space aliens. Fortunately, by the time any of us are likely to see it, the monkfish has been decapitated, scaled, cleaned, and cut into nice, benign fillets.

Now, what about this lobster business? Eating monkfish, it's easy to see why it's compared to lobster. It's much firmer and more succulent than other white fishes, and its texture is closer to lobster than sole or snapper. The taste, however, is mild and fishy, and nothing like lobster.

The nonfishy nature of monkfish's texture needs to be taken into account in deciding how to cook it. While pan-frying is great for a quick-cooking flaky fish, monkfish requires cooking times too long for convenient pan-frying. Roasting, steaming, and poaching, however, all work well.

Be warned that whatever the cooking method, monkfish tends to curl up as it cooks. If it curls too much, the inner part of the curl won't cook all the way through. To avoid this, score the thickest parts of long fillets before cooking.

There's another reason it's good to be forewarned of monkfish's curling tendency—it can be startling. I remember a dinner many years ago when a boyfriend of mine decided to cook monkfish. He marinated it and put it in a pan in the oven to roast. After the prescribed 25 minutes, he opened the oven door, let out a sound that could only be described as a squawk, and shut the door again—quickly. The monkfish fillets had been particularly long and thin, and as they cooked they curled up until they resembled giant white worms. Under no circumstances could he be induced to eat them, and we went out for Chinese. He didn't last long.

ROASTED MONKFISH WITH MUSHROOMS
Makes 4 to 6 servings

2 pounds monkfish fillets

½ cup all-purpose flour

½ teaspoon freshly ground black pepper

2 teaspoons olive oil

3 garlic cloves, chopped

2 shallots or scallions, chopped

¾ pound mushrooms (shiitakes work well
    but regular mushrooms are just fine), sliced

¼ cup balsamic vinegar

1 cup fish or chicken stock

½ teaspoon sugar (optional)

¼ cup chopped Italian parsley

1. Preheat the oven to 425°F. Lightly oil a roasting pan.
2. Trim the monkfish, removing the translucent membrane and, if you find them offensive, any dark purple sections. Score the fillets if you're frightened by curled-up fish.
3. Mix the flour and pepper on a plate and lightly coat the fish fillets with it.
4. Heat 1 teaspoon of the olive oil in a large nonstick skillet over medium heat. When it's hot, add the monkfish and sear until slightly browned on all sides, another 5 minutes or so. Put the monkfish in the roasting pan and roast in the oven until it is opaque in the center, about 20 minutes.
5. Meanwhile, add the remaining olive oil to the same skillet. Add the garlic and shallots and sauté over medium heat until they're soft, about 5 minutes. Add the mushrooms and sauté until they begin to re- lease their liquid, about 5 minutes. Add the vinegar and about half of the fish stock and simmer for about 10 minutes more. By then, the fish should be just coming out of the oven.
6. To finish the sauce, taste it. If it's too acidic, add the sugar. If there's not enough liquid, add a little more stock (you may not need it all). Just before serving, toss in the parsley and pour the sauce over the fish.

160 calories, 4 grams fat, 1 gram saturated fat per serving of 6

MONKFISH AND PEPPER SALAD
Makes about 4 servings

> 1½ pounds monkfish
> Juice of 1 lime
> 3 teaspoons grated fresh ginger
> 1 yellow bell pepper, chopped
> 1 red bell pepper, chopped
> 2 ripe medium tomatoes, chopped
> ¼ cup chopped fresh cilantro
> ¼ cup rice vinegar
> Freshly ground black pepper to taste

1. Trim the monkfish, removing the translucent membrane and any dark purple sections. Cut it into medallions about ¾ inch thick. Combine the monkfish with the lime juice and 2 teaspoons of the ginger. Let it marinate in the refrigerator for at least 1 hour.
2. Remove the monkfish from the marinade and steam it until it's opaque in the center, about 10 minutes. Combine the monkfish, remaining 1 teaspoon of ginger, the bell peppers, tomatoes, cilantro, vinegar, and pepper in a large bowl. Chill.

N O T E : This salad can be made using any firm white fish. Just shorten the cooking time. Precooked, leftover fish also makes a good salad. Instead of marinating the fish, use the lime (combined with a little olive oil) for dressing. Reduce the ginger to 1 teaspoon.

160 calories, 3 grams fat, 0 grams saturated fat per serving

BLUEFISH

The ugliness of the monkfish's physiognomy is more than matched by that of the bluefish's disposition. A work entitled *American Food and Game Fishes* by Jordan and Evermann, published at the beginning of the century, describes the bluefish as "a carnivorous animal of the most pronounced type." They give gory details:

> It has been likened to an animated chopping-machine the business of which is to cut to pieces and otherwise destroy as many fish as possible in a given space of time. Going in large schools, in pursuit of fish not much

inferior to them in size, they move along like a pack of hungry wolves, destroying everything before them. Their trail is marked by fragments of fish and by the stain of blood in the sea.

(No, I haven't been browsing through hundred-year-old treatises on sports fishing. Jordan and Evermann are quoted by Alan Davidson in *North Atlantic Seafood.* This is a classic work—a really comprehensive guide to the fish and shellfish of the North Atlantic with lots of great fishy lore. It was originally published in 1979 and is unfortunately out of print at the moment. Watch for it at used book sales.)

The bluefish, of course, is a favorite of sports fishermen, who love to think that they're wrestling with true monsters of the deep, so descriptions like the one above should be viewed a little skeptically. There's no doubt, however, that bluefish are notably fierce and predatory. If you have trouble eating animals that seem cute and sweet, these guys should pose no problem for you.

I ate many a bluefish before I ever cooked one. Although you would hardly believe it to see him tucking into seafood these days, there were many years when my husband would eat only the mildest and whitest fish, and then only if it had a nice brown coating. So when I wanted a fish that wasn't a fried flounder or haddock, I had to order it in a restaurant. I learned that if there was bluefish on the menu, it was a good bet. Even in restaurants where there was no one in the kitchen especially skilled at fish cookery (which was virtually every restaurant in Dutchess County in the sixties and seventies), bluefish generally emerged in good condition. It's such an oily and assertive fish that it's actually rather difficult to overcook.

Chuck tried bluefish for the first time about ten years ago at a bluefish bake on Cape Cod. The fish were fastened to planks that were set at an angle around the fire so that the oil drained into it. There were a lot of flames, a lot of smoke, and, I predicted, a lot of scorched, dried-out fish. I was wrong. They were delicious—even my husband thought so. Not many fish can tolerate such treatment, but bluefish can.

I have a soft spot in my heart for food that's not delicate. When I make an error in the kitchen, I like my ingredients to forgive me. I'm especially prone to the kind of klutziness that turns lovely white fish fillets into nasty little fishy crumbs. Bluefish will forgive the grossest error. It's durable enough to be turned over—even by me—without disintegrating. And as long as it's impeccably fresh, it will taste good whether you cook it for 5 minutes or 20. If it doesn't, serve it with lots of salsa.

PAN-FRIED BLUEFISH FILLETS

Freshly filleted bluefish, 6 to 8 ounces per person (the fillets should measure about ½ inch at their thickest point)

Freshly ground black pepper to taste

1 to 2 teaspoons olive (not extra-virgin) or canola oil, or use vegetable oil spray

Salt to taste

Salsa or lemon wedges for serving

1. Dry the fillets well and sprinkle them with pepper. If they have skin on one side, score it with a knife so that its shrinkage doesn't curl the fillets as they cook.
2. Heat a nonstick skillet large enough to hold the fillets in a single layer. (If you're using oil spray, apply it to the skillet *before* heating.) Add the oil and heat over medium-high heat. When the oil is hot enough so that it ripples a little, use a plastic utensil to spread it fairly evenly over the surface of the skillet, then add the fillets, skin side down, and sauté for about 5 minutes. You should be hearing sizzling noises. If not, turn up the heat. Using a plastic pancake turner, turn the fish and cook for about 5 minutes more. Turn out on a warm platter. Sprinkle with a little salt and pepper if you wish. Serve with salsa or just wedges of lemon.

310 calories, 14 grams fat, 3 grams saturated fat per serving

A Salmon in Every Pot

I know the pickiest eater on the planet. His name is Hugo. My assertion that Hugo is the pickiest eater on the planet is often challenged. Not by people who know Hugo, but by people who know someone else they think is a better candidate for the Pickiest Eater title. If you are one of those people, let me assure you, whoever it is you have in mind is no match for Hugo.

As a rule, picky eaters are defined by the foods they won't eat. In Hugo's case, however, it's quicker and easier to list the foods he *will* eat. Here they are, all of them:

- Plain pasta (literally plain, not with garlic or olive oil and certainly not with tomato sauce)
- Plain chicken breast

- A few mild-tasting fishes
- Plain hamburgers and hot dogs (just the meat and the bun)
- French fries, French bread, French toast
- Cream cheese
- Cheerios
- Raw carrots, celery, radishes, and parsley
- Rice
- Cookies and some cakes
- Pretzels
- Raisins, apples, and bananas

You may be assuming that Hugo is six; unfortunately, it's been more than thirty years since Hugo was six. In those thirty years, a lot happened. Men walked on the moon. The Iron Curtain fell. Wolfgang Puck opened a restaurant in LAX. But Hugo still won't eat cooked vegetables.

(Let me be clear that Hugo has his good points. He is smart and cheerful, and is not without a certain charm. In fact, he's one of my best friends, and he'll stay that way as long as I don't eat with him too often.)

By now, I'm sure you've conceded that your Pickiest Eater candidate will have to settle for runner-up. Since Hugo is the clear winner, the question is, what does he win? A year's supply of egg noodles? I'd suggest a trip to a place where everyone shares his eating habits, but the only place like that I know of is kindergarten.

I propose that we standardize the measurement of picky eating, and make Hugo the Universal Standard Unit of Food Fussiness. Just as electrical current is measured in amperes, pickiness will be measured in Hugos. Hugo himself is a 1.0. Everyone else is lower. I, for example, am a .005. Your four-year-old may be a .6 or .7, but has some excuse, being four. The pickiest eater you know might rate at a .8. I doubt you know anyone who scores higher than that.

I was tempted to leave this new Standard Unit unnamed in the hopes that the powers that be would name it after me. It worked for Ampere. It also worked for Joule, who defined the unit of work, and Ohm, who defined electrical resistance. But then I thought, Why on earth would I want my name on the Universal Standard Unit of Food Fussiness? Besides, the Hugo sounds so good.

My father tells a story from his MIT days about a freshman classmate of his named Ludwig. Ludwig wasn't dumb, but somehow got a reputation for thickheadedness. One day he came home from class to find a sign on his door, courtesy of his roommate: "Home of the Universal Standard Ludwig: Unit of Stupidity." He took the sign down, but he was stuck with the label. Even as a senior, he still heard of people measuring stupidity in Ludwigs. (Ludwig, if you're out there, I hope you've finally shaken this!)

What does all this have to do with salmon? Well, even Hugo eats salmon. It is a fish with nearly universal appeal. It has a distinctive but mild, nonfishy taste. It has a pleasant, flaky texture and a nice rosy color. Because it's oily, it's a little harder to overcook than other fish, and is still edible even if it's been left on the stove or grill a little too long. It's available almost everywhere.

Even children will often eat salmon. One of my favorite children, a seven-year-old by the name of Aly, is a serious salmon devotee. One day when Aly was about four she, her father Russ, and I went to the supermarket to get dinner. We walked into the store, and Russ asked Aly what she wanted for dinner. She thought for a moment (she takes dinner seriously—a child after my own heart), and said, "Fish!" Russ said that sounded good to him, and we proceeded to the fish counter. Once there, Russ asked, "What kind of fish?" Aly surveyed the goods. "Salmon," she said. We moved toward the salmon. "Steaks or fillets?" Dad needed to know. "Fillets," said Aly, and fillets it was. (It was an exciting shopping trip. We also found an eggplant that looked exactly like Richard Nixon.)

Proof of salmon's near-universal appeal is that it is one of the few fishes that comes in a can. Canned salmon sales will never eclipse canned tuna sales, not because of any inherent inferiority in the fish, but simply because salmon doesn't can well. Tuna is a very large fish, and it's relatively easy to can a small piece of a big fish. Salmon is much smaller (and pink salmon, the kind usually canned, is the smallest type of salmon), so it's nearly impossible to get it in a can without including a certain amount of skin and bones.

One of salmon's drawbacks is that it is often expensive. Depending on the time of year and location, salmon can cost upwards of ten dollars a pound. This wasn't always the case. According to Waverley Root, when salmon was plentiful in the Atlantic it was so cheap as to be the food of choice for servants' rations. Servants, however, demanded that they not be served salmon more than a certain number of times a week. Indentured servants in America had contracts that stipulated no more than once a week. For Brittany farmworkers, it was three times a week. For hapless Norwegian servants, it was five times a week.

Times have changed, and there are neither as many salmon nor as many servants as there used to be. Salmon is now thought of simply as an excellent meal for regular people.

Be aware that salmon is among the fattiest of fish and is relatively high in calories. Most salmon has 5 to 9 grams of fat and 120 to 150 calories in a 3-ounce portion. Swordfish, by contrast, has 3 to 4 fat grams and about 100 calories. Sole has only 60 calories and almost no fat. Fish fat, however, seems to be the only kind of fat that is actually good for you, consisting of omega3 fatty acids, so there's no reason that salmon shouldn't be part of dinner for even the most stringently fat-averse.

Like most fish, salmon is easy to prepare. You can bake it or poach it or grill it, and it tastes great just plain. The only thing you have to be careful about is not to overcook it.

POACHED SALMON
Makes 4 large servings, 1 steak per person

2 cups fish or chicken stock
2 cups white wine
2 tablespoons Dijon-style mustard
Several large dill sprigs
4 salmon steaks (about 3 pounds)

1. Bring the stock, wine, mustard, and dill to a boil in a large pot. If you have a fish poacher, or a pot big enough to accommodate all the steaks in one layer, use it. If not, use a pot that will hold at least two of the steaks and poach them in shifts. Let boil for 5 to 10 minutes.
2. Turn the flame down so the mixture simmers, and add the fish. If the liquid doesn't completely cover the fish, add enough boiling water so the salmon is completely submerged. Cover the pot and let the fish simmer until it is nearly opaque in the center, 8 to 10 minutes for each inch of thickness. Serve hot, warm, or cold.

340 calories, 13 grams fat, 2 grams saturated fat per serving

BAKED SALMON
Makes 2 large servings

2 salmon steaks, about 1 inch thick
½ lemon, thinly sliced
Several fresh cilantro sprigs
⅓ cup dry white wine

1. Preheat the oven to 350°F.
2. Put a large sheet of aluminum foil on a baking sheet and place the steaks near one end of the foil. Arrange the lemon slices and coriander sprigs on top of the fish. Turn the edges of the foil up so you can add the wine without it spilling out. Once you add the wine, fold the end of the foil over so the salmon is loosely covered, then seal the edges to keep the steam in.
3. Bake for about 25 minutes, a little longer if you like your salmon opaque all the way through.

350 calories, 14 grams fat, 3 grams saturated fat per serving

FAUX STUFFED SALMON
Makes 3 or 4 large servings

1 tablespoon olive oil

1 large onion, chopped

2 garlic cloves, chopped

2 tablespoons chopped fresh basil, or 1 teaspoon dried oregano

½ pound fresh shiitake mushrooms, or ¾ pound white mushrooms, stems removed or trimmed, caps sliced

¼ cup dry unflavored bread crumbs (commercial are okay)

2 ripe plum tomatoes, chopped

¼ cup dry red wine

Salt and freshly ground black pepper to taste

2 salmon fillets, approximately the same size and shape, about 12 ounces each

Chopped fresh parsley and lemon wedges for garnish

1. Preheat the oven to 400°F.
2. Heat the oil in a large nonstick skillet. Add the onion and garlic and sauté over medium heat until slightly wilted. Add the dried oregano if using and the mushrooms; sauté slowly, stirring frequently, until the mushrooms are thoroughly cooked, about 15 minutes. Sir in the bread crumbs and then the tomatoes. Cook until the tomatoes are soft and the liquid has evaporated. Raise the heat slightly, add the wine, and cook, stirring constantly, until the mixture barely holds its shape (moist but not soupy). Remove from the heat and stir in the fresh basil if using and salt and pepper.
3. Place one salmon fillet (the larger, heavier one if there's a difference)

skin side down in a nonstick baking dish. Top with the stuffing mixture and then the second fillet skin side up. There is no need to be especially neat. Spilled stuffing can be served along with the fish.

4. Bake just until the top fillet has turned pale pink throughout, about 20 to 25 minutes. Invert the salmon onto a serving platter. The skin of the bottom fillet will be left behind, usually exposing some grayish flesh that was next to the skin. For cosmetic purposes, it's a good idea to remove the gray parts and garnish the dish with some parsley and lemon wedges. Slice all the way through both fillets to serve.

370 calories, 14 grams fat, 2 grams saturated fat per serving of 4

SMOKED

IN THE ELEVEN YEARS I LIVED IN CALIFORNIA, I ate well. San Francisco has great produce, plentiful seafood, and outstanding restaurants. Almost anything I can find in New York I found in San Francisco, although sometimes I had to look hard. The one exception was smoked fish. The only way to get good lox in San Francisco is to fly it in from New York.

One of the first things I did when I moved back to my old New York stomping grounds, the Upper West Side, was to establish myself as a regular at Barney Greengrass, the self-anointed Sturgeon King. I don't quibble with the moniker—I think Barney Greengrass does indeed have some of the best smoked fish in the city. Not just sturgeon, but lox, sable, whitefish, and kippered salmon. Everyone in my family is a regular, and we go in many permutations: Mom and me, Mom and Jake, Jake and Aaron, Mom and Dad. We all frequently bring friends.

As much as I enjoy the fish, I also enjoy the ritual of being a regular. The waiter nods and says good morning; you're part of the in-crowd. One day I went in with a friend from out of town, and Adam the waiter asked whether we wanted the usual (a platter of sable and Nova lox). I said yes, and joked that my family always eats the same things. Adam said, "Actually, sometimes your brother gets Nova, eggs, and onions." You know you're in a food-oriented family when the waiter at Barney Greengrass knows more about your brother than you do.

11.

Moo

**The friendly cow all red and white
I love with all my heart.
She gives me cream with all her might
To eat with apple-tart.**

—Robert Louis Stevenson

THROUGHOUT MY CHILDHOOD milk was the sine qua non of wholesomeness. Times have changed. Many of us look askance at milk these days. Ten years ago, after my husband's heart surgery, his doctor approached his bedside with dietary advice. I told him we already knew the drill, but Chuck, who hadn't yet learned that doctors are a poor source of nutritional information and whose brush with mortality had made him uncharacteristically humble, thought we should listen. So the doctor began the standard litany: No red meat, egg yolks, milk, or other dairy products. *"Milk!"* I interrupted. "Except skim, you mean." "Oh, yes," he replied, "skim's all right."

I wondered how many people he had misled that week, but I refrained from asking. My husband was lying right there and I wanted to keep his recovery stress-free. He was already convinced that I was getting more red meat than was good for me just by biting off the heads of members of the medical profession.

Unfortunately, lots of folks make the same assumption as Chuck's doctor—that to give up dairy fat is tantamount to giving up dairy products altogether. Consumption of milk has declined almost 30 percent in the last thirty-five years, at least partly because many people regard milk as a major source of saturated fat in the diet. They think it makes you fat and clogs up your arteries. Also, there's apparently a widespread belief that removing the fat from milk also removes nutrients. A recent survey of doctors found that nearly half of them believed that skim milk was not as good a source of calcium as whole milk. That, as we nerds say, is exactly wrong. Ounce for ounce, skim milk contains *more* calcium than whole milk. The fat is removed; but the part of the milk with all the nutrients remains. It stands to reason; it also happens to be a fact.

I know I made a solemn promise not to pack this book with Dreaded Nutritional Data, but I think that the power of dairy products is a subject that's gotten short shrift lately. You don't need anyone to tell you you're supposed to be eating your veggies, but you may not know you should also drink your milk. I worry about people who have given up or cut way back on dairy products. Low levels of calcium are linked not only to osteoporosis, but to heart disease and some cancers. It's true that there are good sources of calcium that don't originate in our friend the cow—sardines, some nuts, kale, and collards, for example. But sardines and nuts are too high in fat to eat in large quantities. As for the large leafy greens, not only do few of us eat them regularly and copiously, their calcium is not as accessible to the body as that provided by milk.

On the other hand, a recent humongous study of 4,500 Chinese has demonstrated that a dairy-free lifetime need not end in osteoporosis. In fact, the Chinese showed fewer signs of calcium deficiency than typically occur among Western dairy users. However, it may well be that someone who has always obtained calcium from vegetables develops a capacity for extracting and using it that is not present in a person who decides in mid-life to switch from milk to kale. In the case of the Chinese, this capacity might even have a genetic component. We don't know. The data is simply not there.

On yet another hand (for those of you who have three of them), a recent large study of moderately hypertensive men found that the diet most effective in controlling blood pressure was not only high in vegetables and low in saturated fat, but included three or more servings of low- or nonfat dairy products a day. (It's being touted as the DASH diet. You've probably heard of it.)

My guess is that, unless you're the kind of serious vegan who eats tons of leafy greens and calcium-enriched tofu, you're better off with milk than without it. Don't let trendy diet gurus buffalo you into believing it's not good for you. It's unnatural, they argue; no other adult animals drink milk. Well, no other animals cook their food either. Neither do they practice agriculture. Beware of trendy diet gurus. Tell them you want to see the studies that support their conclusions.

Of course, there's an additional reason lots of adults don't touch milk of any sort. It creates disorder in their lower intestines. Milk contains lactose, a sugar that requires the enzyme lactase to break it down. Once past infancy, human beings produce less and less lactase every year. By adulthood, except for those of us whose ancestors came from the big milk-drinking countries of Northern Europe, most people have very little capacity to digest lactose. But all is not lost.

The enzymes in yogurt break down lactose to some degree, so you may be able to tolerate milk in that form. Also, milk that contains lactase is now widely available, including a skim version. Most interestingly, a recent study of adults who believed they couldn't digest milk at all found that they reported no more symptoms when they consumed a daily cup of milk without added lactase than when they were given milk with the helpful enzyme. It seems that when milk consumption is kept to relatively small amounts most of us can handle it.

Another important reason to keep dairy products in your diet if you're not hypersensitive or allergic to them—or philosophically opposed to the use of all animal products—is that you probably like them. The trick is to find those your low-fat diet can accommodate. The dairy industry is partly to blame for the widespread ignorance about nonfat milk and its lean relatives. Until very recently, the dairy people have failed to keep up with the growing interest in reduced-fat products. Things are improving, however. There's a lot more good-tasting non- and low-fat dairy stuff being produced and widely distributed every year. If it's not in your supermarket, you may find it in a health food store.

I understand that people have a certain resistance to low-fat dairy products. Milk is a primal food. We know exactly how it's supposed to taste and any variation is just wrong. But the human palate is almost scarily malleable. I know whereof I speak.

GETTING ADJUSTED

"The milk tastes funny."

"You'll get used to it."

Every year of my childhood I initiated the foregoing conversation at least twice—once when I arrived at my great-aunt's farm in the spring and again when I returned to the city in the fall. It wasn't that I'd forgotten that I'd said the same thing just a few months earlier. I'm not *that* slow a learner. But I could never believe that the milk could taste quite so different from what I'd just been drinking elsewhere and still be all right. I'd never gotten used to something *this* strange, had I?

It always took about three days of nose wrinkling and being sure I had something handy to take away the taste and then, sure enough, I was used to it. That was how milk tasted. The city milk was, of course, pasteurized, the milk at the farm was not. Many gourmets maintain that pasteurization is an unfortunate necessity that has ruined the taste of milk. I wish I could say I appreciated the taste of the real live milk I drank in the summer and felt deprived back in St. Paul, but I can't. After each period of acclimatization, milk was just milk.

There were other sources of funny milk. We had milk breaks in school. The milk came in little bottles with the cream on top—more cream than I ever saw at home because my grandmother and Aunt Dag both skimmed most of it off for their coffee. I found it cloying and unpleasant but, because I was a skinny child in those days obsessed with the horrors of "underweight," my teachers virtually insisted that I drink it. So I would hold my nose and gulp it down. But, because it wasn't my primary source, I never got used to it. It always tasted funny.

Then homogenized milk came along—staunchly resisted by my grandmother because it dried up her source of coffee cream. I supported her because it tasted funny. But soon it was the only kind the milkman carried and we both adjusted.

My next milk trauma was switching from whole to skim as an adult. It was watery. It turned the coffee gray. It tasted funny. I got used to it. Whole milk tastes funny now.

Fortunately for those who are contemplating the change to nonfat dairy, the bad old days of the fearful dichotomy—good, real milk (not to mention cream, ice cream, butter, etc.) versus unpleasant, bluish-gray watery stuff—are gone. It's definitely worth your while to explore the wonderful world of the lean cows. While it's true that many dairy products—like sour cream and most hard cheeses—are unpalatable in their low-fat versions, there are a lot of skim milk products that you can learn to enjoy in less time than it took me to get used to the milk on the farm.

Moos You Can Use

Fortified Skim Milk. It hasn't got any sinister additives. It's just fortified with more skim milk; that is, milk solids. Like regular skim milk, fortified skim contains no fat, but it does contain additional nutrients: about a third more calcium and protein than the standard product. It may be sold in your area under a name like Skim Plus or Skim Delight and it will cost more than ordinary skim. But it's worth seeking out and paying a little extra for. Although ultrapasteurization gives it a slightly cooked taste that may bother you if you're a serious milk drinker, its mouth feel and appearance are superior to that of ordinary skim. It looks like milk instead of like bluish water, and it won't turn your coffee gray.

You can produce your own fortified skim milk quite easily. When you open your next quart of skim milk, pour about a cup of it into a pitcher containing ⅓ cup of nonfat dry milk solids and stir to dissolve. Add the rest of the quart and stir to mix. Then you can pour it (or nearly all of it) back in the original container if you want to. It's best to refrigerate it for a few hours before you use it. That distinctive dry milk taste and odor become less noticeable with time and thorough chilling.

Organic skim milk has recently become available in New York, and I've found that it too seems much less watery than ordinary skim, although I haven't the faintest idea why. I would never even have tried it if my son Jake hadn't recommended it. It's also fresher tasting than the fortified product.

Evaporated Skim Milk. It looks thick and rich but, not surprisingly, its prevailing flavor is that of cooked milk. Nevertheless, this is a product no low-fat kitchen should be without. Use it in any dish that you think needs a little cream. Do not use it in any dish that you think needs a lot of cream. It works in a potato-leek soup with lots of watercress, but don't try to produce a subtle vichyssoise. White clam sauce with lots of garlic and parsley is enhanced by a little evaporated skim, but you can't make a successful fettuccine Alfredo. The bottom line is that while there is no real substitute for cream, a little evaporated skim can provide some of the mellow quality that we all miss. It cuts the acidity that is the bugbear of so many low-fat dishes.

Buttermilk. Buttermilk is wonderful in soups, salad dressings, and blended fruit shakes. It's my liquid of choice for all no-fat-added pancakes. All buttermilk is low in fat, but try to find a fat-free version. Very little change in flavor or texture seems to occur in the skimming process.

Nonfat Yogurt. Nonfat yogurt may be the greatest blessing the food technologists have brought us in the last decade. Many brands taste good. Look for one with live yogurt cultures and no additives. We eat yogurt with bananas or berries, in blender fruit shakes, and with the whey removed (page 271) as the base for dips, salad dressings, and toppings for baked potatoes.

Soft Cheeses

> Many's the long night I've dreamed of cheese—toasted mostly.
>
> —BEN GUNN, IN *TREASURE ISLAND* (ROBERT LOUIS STEVENSON AGAIN!
> THIS MAN WAS A FRIEND OF THE DAIRY INDUSTRY.)

Quark (there is also a Quark that contains fat, so be careful) and Fromage Blanc are fat-free, soft, smooth, yogurt-style cheeses that are widely available and taste all right as dips or toppings for baked potatoes, fruit desserts, soups, etc. They do have a disconcerting way of just sort of sitting there when you put them on anything hot. (At least you hope they just sit there. They may elect to sit there exuding whey.) They do not soften in the manner of whole-milk products or taste like them. It's best to mix them with lots of some appropriate flavoring agent like salsa or chopped chives. The rather cloying texture is less noticeable that way. Fairway, the famous Upper West Side food market, once displayed one of these cheeses with a sign calling it "a tantalizing blend of cotton wool and library paste."

Cheese snobbery aside, great strides have been made in producing fat-free and nearly fat-free soft cheeses. (Lots of them, though, are still too slimy: watch out for the cream cheese!) If you're looking for a cheese that's not yogurty, fat-free or low-fat ricotta is fresh tasting and palatable, albeit a little wet. If you want to cook with it, de-whey it for a couple of hours using the same process that improves your yogurt (page 271). A 50/50 combination of de-wheyed yogurt and nonfat ricotta mixed with some chopped garlic, scallions, and herbs—served with lots of raw firm vegetables like cucumber, peppers, and radish—makes a great lunch. My husband finds it an acceptable stand-in for the vegetables with pot cheese and sour cream that were a staple of his misspent youth. Chuck is also passionately fond of Breakstone's small-curd tangy cottage cheese. It's very good for him: only ½ percent butterfat. As long as I don't have to eat it. *Chacun à son gout.*

Parmesan Cheese. No, the laboratory has not produced a fat-free substitute for Parmesan cheese. At least if it has, we don't want to try it. Few reduced-fat hard cheeses are worth eating. (See below for a couple of exceptions.) Parmesan isn't significantly leaner ounce for ounce than other hard cheeses, but a little of it goes a long, long way. A tablespoon of freshly grated Parmesan contains less than 2 grams of fat and will enhance your plate of pasta immeasurably. Unless you can get the real stuff, however, don't bother. If your local market offers nothing but canned Parmesan, get your fat grams somewhere else. Anybody with my kind of willpower should buy Parmesan only for company meals and in very small quantities. It's amazing what just an occasional nibble can do to half a pound of it over the course of a day or two.

Hard Cheese. There's not a whole lot of good news here on the reduced-fat front. In fact, until fairly recently, I was saying categorically that if a cheese is labeled "low fat" and you can slice it, don't buy it. But Alpine Lace Swiss doesn't taste bad, and we've recently discovered a French yogurt cheese reminiscent of Muenster that's really good. The rub is that neither of these is all that low in fat. Both contain about 4 grams to the ounce. I hereby revise my rule: If you can slice it and it has less than 3 grams of fat to the ounce and contains nondairy ingredients like vegetable gum, you don't want to take it home. However, if just a moderate reduction in fat is enough for you, experiment. You can probably find a product you like.

Low-Fat Goat Cheese (Baaaa). It's not just the cow that can provide good-tasting dairy products. Goat cheeses in general are lower in fat than those made from cow's milk. Coach Farm makes one with only 2.5 grams of fat to the ounce. This cheese is extremely flavorful and a little does a lot for a pasta dish. It's also good on bread or bagels—its consistency is a little crumbly, but the taste is excellent. In New York, I buy mine at Fairway, Zabar's, or at the Union Square greenmarket. I'm afraid it's not all that widely available, but if you want some, write to Coach Farm, Inc., Pine Plains, NY 12567, for the name of a distributor near you.

Soft-Serve Nonfat Frozen Yogurt. These are available all over and most of them taste pretty good. Honey Hill Farms and Stonyfield Farms are two of my favorites, but lots of others pass muster as well. All these yogurts are best when they contain plenty of air. If you've had some that were cloying and slimy, it may be that the vendor is making them too dense. Try different brands, different flavors, different vendors. You should be able to find something that's worth going out for on a summer evening. (WARNING: We've found all nonfat yogurts and ice creams from the supermarket's frozen-food case unacceptable. Both Tamar and I have had samples of these products hanging out in our freezer for weeks, and *that's* saying something.)

The Way to De-whey

If you shudder at the idea of a dip or a baked-potato topping without sour cream, and shudder even more at the taste and texture of the reduced-fat substitutes, you may find that nonfat yogurt can provide an acceptable alternative. Before putting it on your chips or potato, however, it's best to remove at least some of the whey. The result of this process is generally called yogurt cheese so, although it really bears very little resemblance to cheese of any sort, we'll call it that too.

Line a strainer with a double or triple layer of cheesecloth or use your cone-style coffee filter and put in enough yogurt to make the amount of cheese you want. I use Stonyfield Farms or Dannon yogurt and find that 8 ounces makes about 5 or 6 ounces of cheese. Put the strainer over a container into which the whey can drip, cover it with a piece of plastic wrap, and let it drain in the refrigerator for 6 to 24 hours, depending on how much time you have and how thick you want your cheese. Try to allow plenty of time. Watery dips and toppings are nasty.

When you make your dip or topping from this product it's best to mix in a lot of some appropriate flavoring agent—like salsa or chopped chives (a good rule of thumb is to use twice as much of whatever you're adding for flavor as you would in a full-fat dip or topping). Incidentally, vanilla-, lemon-, and coffee-flavored yogurts can all be de-wheyed by this method and make good desert toppings. But don't try to make yogurt cheese with yogurts that contain gelatin or thickeners.

There is a gadget called a yogurt cheese funnel that will perform the above task, and I find it more effective and less messy than playing around with coffee filters or cheesecloth. This device is simply a plastic funnel lined with a polymer mesh that can be used repeatedly and washed in the dishwasher. It sells for about ten dollars and is available through several mail-order cookware catalogs and in lots of big housewares departments.

I find that if I leave plain nonfat yogurt in the yogurt cheese funnel for two or three days I have an acceptable spreadable product. It can even be eaten on a bagel with lox, although I suggest using a very modest amount. Cream cheese this isn't. I also find that I can mix de-wheyed yogurt with hot foods such as risottos and pastas with much better results than I get with untreated yogurt. The flavor is more intense and you don't have to worry about your dinner being swamped in unwanted liquid.

Incidentally, if, like me, you recycle lots of your leftovers into more or less impromptu soups, don't discard the whey from your yogurt. Not only is it rich in calcium, it's often the right liquid to bring out the flavor of a rather bland set of grains and vegetables. It provides just a bit of an edge without being as assertive as vinegar. It will keep a week or so in the refrigerator.

Fruit Soups/Fruit Smoothies: Separated at Birth?

Cookbook author Melanie Barnard has given fruit soups a new twist—or at least she's publicized a shortcut a lot of us have been using for years. She uses canned fruit. This may not seem like a startling strategy to come up with on a hot afternoon, but it certainly beats cooking Bing cherries and pushing them through a food mill. Barnard blends two 16-ounce cans of apricots (liquid reserved) with a cup of plain low-fat yogurt. She adds ¼ teaspoon ground ginger, nutmeg, or cinnamon, 2 tablespoons orange liqueur, and enough of the reserved liquid to make a thick soup. She sprinkles on some mint leaves for garnish, puts the bowl in the freezer for 20 minutes, and she's got a summer dessert that would certainly pass muster in most circles. She suggests that peaches, pears, mixed fruit, and sweet cherries would work as well as apricots, but I think they'd be blander.

We consume a lot of fruit, both fresh and canned, mixed with yogurt. It's a breakfast favorite here. However, we always drink it. I freeze the fruit, put it in the blender with the yogurt (I use a ratio of approximately two parts fruit to one part yogurt, but the proportions aren't critical), and add a little honey or maple syrup, some cinnamon or nutmeg, and sometimes a little vanilla extract. Some recipes for fruit smoothies recommend using ice cubes to chill the fruit instead of freezing it. I prefer the more intense flavor and thicker consistency of an all-fruit smoothie.

Freeze your fruit in small quantities—it won't blend if it's in one big block. Small plastic yogurt containers filled about halfway can be unmolded easily and the frozen contents digested by most blenders. Fruit smoothies are a great use for less than perfect melons and over-the-hill bananas. (If you forget them in the freezer for several months they'll be dark brown and a little wizened, but they'll still taste fine in your smoothie.) When I use canned fruit I discard the liquid, which is usually low in flavor. And I always use nonfat yogurt, Stonyfield Farms being my favorite.

So drink your puréed fruit or eat it with a spoon. The choice is yours.

BANANA SMOOTHIE
Makes 1 serving

1 large banana, peeled and frozen (see Note)
⅓ cup low-fat or nonfat milk
2 tablespoons maple syrup
3 to 4 ounces vanilla yogurt

1. Put all the ingredients in a blender or food processor and process until smooth.

NOTE: Before you freeze the banana, peel it and break it into several pieces. If you just toss it, peel and all, into the freezer, you will be very sorry. Peeling a frozen banana is a thankless job. If you haven't thought far enough ahead to freeze your banana (or if you prefer your smoothies a little thinner and not as cold), you can also make this with a plain old unfrozen banana.

280 calories, 1 gram fat, 0 grams saturated fat

12.

What's for Dessert?

AH, DESSERT. As much enthusiasm as I can muster for beets—and it's quite a bit—I can unfortunately muster quite a bit more for bread pudding. Or chocolate soufflé. Or pecan pie. But I usually make my dessert enthusiasm take a backseat to my beet (and asparagus and spinach and mushroom) enthusiasm because if I didn't I'd be buying clothes from Omar the Tentmaker.

There are two problems with trying to make dessert compatible with healthful eating. The first is fat, which is an integral part of most desserts. To make things even more difficult, the fat you usually find in dessert is the evil, saturated kind—the butter and cream and eggs kind. You don't find too many desserts made with olive oil.

The second problem is sugar, which is an integral part of *all* desserts. In fact, sweetness is dessert's defining characteristic. The good news, of course, is that sugar isn't actively bad for you—it's just empty calories. Healthful eating requires keeping a close eye on sugar not because there's anything wrong with it, but because of the opportunity cost of consuming calories without nutrition. For each can of Coke you drink, you could be eating a slice of whole-grain bread and an apple. But sometimes you just gotta have the Coke. I understand.

Sometimes I just gotta have the bread pudding, and I have it. Most of the time, however, I make a dessert compromise. I cut down on the fat but leave the sugar. The worst you can say about most of the desserts

I eat is that they would make me fat if I ate a lot of them. They won't, however, increase my risk of cancer or clog my arteries.

If you're looking for ways to cut down on dessert fat, there's no shortage of suggestions out there. Practically every issue of every health-oriented magazine has recipes for low-fat desserts, where cottage cheese substitutes for cream cheese and low-fat margarine for butter. Thinking about trying one? STOP! DON'T DO IT! They are almost universally terrible.

But the problem with these desserts goes beyond their tasting bad. They represent everything healthful eating should not be. It shouldn't be about making second-rate (or third-rate or just plain awful) healthful substitutes for good-tasting food that's bad for you. If you go that route, everything you eat will remind you that there's another, tastier version that you can't have, and each meal will be another step to martyrdom.

You don't want that. Dinner shouldn't be a harsh reminder of the food you can't eat. It should be a celebration of the food you can. And dessert is no exception. There's a wide variety of desserts that can be made with little or no fat, and they can all be enjoyed without the ghosts of their high-fat versions haunting you.

Pie in the Sky

There are some meals that just cry out to be finished with pie. Picnics need apple pie. Thanksgiving needs pumpkin pie (and, in our house, pecan pie). I'm told that Christmas needs pie too, although I'm not an experienced celebrant of that holiday. In fact, the only festive meal that doesn't cry for pie is the Passover seder, for which your desserts aren't made with flour, but with sand, to remind you of the desert the Jews walked through on their way to freedom. (Point of information: Passover desserts aren't really made with sand, but with matzoh meal, which is the next best thing.)

While some pies just can't accommodate themselves to healthful eating (coconut custard, pecan, chocolate chiffon), there's a whole school of pies you can adapt without losing their essence—fruit pies.

The reason you can do so much with fruit pies is that the fat isn't in the filling, but in the crust. Let's look at a standard 9-inch, two-crust apple pie. The total pie has about 3,300 calories, with a little more than a third of those coming from its 135 grams of fat. Not terrible, but not great. But now let's break up the pie into two elements: filling (essentially apples, spices, and sugar) and crust (flour and shortening). The filling has about 1,200 calories with a mere 5 grams of fat, for a scant 4 percent of calories from fat, but the crust has 2,100 calories and 130 fat grams, for a whopping 56 percent of calories from fat.

Almost all the fat in a fruit pie is in the crust, but it's the filling that makes it pie. Find a substitute for the crust and you have a successful low-fat dessert. And that shouldn't be too hard to do since the crust is seldom anyone's favorite part of the pie—it is, after all, really just a container.

Here are some suggestions for dressing up a pie filling without adding a crust:

PUT CRUNCHY THINGS ON TOP.

Toast some chopped nuts and sprinkle them on top of a soufflé dish filled with a fruit filling. (The full-fledged Earth Dog alternative is, of course, Grape Nuts.) While it's true that the best crunchy things (like crumb crusts) are high in fat, even the worst of them is better than a full-fledged crust. Adding crunchy things can even dignify your dessert by giving it a title. If you layer the crunchy things throughout, you've made a betty. If you just sprinkle them on top, it's a crisp. If you add a layer on the top and one on the bottom, it's a crunch.

GARNISH.

If you decorate the tops of your dessert servings, they seem more satisfying and complete than if you just leave a blob on a plate. Bake your fruit filling *sans* crust or topping, and use sliced, dried, or candied fruit, mint leaves, chocolate shavings, powdered sugar, or anything else that appeals to your imagination, to dress up each plate. A whipped-cream substitute that works well is sweetened part-skim ricotta cheese. Sweeten the cheese with honey, in the proportion of three to four parts cheese to one part honey. Mix it up thoroughly in your food processor or blender, and put a dollop on your fruit.

SERVE IN CUTE LITTLE INDIVIDUAL CONTAINERS.

Presentation counts for a lot, and tends to make people forget that there's no fat in their dessert. You can bake your fruit filling in individual ramekins, and then garnish them as above, for a very dessertlike result.

USE A MERINGUE CRUST.

Meringue crusts, made of egg whites and sugar, are fat-free and satisfyingly crunchy and elegant. They can, however, be tricky. You can be thwarted by overbeating, underbeating, insufficient baking, too much baking, a humid day, or the wrath of the meringue gods. (For more on meringues, see page 281.) In the meantime, if you're already an accomplished meringuer, go ahead and try it.

CONFESSIONS OF A FAILED PASTRY COOK

I **RATHER ENJOY PERFORMING MOST** of the procedures (dreaded veggie prep being a major exception) that change raw food into dinner, but I never did take to baking. It's too much like chemistry. I want to be able to alter recipes and poke at things as they cook. Even when I've followed instructions conscientiously, anything I've ever tried to bake has seemed to understand that I was not performing a labor of love and, in retaliation, has turned out badly. I did not persist. A few lopsided cakes and heavy loaves of bread were enough for me.

Back in the days before our house became a pastry-free zone, the only desserts my oven produced regularly were brownies and cheesecake—things that didn't have to rise. For years, however, I did keep trying to make pie crust. I really love good traditional pie: apple, berry, lemon meringue, pumpkin, pecan, whatever. So does my husband. And there was no bakery in Poughkeepsie that could provide one we liked. But alas, as you might expect from a world-class klutz and generally unsuccessful baker, my pies were even worse than the ones we could pick up down at the shopping center. I could manage the fillings all right, but the crusts! After coating the kitchen in flour, I would try to deal with a mess of dough that adhered stubbornly to the pastry board, the rolling pin, the floor, and the dog. The portion that I eventually coaxed into the pie plate would bake into a sort of hard tasteless pie liner obviously unfit for human consumption. I tried every pastry-making trick known to womankind. Nothing helped. So I made graham-cracker crusts or bought frozen pie shells in the supermarket.

Then one day Tamar came home from junior high and said she wanted to make a pie. She had learned how in home economics class. "Of course, dear." I said. I figured it couldn't be any worse than mine. A friend had given me a terrific recipe for pecan pie that, for obvious reasons, I had never tried. The contrast in taste and texture between filling and crust is even more essential to pecan pie than it is to apple or pumpkin. Without a successful crust, you're just eating a rather cloying pecan pudding. But Tamar wanted to make the pecan pie, so we went out and purchased the ingredients.

I hadn't intended to watch, but I couldn't help myself. I was fascinated. My little daughter mixed her pie dough, chilled it briefly, rolled it out, popped it into the pan, and (I could hardly believe my eyes!) fluted the edges. Where was the flour mess? Where were the sticky crumbs of dough? (The second question was the dog's. He had developed quite a taste for pie dough. Now he sat under the table looking deprived.) Then she made the filling. I could handle that. I even helped a little.

The pie was perfect. Every pie Tamar has ever made has been perfect. These days, though, she makes her pecan pie only for special occasions like Thanksgiving. Pecan pie is impressively high in calories and saturated fat. It's not something you want sitting around the house. But even a tiny piece is very satisfying. Just find a young, healthy, thin person to take home the leftovers: a designated eater. Your pecan pie will be a beautiful, festive thing—if you have the pie crust gene.

TAMAR'S KILLER PECAN PIE
**WARNING: This recipe is suitable only for special occasions.
It is *very* nutritionally incorrect.**
Makes 12 servings

4 large eggs
1¼ cups dark corn syrup
1 cup sugar
4 tablespoons melted butter
3 tablespoons dark rum
1 teaspoon vanilla
2 cups coarsely chopped pecans
1 unbaked 9-inch pie crust

1. Preheat the oven to 325°F. Beat the eggs lightly in a large bowl. Stir in the remaining ingredients. Pour into a 9-inch pie plate lined with the unbaked crust.
2. Bake for 1¼ hours. Cool and serve at room temperature.

420 calories, 22 grams fat, 5 grams saturated fat per serving

The Great Pumpkin

I suppose, technically, a pumpkin pie is a fruit pie. A pumpkin is, after all, the fruit of a vine. But in this case as in so many others the technical has little to do with the gastronomic.

I love pumpkin pie—the taste, the color, the texture—and it has the advantages of being easy to make and lending itself well to a low-fat version, which can be baked without a crust. Its ease of preparation, of course, depends on whether you start with canned pumpkin or whole pumpkin.

The disadvantage of using whole pumpkins is pretty obvious—it's a big pain. There are advantages, though. For one, you get to make a really big mess. I love sticking my hands in the pumpkin and pulling out all the goo and the seeds. It's the same sensation I used to get from burying my hands in the barrels of whole-bean coffee at Zabar's. (When I was a child, my mother forbade this. Just as I got old enough so she couldn't really forbid me anymore, my own self-governing impulses annoyingly kicked in and prevented me from doing it. Coincidence? I think not.) I realize that sticking your hands in pumpkin goo isn't everyone's idea of a fine way to spend the afternoon, so for those people I will point out a second advantage—the seeds.

Roasted pumpkin seeds make a great snack. To make them, just separate the seeds from the goo (if you're goophobic, get someone else to do it) and spread them out on a nonstick baking pan. Bake them for about an hour at 250°F. If your seeds aren't brown and crisp enough after an hour, turn the temperature up a bit and leave them in for another 10 to 15 minutes.

Every year at Thanksgiving my brother Jake makes pie filling from whole pumpkins. I get the benefit of the goo, the seeds, and the custard without actually having to do any of the work. I'm happy with this arrangement. If you—or your brother—are tempted to try this, remember there are two kinds of pumpkins. There's eatin' pumpkins and then there's decoratin' pumpkins. If you're going to cook it, find the eating kind (usually called sugar pumpkins). The decorating kind makes distinctly inferior custard.

If you lack either the time or the inclination to deal with fresh pumpkins, use the stuff in the can. Unlike many things in cans, there's absolutely nothing wrong with it. It has one ingredient: pumpkin. If your can has more than one ingredient, find another can.

I'm not ashamed to admit that I not only use Libby's solid pack pumpkin, I also use the recipe on the can, with three egg whites substituted for two of the eggs and the spices beefed up a bit. And a little less sugar. Oh, and a little vanilla. And maybe some nutmeg. Okay, so I guess I don't use the recipe on the Libby's pumpkin can. Fortunately, pumpkin pie filling is very forgiving—the basic ingredients are pumpkin, evaporated milk, eggs, sugar, and spices. If you use them in any kind of sensible proportion, you will end up with a fine pumpkin custard.

These are Mom's proportions, and they are eminently sensible.

PUMPKIN CUSTARD
Makes 6 servings

> 1 cup firmly packed brown sugar
> 1 small chunk fresh ginger, peeled (enough to make about 1 teaspoon minced)
> 1 teaspoon cinnamon
> ½ teaspoon nutmeg
> One 15-ounce can pumpkin purée
> One 12-ounce can evaporated skim milk
> 2 large eggs
> 3 large egg whites
> 2 teaspoons vanilla

1. Preheat the oven to 375°F. Spray a 6-cup baking dish with vegetable oil spray.
2. Place the sugar, ginger, and spices in a food processor and process until the ginger is well minced. Add the remaining ingredients and process until mixed. Pour the pumpkin mixture into the oiled baking dish.

Bake until the center no longer jiggles when you move the dish and the surface is dry to the touch, 45 to 60 minutes. Serve warm or at room temperature.

230 calories, 2 grams fat, 1 gram saturated fat per serving

Meringues: The Thrill of Victory and the Agony of Defeat

There's something very appealing about meringue cookies. They're big and crunchy and sweet. They have no fat and very few calories. In short, the ideal dessert.

So, I said to myself, how hard can it be to make something that has only two ingredients? Pretty damn hard, it turns out. Meringues look simple on paper. You separate some eggs and beat the whites with sugar. Then you form them into cookies, bake them, and—voilà!—meringues. Yeah, right. Now let's look at everything that can go wrong.

1. CHOOSING THE BOWL.

As you may have heard, the bowl you use to whip egg whites has to be clean, but that's not all—it should also be copper. This sounded like cooking superstition to me, so I looked into it. It seems that one of the proteins in the egg whites, conalbumin, actually binds to the metal in the copper bowl and makes a more stable foam that is difficult to overbeat. Hey, if anything actually makes this process easier, I'm all for it. If you don't have copper, use glass. Avoid plastic, which can harbor all sorts of foam-killing demons.

2. SEPARATING THE EGGS.

I am, unfortunately, not the kind of person who pays rigorous attention to detail. I like my proportions approximate, my ingredients fungible, and my cooking times flexible. I seldom use measuring utensils and I don't even own a kitchen timer. If you are also this kind of cook, you might consider skipping this section. Or ask for help from the most meticulous friend you have. If, however, you decide to press on, be very careful in separating your eggs. Even a speck of yolk (or any other fatty material) can keep your egg whites from foaming up. As I mentioned above, make sure the bowl you're using is scrupulously clean.

3. BEATING THE EGGS.

If you use an electric mixer, this process is easier but you will be in danger of overbeating. If you don't use an electric mixer, you will be in danger of overexerting yourself and throwing the whole mixture down the sink in a fit of pique. After weighing these hazards, I opt for the electric mixer. I learned from bitter experience that you cannot use a food processor. Don't even think about it.

4. ADDING THE SUGAR.

The addition of sugar makes egg whites much harder to beat. If you are beating by hand, wait until your whites are almost fully beaten and whip the sugar in at the very end. If, however, you are using a mixer, add the sugar just when the whites begin to foam. Because the sugar slows down the beating process, it makes it easier to gauge when the whites are ready.

A more difficult question is how much sugar to add. After seemingly endless experimentation, I settled on 2 tablespoons per white. Most recipes call for more, but I prefer my meringues less sweet. Feel free to vary the amount.

5. DECIDING WHEN TO STOP BEATING.

This is the hardest part. Stop when the whites form stiff peaks. When you lift the mixer out of the whites, you should get a pointy little wave in the bowl. If the wave isn't pointy, keep beating. You'll know you've gone too far when the foam starts getting lumpy. At that point, the only thing to do is throw it away and start again. Or feed it to the dog, who will enjoy it no end. One thing about experimenting with meringues, you end up with a very happy dog.

6. FORMING THE COOKIES.

You know those nice swirly meringues you get at the bakery? The only way to make those is with a pastry bag. You may be surprised to learn that I have a pastry bag, complete with a set of decorative nozzles. Then why is it that my meringue cookies end up looking like half-melted snow forts? Maybe it has something to do with that attention to detail problem I mentioned earlier. If you have a pastry bag and you want to give it a shot, be my guest. Otherwise, just use a teaspoon.

7. BAKING.

There are only two variables here: time and temperature, and two schools of meringue baking: soft and hard. Soft meringues are crunchy outside and chewy inside. The hard ones are crunchy throughout. Hard meringues are baked at a low temperature (225°F) for a long time (an hour or even more). Soft meringues are baked at a higher temperature (350°F) for a short time (15 minutes or so). Meringue with more sugar is more suitable for soft cookies, and less sweet meringue works better for hard cookies. I prefer hard cookies and have found that an hour at 225°F works in my oven. I've also found that, no matter how low I set the temperature, the meringues will brown. I cannot keep them white. I can prevent meringues with a higher sugar content from browning, so I don't think it's me. I think that less sweet meringues will inevitably brown. I haven't had much luck with soft meringues, but that could be a personal problem.

MERINGUE COOKIES
Makes 36 cookies

2 large egg whites
⅛ teaspoon cream of tartar (optional)
¼ cup sugar
1 teaspoon maple syrup or ¼ teaspoon vanilla (optional)

1. Preheat the oven to 225°F.
2. Beat the egg whites in a metal or glass bowl (copper is best). When the whites begin to foam, add the cream of tartar, if you're using it. If you are mixing by hand, wait until the whites are almost at the stiff peak stage and then beat in the sugar. If you are using an electric mixer, add the sugar when the whites begin to foam. Beat the mixture to stiff peaks. If you are using the maple syrup or vanilla, beat it in at the very end.
3. Using a pastry bag or just a spoon, form the meringue into 1-inch cookies on an ungreased nonstick cookie sheet. Bake for 1 to 2 hours, or until the cookies are crisp and completely set.

10 calories, 0 grams fat, 0 grams saturated fat per cookie

VARIATIONS ON A THEME

Easier than meringues, and tastier in the bargain, are these cookies I first had at the home of my friends the Caplans. They are higher in calories, but also more substantial and interesting.

ITALIAN LEMON COOKIES
Makes 36 cookies

3 large egg whites
1¾ cups sugar
1 teaspoon grated lemon zest
½ teaspoon baking powder
¼ teaspoon almond extract
1¾ cups all-purpose flour
1½ cups chopped nuts or dried fruit

1. Preheat the oven to 375°F.
2. Using an electric mixer, beat the egg whites, sugar, lemon zest, bak-

ing powder, and almond extract until smooth. Add the flour and nuts or fruit, and stir just until the ingredients are thoroughly mixed.

3. Drop tablespoon-size lumps of dough on a greased baking sheet. Bake until the cookies are lightly browned, 10 to 12 minutes.

4. Let them cool completely and store in an airtight container.

80 calories, 2 grams fat, 0 grams saturated fat per cookie

Chocolate: A Permanent Thing

> Caramels are only a fad. Chocolate is a permanent thing.
>
> —CARAMEL MAKER MILTON HERSHEY (1890)

No food inspires rabid fanaticism like chocolate. People who otherwise lead normal, low-key lives have been known to go berserk when it comes to chocolate. They just have to have it.

And chocolate desserts reflect that in their decadence. You'll never see a dessert called Death by Apples—execution-style dessert is always chocolate. And make no mistake, these desserts are really really bad for you. But the culprit isn't chocolate. It's good old saturated fat. Some of that fat comes from the cocoa butter in the chocolate, but more of it comes from butter, eggs, and cream.

Chocolate comes from the cocoa bean, which goes through a series of drying, fermenting, cleaning, roasting, and grinding processes until it emerges as its two component parts: cocoa butter and cocoa powder. Cocoa butter is pure fat, and cocoa powder is mostly lean. These two components can be used separately or combined in different proportions to make the products we're familiar with. Unsweetened baking chocolate preserves the cocoa butter/cocoa powder ratio of the original bean (more than half of which is cocoa butter). Eating chocolate has added cocoa butter. White chocolate *is* cocoa butter (with milk solids and sugar added).

Because the flavor we think of as chocolate is not cocoa butter but cocoa powder, you can have chocolate without most of the fat. Commercial chocolate sauces (like Hershey and Nestlé), for example, are low in fat. They can be drizzled over fruit, angel food cake, or sorbet to make dessert seem more like dessert. If you toast angel food cake, even the supermarket variety, and top it with chocolate sauce, you've got a fine dessert. (Just cut the cake into ½-inch cubes and toast in a 350°F oven for about 10 minutes, or until lightly browned, turning once or twice. It's true that cubes this small bear an unfortunate resemblance to crumbs, but they give you a larger proportion of toasted surface than bigger ones.)

Hot chocolate and chocolate milk made with low-fat or skim milk taste very good. With care, you can even produce satisfying low-fat chocolate baked goods.

I like chocolate, but I'm not a fanatic. However, I'm inordinately fond of chocolate milk. It's not something I like to admit since I am, after all, over eleven. In my defense, I'm not the first adult to confess a fondness for chocolate drinks. Early in the sixteenth century, the Aztec emperor Montezuma introduced Cortez to a thick, rather bitter cocoa-based beverage called *xocotlatl*. Montezuma reputedly drank it for its aphrodisiac properties, but Cortez, ever a practical man, valued the drink as a fatigue fighter.

Neither Montezuma nor Cortez recorded his recipe for posterity, and making the perfect glass of chocolate milk in this day and age is tricky. If you use commercial chocolate sauce, the milk gets too sweet before it gets chocolatey enough. So I use cocoa and sugar to achieve the right balance of chocolate and sweetness.

This is my recipe. It can easily be altered to suit individual tastes.

CHOCOLATE MILK
Makes 1 serving

1 tablespoon unsweetened cocoa
2 teaspoons sugar
¼ cup boiling water
Several ice cubes
1 cup nonfat milk

1. In a glass, dissolve the cocoa and sugar in the boiling water. Let cool slightly. Add the ice cubes and stir until the mixture is cold. Stir in the milk. If you don't like ice cubes in your chocolate milk, remove them.

NOTE: If you prefer your chocolate milk hot (i.e., as cocoa), just heat the milk before you add it to the cocoa mixture and eliminate the ice cubes.

130 calories, 0 grams fat, 0 grams saturated fat

BAKING WITH PRUNES—YES, PRUNES

Having taken an unequivocal stand against low-fat imitations of high-fat foods, I will now equivocate. There are times when the healthful versions are serviceable, and there are even times when they're good. An example of a good one is Mattus low-fat ice cream (page 289). An example of a serviceable one is plain chocolate cake made with fruit purée instead of fat.

You may have read that fruit purée can be used as a one-to-one substitute for butter, shortening, or oil in recipes for baked goods. Sounds like quite a deal, eh? Well, we can't just let a claim like that drift by without testing it, so we tested prune purée as a fat substitute in a classic recipe for one-bowl chocolate cake.

It works. You end up with a serviceable chocolate cake. It certainly isn't identical to its fat-laden brethren, but it can make a perfectly respectable dessert. It's a little rubbery and it doesn't develop much of a crust, but it's flavorful and has a nice texture. We suggest that you not serve this cake all by its lonesome, but load on diversionary accoutrements like fruit and chocolate sauce. That way its shortcomings are much less noticeable. We also suggest that you serve it warm, for the same reason. Its flaws are much more obvious when the cake is cold or room temperature.

We've also seen applesauce as a fat substitute, and we tried that one too. I liked the prune results better—they were less dense and more cake-like—but since personal tastes vary, you might want to try applesauce yourself. Either prune purée (frequently called lekvar) or applesauce can be purchased in jars at the supermarket.

NUTRITIONALLY CORRECT ONE-BOWL CHOCOLATE CAKE
Makes 12 servings

> 2 cups sifted cake flour
> 2 teaspoons baking powder
> ½ teaspoon baking soda
> ¼ teaspoon salt
> ¾ cup unsweetened cocoa
> 1½ cups sugar
> ⅔ cup prune purée
> ½ cup warm water
> ⅔ cup nonfat milk
> 2 large eggs
> 2 teaspoons vanilla

1. Preheat the oven to 350°F. Grease a 13 x 9-inch baking pan.
2. Sift the flour, baking powder, baking soda, salt, cocoa, and sugar to-

gether into a mixing bowl. Add the prune purée, water, milk, eggs, and vanilla. Blend the ingredients thoroughly, using an electric mixer.

3. Pour the mixture into the baking pan and bake 25 to 30 minutes. Serve warm with berries and chocolate sauce (recipe below) or perhaps a scoop of Mattus ice cream.

NOTE: Because the prune purée version of this cake doesn't rise as much as the fatted version, the end result is fairly flat. If you want a thicker cake, increase the recipe by one-third or use a smaller pan.

210 calories, 2 grams fat, 0 grams saturated fat per serving

BUTTERMILK CHOCOLATE SAUCE
Makes 4 to 6 servings

⅓ cup unsweetened cocoa

⅓ cup firmly packed brown sugar

½ cup nonfat buttermilk (see Note)

⅛ to ¼ teaspoon vanilla

1. Combine the ingredients in a small saucepan and heat gently over low heat, stirring frequently, until the sugar and cocoa are dissolved.

NOTE: This sauce has a distinct buttermilk tang, which I like, but which may not be to everyone's taste. If you prefer tangless chocolate sauce, you can substitute low-fat or nonfat milk.

50 calories, 0 grams fat, 0 grams saturated fat per serving of 6

WE ALL SCREAM

Best Flavors

- Original Chocolate
- Coffee
- Chocolate Chocolate Cookie
- Caramel Crunch

IT'S **TOUGH WORK** but someone had to do it. We really had to try *all* the flavors. We've listed the ones we like best above.

Mattus ice cream (except for the sorbet-and-cream flavors, which are a bit leaner) is 3 percent fat by weight (about 16 percent of calories). That means that a half cup of Mattus contains 3 grams of fat, 2 of them saturated. It was started by the same company that created Häagen-Dazs and, for my money, it tastes better. It has about 170 calories per serving, and while lots of them are from sugar, there is also plenty of real milk in this ice cream. A half cup will provide 22 percent of your Daily Value for calcium.

Tamar and I agree that the chocolate and coffee flavors really taste like chocolate and coffee. In addition, the mouth feel is smooth and creamy in the way ice cream should be, rather than in the style of vegetable gum. The chocolate chocolate cookie flavor is good too, chocolatey and satisfying, but I've never really been able to get behind having little bits of cookie in my ice cream, an idiosyncratic taste that mars my enjoyment of a number of Mattus flavors. Their flavors don't need textural contrasts to distract the eater from inferior mouth feel. The original chocolate stands very well on its own.

My husband's favorite is the caramel crunch, and I like it too. It would be excellent with some lightly sweetened pumpkin custard. It contains real pecans and caramel, but the ice cream has a slightly more ice-milky texture than my favorites and is a bit too sweet. For some reason this seems to be true of all the vanilla-based flavors. I hesitate to complain about this problem, because its obvious solution is an infusion of slimy guar gum. Too little guar gum is a far, far better thing than too much.

What I think Mattus needs is an X-rated line. Few adults of my acquaintance want ice cream flavors like mint cookie or chocolate chip cookie dough. How about some really fruity fruit flavors? Or something a bit unusual? Ginger is good. So is cinnamon. I've even had green tea ice cream and found it interesting.

The Mattus sorbet-and-cream flavors we tasted were too sweet and lacked intensity. Sorbet flavors like bitter orange and sour apple, not to mention a really serious raspberry (their present black raspberry is almost there, but it needs more contrast between the sorbet and the ice cream), would provide sophisticated, grown-up desserts. Perhaps the ice cream in such flavors could even contain a bit more cream. Since sorbet is fat free the fat content could remain at 3 grams per half-cup serving.

All in all, however, Mattus deserves a standing ovation. They have produced high-quality ice creams that are low in fat. Although I'm sure they worked long and hard to develop them, there is none of the look, smell, or taste of the food-processing laboratory about these ice creams. They are food.

Mattus ice creams are widely available on both coasts (at least in New York, Miami, and San Francisco) but may be hard to find in the country's interior. Check specialty food stores if Mattus isn't in your supermarket. If you can't find it anywhere, write to The Mattus Group, Fairfield, NJ, 07004, and ask if there's a distributor in your area.

Pasta for Dessert

I avoided noodle kugel for years because I had encountered it only as an accompaniment to the main meal. I have always firmly believed that sweet foods belong to the dessert course. I never considered serving kugel that way. But my husband's Aunt Teddie did. Not only that, she created a palatable low-fat version. This kugel can be made even more dessertlike by adding more sugar or other sweetener. A handful of raisins or some chopped dates also makes a nice addition. You can render it more or less moist with the addition (or subtraction) of milk or eggs. Experiment until you find a version you're happy with. Leftover kugel can be frozen and reheats well in the oven or the microwave. You can even have it for breakfast. Tamar suggests that it could be made using lasagna noodles and layering the ingredients. I suspect that would work just fine, but then it would become the property of another ethnic group.

AUNT TEDDIE'S NOODLE KUGEL
Makes 6 servings

> 6 ounces medium-width regular or no-yolk egg noodles
>
> 1 large egg
>
> 2 large egg whites
>
> 2 cups nonfat milk, yogurt, buttermilk, or a combination
>
> 1 tablespoon sugar, honey, maple syrup, or other sweetener (more if
>   you like a sweeter kugel)
>
> 1 teaspoon vanilla

> **For the topping**
>
> 2 cups Kellogg's Mueslix cereal
>
> One 15-ounce can sliced unsweetened peaches with their
>   juice (an equivalent amount of any other fruit and liquid
>   may be substituted)
>
> 1 cup brown sugar
>
> Juice of 1 lemon
>
> 1 teaspoon cinnamon
>
> ½ teaspoon nutmeg

1. Preheat the oven to 350°F. Grease a 2-quart (8 x 10-inch) baking dish.
2. Cook the noodles in a large pot of boiling water until al dente and drain well.
3. Beat the egg and egg whites lightly with a fork. Add the milk, sugar, and vanilla and stir to blend.
4. Spread the noodles in the baking dish and immediately pour the egg mixture over them.
5. Stir together the topping ingredients (Yeah, use that dirty egg bowl!) and spread topping over the noodles.
6. Bake until the center is firm to the touch, 45 to 60 minutes. Serve warm.

190 calories, 1 gram fat, 0 grams saturated fat per serving

Finally, Fruit

When I was a kid, there was almost always fruit in the house. Whenever there wasn't, it was because my brother Aaron had eaten it all. Not that Aaron was a much bigger fruit consumer than the rest of us, he was just less discriminating. No banana was too green, no pear too crunchy for Aaron to make a snack out of. My mother used to hide the unripe fruit to give the rest of us a fighting chance.

It wasn't that Aaron actually *liked* unripe fruit, he just never paid much attention, to fruit or anything else. If it looked like food and he was hungry, he ate it. If you had to assign Aaron a defining characteristic, it would have to be obliviousness.

My brother Jake had his number, though, and wreaked his revenge. He found a plastic pear (on the street, I think) that was remarkably real-looking. He brought it home and put it with the rest of the pears. And waited. I came home from school and, unsuspecting, picked up the pear. I knew immediately that something was wrong and asked Jake why there was a plastic pear in with the real pears. He replied, "Put it back. It's for Aaron." I told him it was obviously fake, and there was no way even Aaron would fall for it. Jake, sage beyond his years, which at that time numbered about six, said, "Wait."

Aaron came home and headed for the pears. We watched as he washed the plastic pear. He tried to bite into it, looked mildly perplexed, and said, to no one in particular, "This pear is plastic." Then he put it back on the windowsill with the other pears, and chose another one.

We were disappointed that we didn't get more of a rise out of him, but Jake was persistent. About every six months, he would put the same plastic pear in with the fruit, and Aaron would fall for it every time. Eventually, he got really annoyed, and Jake counted it as a victory.

Most fruit in Haspel households, then as now, simply gets eaten. It never sees the inside of an oven or saucepan. Since my mother and I share a reluctance to mix sweet and savory, we almost never put fruit in main dishes or salads. When we cook fruit, it's dessert.

BAKED APPLES
Makes 4 servings

½ cup dry white wine, apple cider, or a combination

1 tablespoon maple syrup or brown sugar

½ teaspoon cinnamon

¼ teaspoon nutmeg

¼ teaspoon clove or allspice

4 large baking apples, preferably Rome or Jonathan

¼ cup raisins (see Note)

¼ cup chopped nuts (pecans are excellent)

1. Preheat the oven to 350°F.
2. Combine the wine, cider, syrup or sugar, and spices in a small saucepan and bring the mixture to a boil. Lower the heat and simmer for 5 minutes, stirring occasionally.
3. Peel the top third of each apple, core them (leaving them whole), and place them, peeled side up, in a baking dish. Combine the raisins and nuts and fill the cavities with the mixture. Pour the wine mixture over the apples, getting as much as possible into the cavities.
4. Bake uncovered, basting occasionally, until the apples are tender but not collapsing, about 1 hour and 20 minutes. Serve warm, chilled, or at room temperature with the pan juices spooned over them. They can be reheated in the microwave—an efficient breakfast strategy.

NOTE: You can substitute chopped crystallized ginger for half the raisins and add ¼ teaspoon ground ginger to the sauce mixture.

190 calories, 5 grams fat, 1 gram saturated fat per serving

POACHED PEARS
Makes 4 to 6 servings

2 pounds slightly underripe pears (Comice are my favorite)
2 cups full-bodied red wine
⅔ cup sugar
One 3-inch piece cinnamon stick
3 small pieces lemon peel

1. Peel, core, and quarter the pears.
2. Combine the wine, sugar, cinnamon, and lemon peel in a saucepan and bring to a boil. Lower the heat so that the mixture simmers and add the pears. Simmer, uncovered, until they are soft, 45 to 60 minutes, depending on the ripeness of the pears. Stir occasionally to coat the pears. The longer they simmer, the softer they become. Doneness is a matter of opinion—taste them, and when you like them, they're done. If you are serving them chilled or at room temperature, keep in mind that the pears will continue to cook in the syrup as it cools, so remove the pears from the heat a few minutes early.
3. Serve warm, chilled, or at room temperature.

190 calories, 1 gram fat, 0 grams saturated fat per serving of 6

BLUEBERRY CLAFOUTIS

Clafoutis is a French dessert that most closely resembles a giant fruit pancake. The traditional clafoutis is made with cherries, but almost any berry can be substituted. This recipe uses blueberries, but don't feel constrained.

Makes 8 servings

4 cups blueberries

¼ cup plus ⅓ cup sugar

¼ cup orange liqueur

1 cup nonfat milk (approximately)

3 large eggs

1 tablespoon vanilla

⅛ teaspoon salt

⅔ cup sifted all-purpose flour

Powdered sugar for dusting

1. Preheat the oven to 350°F. Grease a 9-inch pie plate.
2. Combine the blueberries, ¼ cup sugar, and liqueur and soak for at least 1 hour but preferably overnight.
3. Drain the berries and add enough milk to the liquid to make 1¼ cups. Using a blender or a food processor, process the milk mixture, ⅓ cup sugar, eggs, vanilla, salt, and flour until well blended.
4. Spread the berries into the pie plate and pour the batter over the top. Bake until the clafoutis springs back to the touch, about 1 hour. Sprinkle with powdered sugar and serve warm.

180 calories, 2 grams fat, 1 gram saturated fat per serving

A NUTRITIONAL AFTERWORD

ALTHOUGH **WORDS LIKE HEALTH** and nutrition crop up in this book every once in a while, *Dreaded Broccoli* is not about health and nutrition; it's about food. We don't believe in special foods that work miracles, don't expect broccoli to cure whatever ails you or carrots to slow down your aging process to a crawl. Nevertheless, because a big part of the reason we cook and eat this food is that it's good for us, we think it's important to mention some of the underlying nutritional assumptions we've made.

In thinking about nutrition, it's important to remember that what we know about the complex interaction between food and our bodies is dwarfed by what we don't know. We're just beginning to understand how different substances affect us, and under what circumstances and in what combinations. That doesn't mean we don't know enough to make good decisions, it just means that we should try to put the latest study on broccoli sprouts or oat bran in context.

The preponderance of evidence suggests that a diet rich in a wide variety of fruits and vegetables, high in fiber, and low in saturated fat is best for us. It also makes sense to keep poly- and monounsaturated fats to reasonable levels—not so much because those fats are harmful, but because of the trade-off. A gram of fat has 9 calories and little other nutrition. A gram of protein or carbohydrate has 4 calories and myriad nutritional possibilities. If you cut down on fat, you can eat more, and more healthfully.

If you get in the habit of cooking with vegetables and whole grains, eating more fish and less meat, and not using oil to excess, you can worry less about nutrition and focus on cooking and eating what you really enjoy. As long as you choose foods that are good for you and consume them in quantities that keep you fairly trim, you'll be okay.

WITH THAT SAID . . .

We like to consider *Dreaded Broccoli* recipes guidelines, to be modified, adapted, or turned on their heads in accordance with the cook's taste and the ingredients' availability. In addition, all our recipes, both in their original versions and their suggested variations, are very low in saturated fat. You won't break your fat gram bank cooking out of this book. Nevertheless, operating under the assumption that most people like to have at least a general idea of the calories and fat they're consuming, we've given some basic nutritional information.

This information—calories, fat grams, and saturated fat grams—is necessarily approximate. Your asparagus spear won't have exactly the same number of calories as my asparagus spear; your chicken breast may be smaller and leaner than mine. And once you make changes in the recipe, which we're counting on you to do, all bets are off. However, we still think it's important to keep track of what you're eating, and knowing the calorie and fat content of our recipes will probably help. (For the record, where we give a range of servings, the information is for the smallest serving. We've also rounded calories to the nearest 10, and fat and saturated fat to the nearest gram. Optional ingredients are not included.)

If you're tracking these things carefully, we suggest you buy one of those nutritional encyclopedias with tens of thousands of listings and look up the foods you cook. It won't be long before you develop a good sense of the calorie and fat content of most of what you eat, and you'll be able to size up your dinner nutritionally without any help from us.

But remember, life in the kitchen and at the table shouldn't center on food chemistry, but on flavor and enjoyment. Don't worry too much. Eat your veggies.

A NOTE ON SALT

"It may be that some seek not gold, but there lives not a man that does not need salt."

CASSIODORUS, FIFTH-CENTURY GOTH ADMINISTRATOR

Salt is the most fundamental of flavorings. It's been the cause of wars, mass migrations, and riots. It's been used as currency. It's given its name to cities from Salzburg to Salt Lake City. It's been harvested by man almost since man's beginning.

It's no coincidence that this is true of salt and not, say, basil. Sodium chloride is necessary for most human bodily functions; salt is as essential to us as water. But while a taste for salt makes perfect evolutionary sense, almost no one in today's world is in danger of not getting enough. And since if you don't get enough you'll die, that isn't entirely a bad thing.

A much more relevant question is what happens when you get too much. And the answer is by no means clear. For a long time, salt was universally indicted as the high blood pressure culprit. Many recent studies, however, indicate that only a fairly small percentage of the population has salt-sensitive blood pressure. There's even been one study that showed the highest death rate among those participants who consumed the *least* salt.

In short, it seems clear that some portion of the population benefits from reducing salt intake, but it's very difficult to say how big that portion is or whether you're in it. I can safely say that I'm not. I have disgustingly low blood pressure, I'm not at risk for heart disease, and I eat as many pickles as I want. My father, however, may be one of those who benefits from reducing salt. But even if it doesn't help, it certainly can't hurt, and so my mother cooks with very little salt. "Prudence dictates moderation," she says. She's right, of course, but I nevertheless often end up asking for the salt shaker when I eat at her house.

(Actually, "shaker" lends my parents' salt dispenser a dignity it doesn't deserve. It's a six-inch yellow plastic cylinder, stamped with a picture of a whale and the words *sel de mer*. The top has a disk that rotates over dif-ferent-size holes to allow you to choose your rate of salt flow. The choices correspond roughly to "no salt," "too much salt," and "much too much salt." And, at the rate my parents use salt, it looks like the *sel de mer* is going to see us into the next millennium.)

In our recipes, we've pretty much left the salt decision up to the cook. We occasionally offer guidelines for how much salt to add, but we usu-ally just say "salt to taste."

My parents insist that your tastes change and you get used to eating minimally salted food. I believe them, but I have no intention of finding out for myself. Pass the sauerkraut.

MAIL-ORDER SOURCES:
SHOPPING FROM A PRONE POSITION

A BRIEF ANNOTATED GUIDE TO OUR FAVORITE VENDORS
Computers, credit cards, and 800 numbers have done remarkable things for the mail-order business. You can pick up the telephone and have almost anything delivered to your door. As soon as you do, your mailbox will fill with catalogs. Buy a bag of cornmeal and you immediately become the target of merchants selling everything from Peruvian sweaters to garden tools. I don't especially mind. As I don't watch television I figure I need some kind of window on the world. Just so the vendors don't phone me or ring my doorbell.

Some of the products below, such as world-class smoked fish, are available off the shelves in New York, but that may not be the case where you live. All these vendors accept major credit cards. Most use UPS for shipping. No way is this list a result of serious research. These are just some vendors who have stuff we like and seem to distribute it courteously and efficiently.

Mail-order food is expensive. (I occasionally reflect that what we are eating is an extremely pricey third-world diet.) However, a shipment of beautiful citrus fruit, intensely flavorful dried tomatoes, or fragrant ripe pears can ward off clinical depression when you're struggling to sustain a healthful diet in the depths of winter.

DREADED BROCCOLI
235 West End Avenue
New York, NY 10023
(212) 496-1606
Fax: (212) 496-2488
E-mail: thaspel@worldnet.att.net

If you're going to shop from home, it is our (completely unbiased) opinion that your very first purchase should be the *Dreaded Broccoli* newsletter. Issued quarterly, it is a wry, witty (if we do say so ourselves) compendium of cooking strategies, recipes, nutrition information, and irreverent commentary. If you've gotten this far in the book, you probably have a good idea of what the newsletter is like. A subscription is $14 for one year, $26 for two. Call, fax, or e-mail us your credit card information, or just send us a check via snail mail.

BARNEY GREENGRASS "THE STURGEON KING"
541 Amsterdam Avenue (at 86th St.)
New York, NY 10024
(212) 724-4707 (Call in orders Tuesday through Friday,
8 a.m. to 6:30 p.m.)

Barney Greengrass started in the smoked fish business in Harlem in 1908 and moved his store to its present location in 1929. Today, under the management of his son and grandson, it probably looks pretty much as it did back then. It's impossible to equal the experience of sitting in the shabby dining room and scarfing up a platter of assorted smoked fish. Tamar and I love the Eastern Nova and the sable; Chuck is partial to the kippered salmon; Jake favors the whitefish. The lake sturgeon is great, too. Barney didn't get crowned "The Sturgeon King" for nothing. And the place is full of New York Jews. Nobody cares how loud you talk.

But if you can't get to Barney's, you can order the extraordinary smoked fish and have it delivered to your door the next day. Packing in dry ice and shipping UPS Next Day Air is expensive. Shipping and handling on a 10-pound order is about $40. The fish isn't cheap either. But what a brunch you can have!

CHEF'S CATALOG
P.O. Box 620048
Dallas, TX 75262-0048
(800) 338-3232
Fax: (800) 967-3291
Web site: www.chefscatalog.com

A reliable source for a wide selection of kitchen equipment. They aren't as cheap as Zabar's (page 304), but they stock more stuff and they've got the mail-order gig down pat. It's fun to browse the catalog and wonder what kind of person would buy an electric ice shaver or a $219.00 wine-bottle opener. Most items are useful, though. They carry full lines of all the major brands of high-end cookware and small appliances. The main reason the Chef's Catalog guys are in the book, however, is that they sell the Römertopf clay pot that we recommend for baking chicken and vegetables. I own the medium (14-pound) clay cooker, and that is the size you'll probably want too. It holds a gallon and is big enough for a large chicken and a lot of vegetables without being prohibitively heavy and unwieldy.

CUSHMAN'S
3325 Forest Hill Blvd.
P.O. Box 24711
West Palm Beach, FL 33416-4711
(800) 776-7575

In January, Cushman's offers honeybells, a cross between grapefruit and oranges that is somehow both sweeter and more acidic than oranges. They are best eaten in sections, but make a good change for juice too. In August, Cushman's has mangoes to die for. The company is efficient and remarkably pleasant to deal with.

EAST COAST EXOTICS
Toughkenamon, PA
(800) 325-0664

I was introduced to East Coast Exotics fresh and dried mushrooms at one of the New York City greenmarkets and I was hooked. Cultivated exotic mushrooms are reputed to have less flavor than the ones you find in the woods, but the one time I accompanied some experts into the woods to look for mushrooms we didn't find even one. You can always find them at East Coast Exotics. The shiitakes (which you won't find in the woods even if you're luckier than I was) are especially good. Call them for a product list. You'll be amazed at the high quality and reasonable prices.

THE INCREDIBLE LINK
1511 Pike Place Market
Seattle, WA 98101
800-57-LINKS (Next-day delivery; minimum order 5 pounds,
one flavor or assorted)

Several years ago, Tamar and I visited the Pike Place Market in Seattle. The market was full of good food smells and some of the most enticing came from a booth where sausages were being grilled. We figured we should avert our eyes and pass by quickly, but we couldn't. We peeked. When we did, we discovered that some of the sausages on the grill at the Incredible Link were truly low in fat. The salmon sausage claims only a 2 percent fat content, the buffalo and smoked turkey sausages less then 5 percent. Their chicken, lamb, and vegetable sausages also contain relatively little fat.

So, right there at the market, we tried the salmon and buffalo sausages and we were sold. They were spicy, flavorful, and not at all greasy. I've since purchased many pounds of these sausages and they've always arrived promptly and solidly frozen, even in midsummer.

If you're really eating ultra-low-fat, and you want a whole sausage in your sandwich, choose the salmon. The other varieties, while lean by sausage standards, still contain about 6 to 8 grams of fat per link, and it's best to cut them up and use them to enhance grain/legume combos and pasta sauces. I've found that if I slice them while they're at least partially frozen they hold together very well.

THE JUST TOMATOES COMPANY
P.O. Box 807
Westley, CA 95387
(800) 537-1985
Fax: (800) 537-1986

These dried tomatoes, a staple food in our house, aren't salted or packed in oil. They taste good cooked, in salads, or just eaten out of the bag. Ditto for their other dried stuff—like the bell peppers, corn, and mixed vegetables. The dried apples and persimmons are also excellent and make wonderful additions to hot cereal. (Add during the last five minutes of cooking.)

I recommend the "Just Fruit" dried fruit snacks for children; the individual portions are plastic-wrapped with cute labels so they look like something a kid would think might be okay to eat. Someone at school will probably trade a Twinkie for one. Expensive, sure, but remember there's no waste or spoilage with these products. Also, everything is intensely flavored so a small portion goes a long way. This stuff is excellent. If you've got any discretionary food money, go for it.

MEACHAM MILLS
1305 Main Street
Lewiston, ID 83501
(208) 743-0505

Delicious, American-grown lentils at reasonable prices. When I ordered, they were stocking 16 different varieties. I especially like the Pardina—a unique American type. And, like lentils everywhere, they are cheap. Including cross-country shipping, my 16 pounds set me back only about $25.

PENZEYS, LTD.
P.O. Box 933
Muskego, WI 53150
(414) 679-7207
Fax: (414) 679-7878

Penzeys sells every spice or herb you've ever even thought about using, all fresh and costing less than in the supermarket. In addition, the
catalog is full of herb and spice lore—not to mention cooking ideas and
recipes from people who seem to know what they're talking about.

Most Penzeys products come packaged in plastic bags. Although the
bags are the good resealable kind, you'll probably find your flavor enhancers more convenient to store and use if you decant them into jars.

PINNACLE ORCHARDS
P.O. Box 1068
Medford, OR 97501
(800) 759-1232
Fax: 419-893-2660
Web Site: www.mission-orchards.com

An order-taker asked me, "Do you have pears in New York?" Probably
not what she would call a pear—these are unusually juicy and flavorful.
Order the Comice pears—also a good purchase at your local fruit store
when available. This variety can be picked green and continues to ripen
without deterioration in quality. Comice are available in the late fall and
early winter.

THE VERMONT COUNTRY STORE
P.O. Box 3000
Manchester Ctr., VT 05255-3000
(802) 362-8440
Fax: (802) 362-0285

If you want a crockpot to slow-cook your beans, this place has it.
They've also got a lot of other stuff you haven't seen for years—everything from manual typewriters to embroidered hankies. It's worth ordering something just to get the catalog. They also sell some foods that
merit your consideration: dried Bing cherries, McCann's Irish oatmeal,
and powdered egg whites. If these things aren't available where you
shop, consider getting them here.

WALNUT ACRES ORGANIC FARMS
Penns Creek, PA 17862-0800
(800) 433-3998
Fax: (717) 837-1146
Web site: walnutacres.com

Unparallelled pineapple (dried). Thrilling* almond and peanut butters. The company has a large selection of organic and whole-grain foods. We've tried a lot of the cereals and pancake mixes and found them all excellent. I love the twenty-grain cereal; or maybe I just love the idea that there can be such a thing. Avoid the overpriced vitamins and (ugh) "nutritional supplements."

*That's my son Jake's word and he knows his nut butters.

ZABAR'S
2245 Broadway (at 80th St.)
New York, NY 10024
(212) 496-1234
(800) 697-6301 (for out-of-state customers)
Fax: (212) 580-4477
E-mail: info@zabars.com

Like Barney Greengrass, Zabar's is just a short walk from my house, and I've spent many happy hours there, but never used their mail-order service. But they're a high-class operation, and I'm sure they treat their remote customers right. They have excellent prices on cookware and small kitchen appliances and you may find that, even with the shipping charges of 10 percent (more for a small order), you can get a good buy on the set of pots or food processor of your dreams. They also ship their fine smoked fish and their excellent coffees.

INDEX

About the Authors

In 1992, concerned citizens began subscribing to a quarterly newsletter called *Dreaded Broccoli,* begun by Barbara Haspel when her husband's heart attack prompted a radical overhaul of her cooking style. The newsletter—like this book—is full of recipes, food strategies, and lots of no-punches-pulled opinion.

Maintaining their own separate busy kitchens and lifestyles, Barbara and Tamar Haspel still manage to talk about food every day. The press has recognized the newsletter that resulted from these conversations as "witty and substantial" *(Chicago Sun Times)* and "whimsical and encouraging" *(Los Angeles Times). USA Today* especially admired its sense of humor. Both mother and daughter live, cook, and write in New York City.